Lecture Notes
in Business Information Processing   **349**

Series Editors

Wil van der Aalst
RWTH Aachen University, Aachen, Germany
John Mylopoulos
University of Trento, Trento, Italy
Michael Rosemann
Queensland University of Technology, Brisbane, QLD, Australia
Michael J. Shaw
University of Illinois, Urbana-Champaign, IL, USA
Clemens Szyperski
Microsoft Research, Redmond, WA, USA

More information about this series at http://www.springer.com/series/7911

Henderik A. Proper · Janis Stirna (Eds.)

Advanced Information Systems Engineering Workshops

CAiSE 2019 International Workshops
Rome, Italy, June 3–7, 2019
Proceedings

 Springer

Editors
Henderik A. Proper ⓘ
Luxembourg Institute of Science
and Technology
Esch-sur-Alzette, Luxembourg

Janis Stirna ⓘ
Stockholm University
Kista, Sweden

ISSN 1865-1348   ISSN 1865-1356   (electronic)
Lecture Notes in Business Information Processing
ISBN 978-3-030-20947-6   ISBN 978-3-030-20948-3   (eBook)
https://doi.org/10.1007/978-3-030-20948-3

This Springer imprint is published by the registered company Springer Nature Switzerland AG
The registered company address is: Gewerbestrasse 11, 6330 Cham, Switzerland

Preface

CAiSE is a well-established and highly visible conference series on advanced information systems engineering. It addresses contemporary topics in information systems (IS) engineering such as methodologies and approaches for IS engineering, innovative platforms, architectures and technologies, as well as engineering of specific kinds of IS. It is an established tradition that each CAiSE conference is accompanied by a significant number of high-quality workshops. Their aim is to address specific emerging challenges in the field, to facilitate interaction between stakeholders and researchers, to discuss innovative ideas, as well as to present new approaches and tools.

This year the CAiSE conference was held in Rome, Italy, during June 3–7, 2019. The theme of this 31st CAiSE conference was responsible information systems including topics such as digitalization and the new economic models it enables, and the resulting transformation of organizations and industries. Many contributions at CAiSE 2019 addressed trends such as the Internet of Things (IoT), big data analytics, business process management, flexible information systems, as well as blockchain technologies. This year, CAiSE was accompanied by its two long-standing associated working conferences (BPMDS and EMMSAD) as well as six workshops. The workshops were chosen after careful consideration, based on maturity and compliance with our usual quality and consistency criteria.

Each workshop adhered to the CAiSE 2019 submission and acceptance guidelines. The paper acceptance rate for the workshops included in this volume was approximately 49%.

This volume contains the proceedings of the following three workshops associated with CAiSE 2019:

- The 7th International Workshop on Cognitive Aspects of Information Systems Engineering (COGNISE)
- The First International Workshop on Key Enabling Technologies for Digital Factories (KET4DF)
- The Joint Workshop on Blockchains for Inter-Organizational Collaboration and Flexible Advanced Information Systems (BIOC&FAiSE)

The 15th International Workshop on Enterprise and Organizational Modeling and Simulation (EOMAS) published proceedings in a separate Springer LNBIP volume, while the First International Workshop on Processing Information Ethically (PIE) and The First International Workshop on Open Data and Ontologies for Cultural Heritage (ODOCH) published their proceedings in the CEUR Workshop Proceedings series.

As workshop chairs of CAiSE 2019, we would like to express our gratitude to all workshop organizers and to all corresponding scientific committees of the workshops for their valuable contribution.

April 2019

Henderik A. Proper
Janis Stirna

Contents

BIOC & FAiSE 2019

COGNISE 2019

The 7th International Workshop on Cognitive Aspects of Information Systems Engineering COGNISE 2019

Preface

Cognitive aspects of software and information systems engineering have received increasing attention in literature and conferences in recent years, acknowledging that these aspects are as important as the technical ones, which have traditionally been in the center of attention. This workshop serves as a stage for new research and vivid discussions on this topic, involving both academics and practitioners.

The goal of this workshop is to provide a better understanding and more appropriate support of the cognitive processes and challenges practitioners experience when performing information systems development activities, including traditional as well as new and emerging information technologies. Understanding the challenges and needs, educational programs as well as development supporting tools and notations may be enhanced for a better fit to our natural cognition, leading to better performance of engineers and higher systems' quality.

The workshop aims to bring together researchers from different communities such as requirements engineering, software architecture, modeling, design and programming, and information systems education, who share interest in cognitive aspects, for identifying the cognitive challenges in the diverse development related activities and proposing relevant solutions.

The 7th edition of this workshop, held in Rome on June 4, 2019, was organized in conjunction with the 31st International Conference on Advanced Information Systems Engineering (CAiSE 2019).

This edition of COGNISE attracted ten international submissions. Each paper was reviewed by three members of the Program Committee. Of these submissions, four papers were accepted for inclusion in the proceedings (40%). The papers presented at the workshop provide a mix of novel research ideas, presenting full research or research in progress. In addition, the workshop hosted a keynote speech by Prof. Gil Luria: How does organizational climate affect cognitive processes of IS engineers?

We hope that the reader will find this selection of papers useful to be informed and inspired by new ideas in the area of Cognitive Aspects of Information Systems Engineering.

March 2019

Irit Hadar
Irene Vanderfeesten
Barbara Weber

COGNISE 2019 Organization

Organizing Committee

Irit Hadar	University of Haifa, Israel
Irene Vanderfeesten	Eindhoven University of Technology, The Netherlands
Barbara Weber	University of St. Gallen, Switzerland

Program Committee

Banu Aysolmaz	Maastricht University, The Netherlands
Daniel M. Berry	University of Waterloo, Canada
Jan Claes	Ghent University, Belgium
Kathrin Figl	University of Innsbruck, Austria
Jonas Bulegon Gassen	Austria
Stijn Hoppenbrouwers	HAN University of Applied Sciences, The Netherlands
	Radboud University, Nijmegen, The Netherlands
Marta Indulska	University of Queensland, Australia
Meira Levy	Shenkar College of Engineering and Design, Israel
Jeffrey Parsons	Memorial University, Canada
Geert Poels	Ghent University, Belgium
Maryam Razavian	Eindhoven University of Technology, The Netherlands
Alexander Serebrenik	Eindhoven University of Technology, The Netherlands
Sofia Sherman	Tel Aviv – Jaffa Academic College, Israel
Pnina Soffer	University of Haifa, Israel
Dirk van der Linden	University of Bristol, UK
Anna Zamansky	University of Haifa, Israel

COGNISE 2019 Organization

Organizing Committee

The Impact of Confusion on Syntax Errors in Simple Sequence Flow Models in BPMN

Jan Claes[✉] and Gilles Vandecaveye

Department of Business Informatics and Operations Management,
Ghent University, Tweekerkenstraat 2, 9000 Ghent, Belgium
{jan.claes,gilles.vandecaveye}@ugent.be

Abstract. With the growing investments in getting to know and controlling their business processes, organizations produce many business process models. These models have become crucial instruments in the process lifecycle and therefore it is important that they are correct and clear representations of reality. They should contain as few errors and confusions as possible. Because we assume a causal relation between confusion and errors, we investigated it empirically. For our observation group, the data shows a correlation and temporal ordering between both. More in detail, avoiding implicit and redundant events and gateways is related with making less errors.

Keywords: Process of process modeling · Process model quality · Syntactic quality · Syntax error · Confusion

1 Introduction

Nowadays, organizations put a lot of effort in documenting and analyzing their processes with the aid of graphical representations, i.e., with business process models [1, 2]. The de facto standard language they use for these models is BPMN [3]. The models are typically constructed by someone who has gained expertise in modeling through training and practice ("a modeler"), and with the input of people who know the process very well ("the process owners") [4]. Unfortunately, case studies show that the quality of the produced models is poor, because they are often ambiguous, incomplete, or wrong [5–7]. Causes for these issues are categorized in two types: *knowledge problems* (the modeler has imperfect knowledge of the goal, the end users, the process, or the modeling language) and *cognitive problems* (the modeler does not succeed in externalizing their knowledge about the process perfectly in the model) [8]. This paper aims to provide a contribution towards solving the latter kind of problems by analyzing the impact of confusion during modeling on making errors.

Because of the complexity of the study topic, the scope is limited in several ways in order to provide initial knowledge that may be of importance when working towards a solution.

- The language was reduced to its minimum by excluding all but the 6 fundamental constructs for modeling the control flow of processes [9] in order to focus first on essential aspects only.

© Springer Nature Switzerland AG 2019
H. A. Proper and J. Stirna (Eds.): CAiSE 2019 Workshops, LNBIP 349, pp. 5–16, 2019.
https://doi.org/10.1007/978-3-030-20948-3_1

- The modeling was reduced to an assignment of translating a pre-structured textual description of a process into a graphical business process model in order to focus first on cognitive problems and the task of the modeler only.
- The analysis concerns *syntax* issues only in order to focus first on the type of issues that can be determined most objectively.
- The study used observational data of master students as a proxy for *novice* modelers in order to reduce the variability of modeling experience, domain knowledge, problem solving skills, etc. in the dataset.

In our study of the impact of confusion on making errors during modeling, an existing dataset was explored. It contains tool operations of 146 modelers and it was enriched with the timing of adding/removing confusing constructs and of adding/removing syntactical errors in the model. Next, the relation between confusion and errors was studied in detail. The conclusion is not surprising: confusion correlates with making more and solving less errors. More in particular, the study confirms the importance of using explicit events and gateways in a well-structured way.

Yet, since completing the data and constructing the proof for this conclusion proved to be challenging (even under the complexity-reducing limitations mentioned above), we believe that it is important to publish this study. In fact, this is the first paper to provide such detailed explanatory and statistical material on the relation between confusion and errors during modeling. It answers to the criticism in literature about process modeling guidelines, some of which lack an empirical foundation. It provides input for teachers who may now be able to teach their students how to *avoid* certain errors instead of *detecting and correcting* them. It provides useful input for tool developers who can improve their syntax support during modeling. On the other hand, the external validity of the research is not investigated, and readers should be cautious when generalizing the results of this paper.

This paper is structured as follows. Section 2 presents related work. Section 3 describes the data collection and Sect. 4 discusses the data analysis. Section 5 provides a discussion. Section 6 provides a summarizing conclusion.

2   Background and Related Work

The research described in this article builds further on the work of De Bock and Claes [10], who studied the origin and evolution of syntax issues in simple BPMN models. They introduced a classification scheme, which is partially adopted here. The scheme makes a distinction between errors, irresolutions, and confusions (cf. Table 1). A syntax *error* is a clear fault against the specified syntax of the modeling language. Further, since some constructs or their meaning are not clearly or consistently defined in the BPMN syntax specification, the paper distinguishes these from errors and calls them *irresolutions*. Next, some constructs are clearly syntactically correct, but they are still considered as constructions to avoid. These are called *confusions*. For this paper, because of their ambiguity, we decided to consider *irresolutions* also as confusing syntactical constructs.

Table 1. List of identified syntax issues and their occurrence in the dataset

	Construction	Code	#made	#solved
Confusion	Contains no start event	0s	0	0
	Contains no end event	0e	1	0
	Contains multiple start events	S	94	20
	Contains multiple end events	E	85	8
	Multiple parallel sequence flows from non-gateway	Sa	7	5
	Multiple optional sequence flows towards non-gateway	Jx	244	34
	No label for edge departing from XOR splits	Lx	358	269
Irresolution	One gateway combines a join and split feature	C	164	14
	Wrong type of join combined with a certain split	W	22	7
	No join gateways in case of optional iterations	I	0	0
	Wrong nesting of gateways	N	19	3
	AND and XOR are joined together in one join gateway	T	13	0
	No label for activity	La	2	2
	Sequence flow with arrow at each side	DS	22	11
Error	Implicit start event without implicit end event	0se	0	0
	Implicit end event without implicit start event	0es	1	0
	Not all of the paths are closed (missing end event?)	P	57	36
	Condition at sequence flow originating from start event	Ls	0	0
	Sequence flow to start event	Bs	9	0
	Sequence flow from end event	Be	0	0
	Sequence flow from start event missing	Ms	0	0
	Sequence flow to end event missing	Me	0	0
	Multiple optional sequence flows from non-gateway	Sx	99	31
	Multiple parallel sequence flows towards non-gateway	Ja	4	0
	Gateway with only 1 incoming and 1 outgoing sequence flow	1e	373	359

Second, the scheme recognizes the fact that at certain times during modeling one cannot be sure whether a *missing* construct is an issue, since its placement can be deliberately postponed or unintentionally forgotten. The proposed way of dealing with this, is to make a distinction between uncertain issues (certain *missing* constructs in incomplete parts of the model) and definite issues (*missing* constructs in completed parts of the model, and *wrong* constructs). For this paper, we consider both the making and solving of issues, further neglecting the difference between uncertain and definite. Only when an uncertain issue evolves into its definite issue equivalent, we disregarded the "solving of the uncertain issue" and the "making of the definite issue" in order to capture the making of the issues at the earliest time.

This paper contributes to the process model quality literature. Since there are ample papers about this topic, we refer to the recent, extensive literature reviews of Figl [11] and De Meyer and Claes [12]. Besides literature about *what* is a high-quality process model, there is also a growing body of literature about *how* process models of high quality can be constructed. For example, Guidelines of Modeling provides high-level recommendations such as to optimize correctness, relevance, economic efficiency, clarity, comparability, and systematic design [13]. Nevertheless, it was criticized for its lack of concrete, operational support and the lack of empirical evidence. On the other extreme, the Seven Process Modeling Guidelines [14], Ten Process Modeling Guidelines [15], and Quality Indicators related to Gateway Complexity [16] take a dominantly empirical angle as to finding the optimal thresholds for certain process model metrics such as the size of the model, the number and nesting depth of gateways, etc. Further, Concrete [17] and Abstract Syntax modification Patterns [18] bundled detailed guidelines for process modeling from existing literature, software, and cases. What they all have in common, is that the focus is on *how* to improve process models, and less on *why* certain guidelines have certain effects on the quality of the produced models (i.e., the cognitive aspect). The current paper aims to address this gap by studying the relations between different factors of process model quality. More in particular, it relates the amount of syntactical confusion in a model with making and solving errors during modeling.

3 Data Collection

As mentioned, this study builds on an existing dataset used in previous research [8, 10]. The dataset contains all the operations of 146 modelers in our modeling tool while constructing a graphical model from a textual process description.[1] For each operation, the dataset contains, the type (e.g. 'create activity', 'move xor gateway', 'delete edge'), the time, the id of the model element to which it applies, and the code(s) of the issue(s) that is/are made or solved by the operation. For this study, we could use only 122 of the 146 modeling sessions, disregarding the models that contain no confusions nor errors, and Petri-Net-style models (using *event* symbols for *places*).

From these data, we derived for each modeling session the measures presented in Table 2. When considering *operations* in our study, the '*move*' operations are disregarded. They are not relevant, because they have no impact on syntax issues.

---

[1] For details, see the 2015 experiment at https://www.janclaes.info/experiments.

Table 2. Measures per modeling session

Code	Formula	Definition
CI+		The number of confusions and irresolutions made during modeling
CI−		The number of confusions and irresolutions solved during modeling
CI	CI+ − CI−	The number of confusions and irresolutions remaining after modeling
E+		The number of errors made during modeling
E−		The number of errors solved during modeling
E	E+ − E−	The number of errors remaining after modeling
Op		The number of relevant operations used to create the model
T		The number of minutes used to create the model (T stands for *time*)

The above measures represent totals over the whole session. At each operation that created or removed a syntax issue, the measures in Table 3 were calculated as well.

Table 3. Measures per syntax issue influencing operation

Code	Formula	Definition
ci		The number of confusions and irresolutions currently in the partial model
[ci]	ci/max (ci)	The relative ci expressed as a percentage of the maximum ci in the model
e+		The number of errors made by the current operation
e−		The number of errors solved by the current operation
e		The number of errors currently in the partial model
[e−]	e−/e	The *relative* number of *existing* errors solved by the current operation
op		The number of operations since the previous syntax issue operation
t		The number of minutes since the previous syntax issue operation
p_{e+}	e+/op	The current chance to make an error: the number of errors made divided by the number of operations since the previous issue operation
$p_{[e−]}$	[e−]/op	The current chance to solve an error: the *relative* number of errors solved divided by the number of operations since the previous issue operation

4 Data Analysis

4.1 General Relations Between Confusion and Errors

First, we look at the relation between confusion (CI) and errors (E) at the model level. Correlations are calculated between the variables of Table 2. The results are displayed in Table 4.

Table 4. Correlations at model level (displaying Spearman's rho and the 2-tailed significance)

N = 122	CI+	CI−	CI	E+	E−	E	Op	T
CI+	–	,731**	,759**	0,046	−,218*	,316**	−0,113	−0,05
	.	0,000	0,000	0,615	0,016	0,000	0,217	0,587
CI−	,731**	–	,187*	0,011	−0,042	0,044	0,085	,179*
	0,000	.	0,039	0,907	0,644	0,630	0,353	0,048
CI	,759**	,187*	–	0,142	−0,151	,431**	−,232*	−,216*
	0,000	0,039	.	0,118	0,096	0,000	0,010	0,017
E+	0,046	0,011	0,142	–	,776**	,472**	,208*	0,036
	0,615	0,907	0,118	.	0,000	0,000	0,021	0,696
E−	-,218*	−0,042	−0,151	,776**	–	−0,054	,262**	0,109
	0,016	0,644	0,096	0,000	.	0,555	0,003	0,231
E	,316**	0,044	,431**	,472**	−0,054	–	−0,086	−0,136
	0,000	0,630	0,000	0,000	0,555	.	0,347	0,136
Op	−0,113	0,085	−,232*	,208*	,262**	−0,086	–	,561**
	0,217	0,353	0,010	0,021	0,003	0,347	.	0,000
T	−0,05	,179*	−,216*	0,036	0,109	−0,136	,561**	–
	0,587	0,048	0,017	0,696	0,231	0,136	0,000	.

** Correlation is significant at the 0.01 level (2-tailed).
* Correlation is significant at the 0.05 level (2-tailed).

The next conclusions can be drawn from Table 4.

Made Versus Solved. It can be noted that the more confusions are made (CI+), the more[2] confusions are solved (CI−). Similarly, the more errors made (E+), the more (see Footnote 2) errors solved (E−). This makes sense, since issues that are not made cannot be solved. Yet, these two correlations are important to interpret the following results.

Made/solved Versus Total. The more confusions made (CI+), the more (see Footnote 2) remain in the final model (CI). The more errors made (E+), the more (see Footnote 2) remain in the final model (E). This appears to be obvious but given the previously discussed correlation between confusions/errors made and confusions/errors solved, it is important to verify that not all issues are solved in the end. This also explains why solving more confusions/errors (CI−/E−) does not result in less confusions/errors in the final model (CI/E).

Making/Solving Versus Operations and Time. Making more confusions (CI+) does not per se cost more operations (Op) or time (T). Solving more confusions (CI−) costs more[3] operations (Op) and more (see Footnote 2) time (T). Interestingly, making and solving errors are both related with more (see Footnote 2) operations (Op), and more (see Footnote 3) time (T). This is consistent with the findings by Bolle and Claes [19].

---

[2] Statistically significant result.
[3] Results are not statistically significant.

Confusions Versus Errors. The most interesting part of Table 4 however, is the relation between confusions and errors. Making more confusions (CI+) is related to making more (see Footnote 3) errors (E+), solving less (see Footnote 2) errors (E−) and more (see Footnote 2) errors remaining (E). Solving confusions (CI−) is not found to be related to making, solving, or remaining errors. Remaining confusions (CI) is related to making more (see Footnote 3) errors (E+), solving less (see Footnote 3) errors (E−), and to more (see Footnote 2) errors remaining (E).

In summary, these are statistically (in)significant indications of a positive relation between confusions (CI+/CI−/CI) and errors (E+/E−/E). However, the above tests neglect the *timing* of confusions and errors. Since we assume a causal relation between confusion and errors, it is more precise to verify whether more errors are made/solved *at the time* that more confusion exists in the model. This does not proof causality, but temporal ordering is a necessary condition for causality (on top of correlation). Let us now examine this in more detail.

4.2 More Errors are Made when More Confusion Exists in the Model

For the analysis of the relation between errors made (e+) during modeling and the number of confusions existing in the model (ci), only those entries in the dataset are selected where errors are made. Note that a single operation can make one error and at the same time solve another one. The net effect on e is zero, but this record is still included. The correlation results are summarized in Table 5.

Table 5. Relation between confusion and errors made (displaying Spearman's rho and the 2-tailed significance)

N=493	e+	p_{e+}
ci	0	,312**
	0,992	0,000
[ci]	0,044	,177**
	0,328	0,000

** *Correlation is significant at the 0.01 level.*

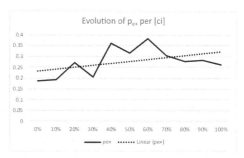

As can be seen, there is no statistically significant relation in our dataset between the number of errors made (e+) and the absolute number of confusions present in the partial models at the time of the error (ci). The reason for this may be because the number of errors that can be made is dependent on the number of operations of the modeler. Therefore, the data was normalized. The number of errors made is considered per operation made (p_{e+} = e+/op). It represents the chance for an operation to be an error. The number of confusions in the partial models is considered relative to the maximum number in the model ([ci] = ci/max(ci)). This gives a more correct comparison between models and between number of operations. The correlation analysis now shows a sta-tistically significant relation.

The chart in Table 5 shows a more detailed view of the relation in our dataset. It represents the deciles of the confusion level ([ci]) and sets out the average chance to make errors (p_{e+}), as well as a linear trendline of this relation. In general, it can be concluded that the more relative confusions were present in the partial model, the more (see Footnote 2) the chance was to make errors.

4.3 Less Errors are Solved when More Confusion Exists in the Model

For the analysis of the relation between errors solved ($e-$) during modeling and the number of confusions existing in the model (ci), only those entries in the dataset are selected when errors are solved. The correlation results are summarized in Table 6.

Table 6. Relation between confusion and errors solved (displaying Spearman's rho and the 2-tailed significance)

N=397	e-	[e-]	$p_{[e-]}$
ci	-0,022	-,228**	-0,046
	0,661	0,000	0,363
[ci]	-0,017	-,173**	-,147**
	0,739	0,001	0,003

** Correlation is significant at the 0.01 level.

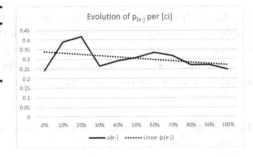

Again, there is no statistically significant relation in the dataset between the number of errors solved ($e-$) and the absolute number of confusions in the partial models (ci). The number of errors that can be solved depends on the number of errors existing in the model and on the number of operations of the modeler. The data was again normalized for more correct comparison. The number of errors solved is considered per number of errors existing ([$e-$] = $e-/e$) and per operation made ($p_{[e-]}$ = [$e-$]/op). The correlation analysis now shows statistically significant relations.

The chart in Table 6 shows the more detailed view of the relation in our dataset. It represents the deciles of the confusion level ([ci]) and sets out the average chance to solve errors ($p_{[e-]}$), as well as a linear trendline of this relation. In general, it can be concluded that the more relative confusions were present in the partial model, the less (see Footnote 2) chance there was to solve errors.

4.4 Which Confusions Cause which Errors?

Next, the effects of individual confusions, irresolutions, and errors are studied. We limited the study to those variables who have been observed at least 50 times, which can be derived from Table 1. As such, the effect of confusions *multiple start events*

(c_S), *multiple end events* (c_E), *multiple optional sequence flows towards non-gateway* (c_{Jx}), *no label for edge departing from XOR splits* (c_{Lx}), and irresolution *one gateway combines a join and split feature* (i_C) on the errors *not all paths are closed* (e_P), *multiple optional sequence flows from non-gateway* (e_{Sx}), and *gateway with only 1 incoming and 1 outgoing sequence flow* (e_{1e}) are calculated. The results are summarized in Table 7. They are discussed below, column per column.

Table 7. Correlations at issue level (unexpected signs are marked in grey) (displaying Spearman's rho and the 2-tailed significance)

	pe$_{P+}$	pe$_{Sx+}$	Pe$_{1e+}$	pe+	p[e$_{P-}$]	p[e$_{Sx-}$]	p[e$_{1e-}$]	p[e-]
c_S	0,155	,222*	,108*	,216**	0,166	,448*	0,044	-,203**
	0,267	0,04	0,043	0	0,347	0,017	0,418	0
c_E	,422**	-0,028	,177**	,162**	-0,152	-0,228	0,099	0,031
	0,002	0,796	0,001	0	0,392	0,243	0,069	0,543
c_{Jx}	0,1	,255*	-0,012	0,037	-0,294	0,146	-0,07	-,107*
	0,477	0,018	0,819	0,409	0,091	0,46	0,2	0,032
c_{Lx}	,353**	0,141	,206**	,239**	0,079	0,15	,220**	,275**
	0,01	0,197	0	0	0,657	0,447	0	0
i_C	0,136	,216*	0,003	0,068	-0,275	-0,134	-0,008	-0,08
	0,331	0,046	0,951	0,132	0,115	0,498	0,879	0,111
[ci]	,496**	,247*	,126*	,177**	-,517**	0,134	0,025	-,147**
	0	0,026	0,018	0	0,002	0,522	0,644	0,003

** Correlation is significant at the 0.01 level.
* Correlation is significant at the 0.05 level (2-tailed).

Not closing all paths of the model (e_{P+}) happens more (see Footnote 2) when there are multiple end events in the model (c_E) and when more edges from xor gateways are not labeled (c_{Lx}). We expect that **using multiple end events *causes* the modeler to forget to close all paths in the model (H1)**, whereas we do not assume a *causal* relation between not labeling edges and forgetting to close all paths. On the other hand, these confusions do not appear to relate (see Footnote 3) with *solving* this error.

Using an implicit xor split gateway (e_{Sx+}) is not allowed by the BPMN syntax. This error was made more (see Footnote 2) when there were multiple start events (c_S), when the modeler used also more implicit xor join gateways (c_{Jx}) and gateways that combined split and join functionalities (i_C). We propose that **people who use implicit gateways are not always aware of when this is allowed (c_S, c_{Jx}, i_C) and when not (e_{Sx}) (H2)**. Surprisingly, these errors are more (see Footnote 2) *solved* when there are more start events in the model.

Having gateways in the model that are not used for splitting or joining multiple paths (e_{1e+}) happens more (see Footnote 2) when there are multiple start events (c_S) or multiple end events (c_E) in the model, and when there are more edges from xor gateways without labels (c_{Lx}). **Perhaps having multiple start and end events increases the structural complexity of the model, *causing* the modeler to forget adding the postponed paths for which a gateway was already created (H3)**. We do not assume a *causal* relation between the labels of edges and forgetting some paths at gateways, which is supported by the unexpected correlation with *solving* these errors.

This more detailed analysis does not bring conclusive answers. It contributes to the study by adding preliminary insights that can be derived from the statistics. They are formulated in the form of hypotheses (H1-H3), which can be studied in future work.

5   Discussion

5.1   Impact

The impact on research of this study is that it provides (additional) empirical evidence for a number of proposed process modeling guidelines of the Seven Process Modeling Guidelines (7PMG) [14], Ten Process Modeling Guidelines (10PMG) [15], Concrete Syntax Patterns (CSP) [17], Abstract Syntax Patterns (ASP) [18], and Quality Indicators (QI) [16]. The general lack of such evidence on the content, interrelations, and relevance of these guidelines is denounced in multiple critiques [20–23]. The guidelines to which supporting (additional) evidence is formulated in this paper, are listed below.

- *Use 1 start and 1 end event* (7PMG) and *Use no more than 2 start and end events* (10PMG). This relates to confusions S, E, Os, Oe; errors Ose, Oes; and hypotheses H1, H2, H3.
- *Model as structured as possible* (7PMG, 10PMG, ASP) and *Use design patterns to avoid mismatch* (10PMG). This proposes to use explicit and paired gateways, which should avoid confusions Sa, Jx; irresolutions C, W, I, N, T, DS; and errors Sx, Ja, 1e; and it relates to hypothesis H2.
- *Use explicit representation* (CSP). This may refer to avoiding implicit events and gateways, which is related to confusions Os, Oe, Sa, Jx; irresolutions C, I, T, DS; errors Ose, Oes, Sx, Ja; and hypothesis H2.
- *Limit the difference in the number of input/output flows between splits and joins* (QI) refers to both pervious examples, because it is realized by structured modeling and/or using explicit gateways.
- *Use of textual annotation* (CSP) and *Naming guidance* (CSP). This links to the use and format of text in models, which relates to the confusion Lx, the irresolution La, the error Ls, and the discussion about Lx in Sect. 4.4.

The impact on practice is that the research provides extra insights into the relation between confusion and errors to practitioners. Even in models that are made as input for computer programs, where only pure syntax errors could seem to be important, it now appears to be important to avoid confusing constructs as well, since they may cause modeling errors during modeling. Besides the modelers, this research should also support teachers. It is always easier to train modelers to apply certain guidelines when the reason *why* they are important can be illustrated. This paper contributes to such illustration of the importance to also focus on avoiding confusion, being a potential cause for errors. Third, tool developers have spent a great deal of effort to support modelers in avoiding syntax errors by highlighting them or by providing an overview of the syntax errors after modeling. The current study provides input to add a level of *warnings* to their support features (just as programming editors do).

5.2 Limitations and Future Work

As discussed in the introduction, the scope of the research is limited. The reduced language, the artificial case and artificial modelers limit the ecological validity of the research. The focus on syntax only, on the modeler's contribution only, on one case only, and the lack of focus on consequences for the readers of a model put a limit to the external validity of the research. Therefore, one should be cautious to generalize the relations discussed above. The research should be considered as an explorative empirical study that provides initial insights and hypotheses for further research.

In Sect. 4.4, three hypotheses are formulated, which can be studied further. But more generally, it would be useful to study systematically the effect of all listed confusions and irresolutions, both on making errors during modeling and on the final user understandability of the model. Further, although methodologically more challenging, it is advised to include not only pragmatic (cf. user-understanding), but also semantic quality into the research. Using the same artificial setup where a modeler is instructed to create a diagram representing the knowledge described in a textual description, it is possible to use a similar methodology as the one applied here to derive the timing and type of semantic errors (missing, wrong, redundant, inconsistent, and unnecessary constructs), and to study their interrelations and links with syntax and understanding.

6 Conclusion

The data of 122 (of 146) modeling sessions was used to build a dataset containing the timing of all operations to construct the model. By adding whether each operation initiated or solved certain types of syntax issues, we were able to study the relation between confusing and wrong syntax constructs. In general, the conclusion is that confusion may lead to errors and therefore it should be avoided as much as real errors. The contribution of this paper is not in this conclusion per se, but in its detailed proof (31.588 operations were analyzed, and 2.489 syntax issues were documented), and explanatory knowledge that is added to this conclusion. It provides interesting knowledge about the presence of various types of confusing constructs and syntax errors and their potential (causal) relations.

References

1. Moreno-Montes De Oca, I., Snoeck, M., Reijers, H.A., et al.: A systematic literature review of studies on business process modeling quality. Inf. Softw. Technol. **58**, 187–205 (2015)
2. Aguilar-Savén, R.S.: Business process modelling: review and framework. Int. J. Prod. Econ. **90**, 129–149 (2004)
3. Recker, J.: Opportunities and constraints: the current struggle with BPMN. Bus. Process Manag. J. **16**, 181–201 (2010)

4. Grosskopf, A., Edelman, J., Weske, M.: Tangible business process modeling – methodology and experiment design. In: Rinderle-Ma, S., Sadiq, S., Leymann, F. (eds.) BPM 2009. LNBIP, vol. 43, pp. 489–500. Springer, Heidelberg (2010). https://doi.org/10.1007/978-3-642-12186-9_46

5. Hassan, N., Recker, J., Bernhard, E.: A study of the use of business process modelling at Suncorp, Brisbane, Australia (2011)

6. Gruhn, V., Laue, R.: What business process modelers can learn from programmers. Sci. Comput. Program. **65**, 4–13 (2007)

7. Mendling, J., Verbeek, H.M.W., Van Dongen, B.F., et al.: Detection and prediction of errors in EPCs of the SAP reference model. Data Knowl. Eng. **64**, 312–329 (2008)

8. Claes, J., Vanderfeesten, I., Gailly, F., et al.: The structured process modeling method (SPMM) - what is the best way for me to construct a process model? Decis. Support Syst. **100**, 57–76 (2017)

9. zur Muehlen, M., Recker, J.: How much language is enough? theoretical and practical use of the business process modeling notation. In: Bellahsène, Z., Léonard, M. (eds.) CAiSE 2008. LNCS, vol. 5074, pp. 465–479. Springer, Heidelberg (2008). https://doi.org/10.1007/978-3-540-69534-9_35

10. De Bock, J., Claes, J.: The origin and evolution of syntax errors in simple sequence flow models in BPMN. In: Matulevičius, R., Dijkman, R. (eds.) CAiSE 2018. LNBIP, vol. 316, pp. 155–166. Springer, Cham (2018). https://doi.org/10.1007/978-3-319-92898-2_13

11. Figl, K.: Comprehension of procedural visual business process models - a literature review. Bus. Inf. Syst. Eng. **59**, 41–71 (2017)

12. De Meyer, P., Claes, J.: An overview of process model quality literature - The Comprehensive Process Model Quality Framework (2018)

13. Becker, J., Rosemann, M., von Uthmann, C.: Guidelines of business process modeling. In: van der Aalst, W., Desel, J., Oberweis, A. (eds.) Business Process Management. LNCS, vol. 1806, pp. 30–49. Springer, Heidelberg (2000). https://doi.org/10.1007/3-540-45594-9_3

14. Mendling, J., Reijers, H.A., Van der Aalst, W.M.P.: Seven process modeling guidelines (7PMG). Inf. Softw. Technol. **52**, 127–136 (2010)

15. Mendling, J., Sánchez-González, L., García, F., et al.: Thresholds for error probability measures of business process models. J. Syst. Softw. **85**, 1188–1197 (2012)

16. Sánchez-González, L., García, F., Ruiz, F., et al.: Quality indicators for business process models from a gateway complexity perspective. Inf. Softw. Technol. **54**, 1159–1174 (2012)

17. La Rosa, M., Ter Hofstede, A.H.M., Wohed, P., et al.: Managing process model complexity via concrete syntax modifications. IEEE Trans. Ind. Informatics. **7**, 255–265 (2011)

18. La Rosa, M., Wohed, P., Mendling, J., et al.: Managing process model complexity via abstract syntax modifications. IEEE Trans. Ind. Informatics. **7**, 614–629 (2011)

19. Bolle, J., Claes, J.: Investigating the trade-off between the effectiveness and efficiency of process modeling. In: Daniel, F., Sheng, Quan Z., Motahari, H. (eds.) BPM 2018. LNBIP, vol. 342, pp. 121–132. Springer, Cham (2019). https://doi.org/10.1007/978-3-030-11641-5_10

20. Chen, C.: Top 10 unsolved information visualization problems. IEEE Comput. Graph. Appl. **25**, 12–16 (2005)

21. Nelson, H.J., Poels, G., Genero, M., et al.: A conceptual modeling quality framework. Softw. Qual. J. **20**, 201–228 (2012)

22. Rockwell, S., Bajaj, A.: COGEVAL: applying cognitive theories to evaluate conceptual models. Adv. Top. Database Res. **4**, 255–282 (2005)

23. Rogers, Y., Scaife, M.: How can interactive multimedia facilitate learning? In: Lee, J. (ed.) 1st International Workshop on Intelligence and Multimodality in Multimedia Interfaces. Research and Applications, pp. 1–25. AAAI (1998)

A Case Study of Executive Functions in Real Process Modeling Sessions

Ilona Wilmont[1,2(✉)], Erik Barendsen[1], and Stijn Hoppenbrouwers[1,2]

[1] Institute for Computing and Information Sciences, Radboud University Nijmegen,
P.O. Box 9010, 6500 GL Nijmegen, The Netherlands
{i.wilmont,e.barendsen}@cs.ru.nl
[2] HAN University of Applied Sciences,
P.O. Box 2217, 6802 CE Arnhem, The Netherlands
stijn.hoppenbrouwers@han.nl

Abstract. Cognitive aspects like executive control functions, reasoning and abstraction have a crucial influence on modeling performance. Yet how are executive functions used in real modeling sessions and what individual differences exist? In this case study we analyse observations of three modeling sessions according to a coding scheme for behavioural observation of executive functions, reasoning and abstraction. We complement the findings with a qualitative, thick description of the sessions. We find that the modelers have unique styles in how they use executive control, that there appears to be a hierarchy in when specific executive functions are used, and that the use of executive control alone does not guarantee modeling progress. Greater awareness of the effects of executive control use in real modeling settings can be very helpful in training modelers to optimize their skills.

Keywords: Executive functions · Process modeling · Individual differences

1 Introduction

What happens in terms of complex cognitive processes during the progression of a modeling session? High-quality modeling performance is associated with behaviours like reflection, elaborate relational reasoning, monitoring model structure, monitoring goals, testing hypotheses and scoping of variables. Low-quality modeling behaviour, on the contrary, is characterized by a lack of the aforementioned behaviours and a strong focus only on visible output [11,16,17]. High-quality modeling behaviours show significant overlap with *executive control functions*: an umbrella term for both fundamental cognitive operations that allow organized behaviour to emerge, as well as complex metacognitive behaviours such as monitoring, planning, reasoning and abstracting [20]. The role of executive control in modeling is still elusive, but has the potential to provide valuable insights in how to optimize modeling training. We therefore pose the following

© Springer Nature Switzerland AG 2019
H. A. Proper and J. Stirna (Eds.): CAiSE 2019 Workshops, LNBIP 349, pp. 17–28, 2019.
https://doi.org/10.1007/978-3-030-20948-3_2

research question: *How is executive control used in real modeling sessions and what individual differences exist?* In this study, we analyse executive control in relation to the process quality variables 'shared understanding' and 'shared consent'. We perform a comparative qualitative analysis of a small set of modeling sessions in which we triangulate the results from applying a coding method [21] with thick descriptions [10].

2   The Question of a Good Model

What constitutes a high-quality modeling result is subject to intense debate. Different types of human behaviour lead to a certain model quality, which can be theoretically described. However, the ultimate purpose of a model is to convey a message to the stakeholders for whom it was made. If this is not minimally achieved, one can question the relevance of all other aspects of model quality. In this brief literature overview, we describe our variables of interest.

Shared Understanding and Consent: One answer is that quality can never be objectively determined without considering the context, in this case the modeling process and the people performing it. The quality of any creative process can be defined by studying the flow of the *process* itself, its *content* and the *skills* required [2]. This is observable from the modelers' interactions, during which they reflect on content using their skills. To create a model that conveys effective communication, modelers firstly need to achieve the quality goal of *shared understanding* [13]. Do they comprehend that which is being expressed in their diagram? Secondly, *shared consent* becomes relevant. Are modelers in agreement that the model meets its intended purpose? In this study we limit modeling process quality to these two goals.

Reasoning and Monitoring: High quality modeling performance, associated with reasoning and monitoring [16], may be said to either lead directly to increased shared understanding and possibly consent, or lead to a better model which facilitates shared understanding and consent. Reasoning and Monitoring are the executive functions most directly concerned with manipulation of the content of the modeling discussion, and they likely have intricate, bi-directional relations. Reasoning facilitates the translation of domain knowledge into modeling notation [14] and makes the modeler consciously aware of his domain knowledge. Explanations, discussions about model structure, hypothesis testing, interaction with peers, inconsistency detection and prompts for model revisions are all correlated with strong modeling skills [16]. Using these skills to explain complicated mechanisms helps to create metacognitive awareness of potential faulty logic behind a mental model, facilitating attempts to correct it [15,16]. Monitoring allows the modeler to pay attention to abstract goals and procedures and to keep the model structure in mind [12,16,17]. Directly related to structure is the ability to determine the relevant scope, which provides a focus for the entire modeling process and allows the modelers to define their goals and purposes [19]. This may contribute greatly to shared understanding and consent.

Abstraction: In general, strong abstraction skills allow modelers to enhance their reasoning [14]. But how might we observe strong abstraction skills? The brain has dedicated areas for responding to challenges on different levels of abstraction [4]. Also, the higher the abstraction level on which reasoning is required, the more brainpower it costs and the harder it is to perform the task. Modelers use abstraction skills to actively connect generic concepts to concrete activities and objects through generalisation and instantiation [18]. This allows a model to become meaningful, which is vital to comprehension [1,9]. Whether comprehension is achieved typically requires acts of monitoring that relate concrete knowledge to model structure, such as testing hypotheses and asking questions. Additionally, concrete knowledge must be available in order to instantiate. The better the integrity of the memory representing this knowledge, the easier it is to form an abstraction [6]. However, concrete knowledge gaps can result in faulty conceptions of a domain, a failure to monitor understanding and progress, and thereby hamper success at problem solving [3,5]. Additionally, if concepts turn out to be too abstract to understand, unconscious reduction of abstraction level may take place by retreating to familiar mental structures, relying on fixed procedures while working, and discussing specific examples rather than a whole set [7].

Initiation and Switching: Initiation and switching are not primarily concerned with manipulating the content of the modeling discussion. Rather, they influence the structure of a discussion, based on an abstraction of what the content is about, and whether the discussion is moving towards its goal or not. So in essence, they can be said to build on Reasoning and Monitoring. Initiating a task can mean engaging in new topics, proposing new or alternative ideas and problem solutions or initiating a corrective action. The modeler must have a solid understanding of the situation at hand. Based on that he must judge whether the task he is about to propose is relevant or not. The same argument can be made for switching focus during a modeling task. Often, switching focus and initiating tasks go hand in hand. These strategies can prevent a modeler from getting stuck on problem features or missing out relevant opportunities [9]. The challenge about observing initiation and switching is to determine where the action happens, and whether the action is deemed relevant by the other session participants.

Planning: This is a metacognitive skill building on all other executive functions to guide the modeling process and consecutive actions. It requires a proactive attitude, which means that the modeler should anticipate to prepare for, intervene in or control an expected occurrence or situation, especially a complex one [8]. It stands to reason that planning skills, given that they require an overview of the situation, would be related to having stronger executive control skills in the other domains as well.

From this brief literature overview, we deduce the following questions to guide data analysis:

- How are instances of the Reasoning, Monitoring, Abstraction, Initiation and Switching groups used in a real modeling session?
- What individual differences in use of Reasoning, Monitoring, Abstraction, Initiation and Switching can be observed?
- How is Planning used in relation to Reasoning and Monitoring in a real modeling session?
- How can the process of achieving shared understanding be characterized in terms of executive functions in a real modeling session?
- How can the process of achieving shared consent be characterized in terms of executive functions in a real modeling session?

3 Method

This is an inductive, qualitative study, centred around the individual, who makes small contributions to a group. Data was collected within a series of unstructured observations of modeling sessions. Observations took place within a Dutch organisation in the collective sector for six months. The organisation's task was to monitor retirement funds. The observed projects' goals were to chart the organisation's business processes, currently executed mostly by hand, and to design new ones for the purpose of automation. The first author spent time at the company both during and outside of the modeling sessions, to get to know the participants and observe them in different settings. Observations were entirely passive, no interventions were done.

Participants and Sessions: For the scope of this study, we included three modeling sessions performed by three experts in different configurations: the project leader, the business analyst and the lead architect. They were externally hired from different companies and had between 2–5 years of relevant experience in business analysis. Modeling sessions lasted for 1–2 h each, with a minimum group size of two. They were recorded in video format with the participants' consent. Furthermore, written documentation resulting from sessions was collected and photos of the final models were taken to complement the session recordings. The sessions took place in rooms equipped with a beamer and a flip chart board. The models under discussion had been printed and put up on the walls. These external working memory offloading opportunities were used extensively. Interaction during the session was not explicitly structured. Models were adapted and contradictory issues discussed.

Data Analysis: We analysed our data from two different perspectives. Firstly, we used the coding scheme we developed in an earlier study [21]. All recordings were fully transcribed, loaded into Atlas.ti and coded. The unit of analysis, represented by a single quotation, was a participant's full turn, terminated only by an interruption or a natural reaction from another participant. Pauses between utterances were taken to belong to a single turn unless they exceeded 10 s. Each quotation was assigned a selection of the following codes:

- a unique identifier for the modeler
- a level of relational abstraction
- a level of semantic abstraction
- instances of the reasoning, monitoring, planning, initiation or switching groups

Semantic and relational abstraction were compulsory for every quotation including more than backchanneling or responses using simply 'yes' or 'no'. Instances of the other groups were assigned as was deemed relevant. After coding, the total number of occurrences of codes were counted and compared per session, for each participant.

Secondly, to complement the coded data with contextual data, interesting episodes were manually selected from the sessions and subjected to thick description [10] according to the following template:

- Session no
- Episode timestamp
- Characterisation tag
- Episode description
- What is remarkable about this episode?
- What precedes the episode?
- Relation to episode events?
- What follows the episode
- Relation to episode events?
- Do they achieve shared understanding? How does this become apparent?
- Do they achieve shared consent (explicit agreement)? How does this become apparent?
- Fragment lead

The characterisation tag is a one-line summary of the episode based on the episode description, which emerged during analysis and was reused whenever possible for similar episodes. The aspects of interest in relation to executive control, reasoning or abstraction were explicitly recorded. For the purpose of context, events preceding and following aspects of interest were noted. 'Fragment lead' refers to the person who mostly leads the discussion. In total, 22 relevant episodes were selected from the 3 sessions; 15 from the first session with all 3 modelers, 4 from the second session with the lead architect and the project leader, and 3 from the third session involving the business analyst and the project leader. The shortest episode lasted 1:52:43 min, whereas the longest episode has a duration of 24:22:24 min.

Validity: We used naturalistic observation to minimize validity threats associated with studying complex skills in isolation, such as oversimplification for ease of measurement, not considering its larger context and removing the true incentive for performing a skill optimally. We used a predefined executive functions scheme, based on both prior observations and the enormous existing body of literature on the topic. However, using a predefined scheme carries a risk of missing relevant aspects, and it does not provide a level of detail that allows one to see how consecutive interactions between participants lead to certain outcomes. Therefore we triangulated the code counts with thick descriptions of interesting episodes. Non-random selection of episodes carries a risk of bias, but in this case we were particularly interested in the moments of disagreement or active peer refinement as opposed to a well-structured discussion flow to see how abstraction and executive functions were used. For the purpose of hypothesis generation, we considered this to be acceptable.

4 Results

Figure 1 shows how many times the project leader, business analyst and architect used the annotated executive functions during the entire durations of the three analyzed sessions. This figure will be referenced throughout the description of the results.

How are Instances of the Reasoning, Monitoring, Abstraction, Initiation and Switching Groups Used in a Real Modeling Session? We found the use of these executive functions to differ with the phase of the discussion and the modelers' goals. However, we observed several prominently recurring patterns. First of all, the use of instantiation with highly concrete examples worked successfully to clarify complex issues. This requires the modeler to have a structured mental model of the context, and sound working memory capacity to make assumptions to fill up potential mental model gaps. If the modeler lacks a solid mental model, he will be able to perform the strategy but the content is less relevant. Second, the Reasoning functions of *Inference*, *Instantiate* and *Case discrimination* were favorites, as well as the Monitoring functions *Refine peer*, *Reflect* and *Test proposition* (Fig. 1). These functions were combined to ensure that all participants were still on the same track. Third, Monitoring functions like *Scoping*, *Inconsistency detection* and *Refine peer* were mostly used once comprehension of both content and context had been achieved. Fourth, rephrasing information and using it in a new line of reasoning was a good way to ensure that comprehension was truly achieved. Rephrasing alone was not enough to bring out potential inconsistencies. Fifth, the modeler initiating the most model writing was often the same person who was in the lead and had the best mental model at that point in time. Finally, extensive use of Switching may point to a deviation in focus. Therefore, evaluation of context with Monitoring functions and Instantiation was crucial when discussing switches.

What Individual Differences in Use of Reasoning, Monitoring, Abstraction, Initiation and Switching Can Be Observed? Three participants were observed across three sessions. The architect showed a clear leading role, expressing a lot of structure and working in a highly goal-oriented fashion. He was the only one to speak of goals at the start of a session. He used *Inference*, *Explain*, *Case discrimination* and *Instantiate*, used Abstraction functionally, to

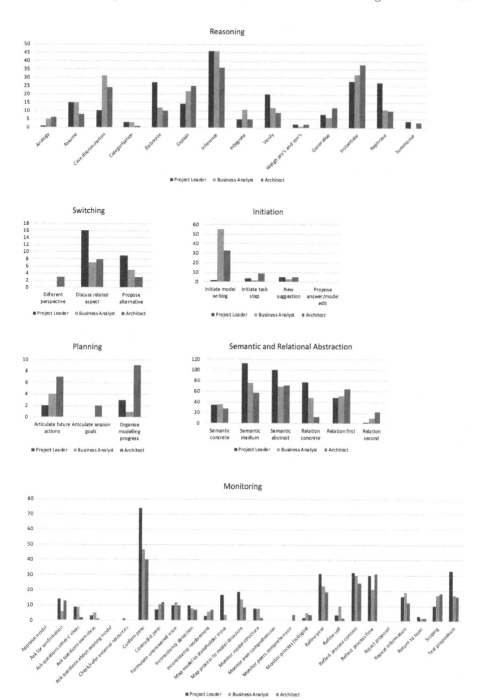

Fig. 1. Code counts for Reasoning, Switching, Initiation, Planning, Abstraction and Monitoring for each modeler.

test hypotheses and to create comprehension of the generic context. Interestingly, he used the least concrete relations and concepts, although for the concepts, this difference is negligible. It could be because he used his concrete concepts only in very targeted cases of trying to clarify something. He was the only one to continuously monitor his peers' comprehension, paid attention to *Scoping*, and would not continue a discussion until he was satisfied, even if it cost extra time. He made effective use of model writing, and whenever his mental model was incomplete, he would make and test assumptions to fill the gaps (Fig. 1).

The business analyst began sessions by silently processing information, but once he detected an inconsistency or had achieved comprehension of something, he would immediately take the lead. He effectively used Monitoring functions, and was particularly strong on *Test proposition* and *Scoping*, along with *Inference*, *Instantiate* and *Explain*, to explain himself and to safeguard the relevance of all that was being discussed (Fig. 1). He too monitored his own and his peers' comprehension well, albeit not as often or as explicitly as the architect. He did use model writing effectively, particularly in the session without the architect. Both higher-level and concrete abstractions were used easily and effectively.

The project leader showed the least functional Reasoning and Monitoring of all participants, but appeared to be in continuous search of comprehension by asking questions, proposing alternatives and offering input, waiting for his peers to provide confirmation, refinement or rejection. Many times, his input was unstructured and came as a surprise to his peers. He used *Elaborate*, *Rephrase* and *Test proposition* significantly more often than his peers (Fig. 1). Unfortunately, *Elaborate* invited him to deviate from the topic, while he used *Rephrase* and *Test proposition* to try and comprehend his peers' explanations. But he provided few contributions out of his own initiative. His use of Abstraction was curious, making instantiations with semantically abstract concepts, which bypassed the point of hypothesis testing. Although his actual use of executive functions does not differ significantly from the others, it is remarkable that his contributions appear to have the least impact on the discussion, even slowing it down, receiving continuous corrections and refinements from his peers, which he accepts. However, in many instances, he still failed to use the new knowledge in future utterances.

How is Planning Used in Relation to Reasoning and Monitoring in a Real Modeling Session? In all three sessions, Planning had only a minimal role in the session, not becoming relevant until the end when decisions about the follow-ups had to be made. Occasionally, a future act would be formulated during the session, and during one session goal planning was done at the start of the session, by the modeler with the strongest mental model. It appeared that Planning required a form of structure and an activated mental goal. If doing this at the start of a session, it implies that the modeler is strong in structuring and aware of his goals. However, it appeared that the end of the session was the most natural moment to engage in acts of planning. For one, the primary goal of shared understanding had been achieved, and a complete structure had been formed. Also, at the end of the session the need to formulate next steps was most pressing, so there was an external stimulus. In practical use, Planning appeared to be the most metacognitive of all executive functions, being engaged in only once the other ones have 'done the work', so to speak. The architect was strongest on Planning aspects (Fig. 1), which matches with his continuous leading role in the sessions.

How Can the Process of Achieving Shared Understanding Be Characterized in Terms of Executive Functions in a Real Modeling Session? Shared understanding appeared to be the main, if often unspoken, goal of every session. As long as any single modeler in the group sensed a discrepancy in comprehension, the entire discussion would be geared towards achieving a uniform idea, even if it thoroughly disrupted the flow of the session. Most surprisingly, the modelers went to great lengths to explain issues even if they had already been marked as irrelevant. However, as long as the modelers were still searching for shared understanding, the discussion was less structured, many options were being explored, modelers were making alternative proposals, or simply were silently processing information. Reasoning was less prominently used when the modelers were indecisive and hesitant. If the mental model was not clear, Instantiation and Monitoring functions were used in order to fix the mental model, after which Reasoning and the use of higher abstraction levels could take place. Planning, Initiation and Switching did not yet have any role during this phase. However, if some had achieved shared understanding and others had not, highly concrete instantiations of the aspects under discussion were made to clarify issues. Occasionally, generalisation was also used to draw a more complete picture of the situation. During these moments, abstraction switches became most clearly visible. Once shared understanding had been achieved, those with a strong mental model became very structured, made notes, drew diagrams on flip-overs and engaged in constructive discussions using a wide variety of Reasoning and Monitoring functions. Abstraction switches to higher levels to create context were more prominently used in explanations, which were often tested using concrete examples.

How Can the Process of Achieving Shared Consent Be Characterized in Terms of Executive Functions in a Real Modeling Session? In all three sessions, achieving shared consent remained implicit for most of the session. The only clues we can observe are the fact that the discussion always continues until all participants either explicitly agree or do not explicitly disagree. As consent became related to Planning issues such as next steps or representation of models to stakeholders, it did become more explicitly visible, as modelers made proposals and asked for explicit confirmation. Thus, in a sense we could say that consent follows from understanding, and that any act of asking for confirmation or proposing something in a questioning tone is in fact a prompt for testing shared consent.

5 Discussion

This study is part of a set of studies aiming to generate working hypotheses about how reasoning and executive control are being used in modeling sessions, how they may influence session progress and the final outcome. We make no claims about generic truths. In this study, we asked "How is executive control used in real modeling sessions and what individual differences exist?" There is no single answer to this question, but in Sect. 4 we have described several aspects related to this question. For now, we choose to finish with a set of working hypotheses (WH) which will serve as research questions for future studies.

WH 1: Semantic and Relational Abstraction Do Not Necessarily Correlate. We observed that simply speaking on a high semantic abstraction level did not always lead to successful abstractions, if we take 'acceptance by peers' as a criterion. The project leader in particular used abstract semantic concepts elaborately, but was continuously corrected by his peers with arguments involving explicit switching between semantic abstraction levels, accompanied by explicit relations between the concepts on different abstraction levels through generalisation or instantiation. This could imply that he was speaking the abstract words without truly being aware of their meaning. It was also curious to see that he used hardly any second-level relations at all. When examining abstraction skills, it may therefore be more meaningful to consider relational level abstraction as indicator for abstraction skills, including switches in semantic abstraction levels accompanied by generalisation or instantiation. Additionally, given that the use of all abstraction levels varies a lot between the sessions and the participants, we will perform a further analysis of the abstraction data in a future study.

WH 2: The Use of Executive Control Alone Does Not Necessarily Correlate With Modeling Progress. In educational frameworks, such as [16], and many other executive control observation frameworks, it appears to be enough to pinpoint the occurrence of the behaviour to conclude something about the quality of an individual's entire strategy. In our study, this did not always appear to be the case. For the business analyst and the architect, their goal-oriented, structured behaviour was clearly reflected in their use of executive control. However, for the project leader, this was less so. He did talk a lot, and in doing so, used just as many executive functions as his peers. However, when examining the context of his utterances, in many cases they were peer-refined, corrected or sometimes declared out of scope. They were not being used to further the knowledge building process. The interesting thing is that there are no clear key functions to be pinpointed that he used differently than the others that might explain his less effective behaviour. The only clues might be that he was much less focused on *Scoping* than his peers, and used a lot of *Elaborate* which allowed him to go off topic. So it is crucial to monitor the content of the utterances and their effects on the discussion in addition to which functions are used. Whether this can efficiently be integrated in a coding method is an open question. One difference with existing executive control frameworks is that they all originate from educational research involving children who are still developing executive functions. It might be that adults have learned how to use them regardless of cognitive capacity, but that cognitive capacity is reflected more in the content of utterances rather than actual function use.

WH 3: There is an Implicit Hierarchy in the Use of Executive Control. In all sessions, there appeared to be a generic tendency to use Reasoning and Monitoring functions as the primary executive functions. Most of the sessions were geared towards achieving shared understanding, and Reasoning and Monitoring contribute most directly to that goal. Switches and Initiation were sporadically used during the discussions when necessary, but mostly only after shared understanding had been achieved about a topic. This might make sense, given that one can only consider something in relation to other things once one has comprehended it. This also allows for higher abstractions to be made. Planning only appeared before or after the discussions, to set goals for the session in question or future sessions.

WH 4: Shared Understanding is of Primary Importance to Strong Modelers. It was interesting to see how frequently shared understanding was prioritized over efficiency, even though efficiency is considered a significant process quality goal [13]. In many cases, it was apparent that no knowledge building for the overall discussion would be achieved by giving detailed explanations of irrelevant utterances, but to those who were leading the discussion, creating a solid understanding of *why* the utterance was irrelevant in relation to the entire discussion was more important than waving it away and achieving quick progress. Especially in the light of achieving shared consent, which follows from understanding, this is desirable strategy.

References

1. Barreteau, O.: The joint use of role-playing games and models regarding negotiation processes: characterization of associations. J. Artif. Soc. Soc. Simul. **6**(2) (2003)
2. Basadur, M.: The Power of Innovation: How to Make Innovation a Way of Life and Put Creative Solutions to Work. Financial Times Management, Upper Saddle River (1995)
3. Brown, A.L.: Metacognition, executive control, self-regulation and other more mysterious mechanisms. In: Weinert, F., Kluwe, R.H. (eds.) Metacognition, Motivation, and Understanding, pp. 65–115. Lawrence Erlbaum Associates, Hillsdale (1987)
4. Christoff, K., Keramatian, K., Gordon, A., Smith, R., Mädler, B.: Prefrontal organization of cognitive control according to levels of abstraction. Brain Res. **1286**, 94–105 (2009)
5. Feltovich, P., Spiro, R., Coulson, R., Feltovich, J.: Collaboration within and among minds: mastering complexity, individually and in groups. In: Koschmann, T. (ed.) CSCL: Theory and Practice of An Emerging Paradigm. Computers, Cognition, and Work, pp. 25–44. Lawrence Erlbaum Associates, Inc., Mahwah (1996)
6. Gazzaniga, M.S., Ivry, R.B., Mangun, G.R.: Cognitive Neuroscience: The Biology of the Mind, 2nd edn. W. W. Norton & Company, New York (2002)

7. Hazzan, O.: Reflections on teaching abstraction and other soft ideas. ACM SIGCSE Bull. **40**(2), 40–43 (2008). https://doi.org/10.1145/1383602.1383631
8. Lee, D., Trauth, E., Farwell, D.: Critical skills and knowledge requirements of IS professionals: a joint academic/industry investigation. MIS Q. **19**(3: Special Issue on IS Curricula and Pedagogy), 313–340 (1995)
9. Lehrer, R., Schauble, L.: Developing model-based reasoning in mathematics and science. J. Appl. Dev. Psychol. **21**(1), 39–48 (2000)
10. Lincoln, Y.S., Guba, E.G.: Naturalistic Inquiry, SAGE Focus Editions, vol. 75, 1st edn. SAGE Publications, Thousand Oaks (1985)
11. Mendling, J., Strembeck, M., Recker, J.: Factors of process model comprehension—Findings from a series of experiments. Decis. Support Syst. **53**(1), 195–206 (2012). https://doi.org/10.1016/j.dss.2011.12.013
12. Persson, A.: Enterprise modelling in practice: situational factors and their influence on adopting a participative approach. Ph.D. thesis, Department of Computer and Systems Sciences, Stockholm University (2001)
13. Ross, D., Goodenough, J., Irvine, C.A.: Software engineering: process, principles, and goals. Computer **8**(5), 17–27 (1975)
14. Salles, P., Bredeweg, B.: A case study of collaborative modelling: building qualitative models in ecology. In: Model Based Systems and Qualitative Reasoning for Intelligent Tutoring Systems, pp. 75–84 (2002)
15. Schwarz, C., et al.: Developing a learning progression for scientific modeling: making scientific modeling accessible and meaningful for learners. J. Res. Sci. Teach. **46**(6), 632–654 (2009)
16. Sins, P.H.M., Savelsbergh, E.R., van Joolingen, W.R.: The Difficult Process of Scientific Modelling: an analysis of novices' reasoning during computer-based modelling. Int. J. Sci. Educ. **27**(14), 1695–1721 (2005)
17. Sutcliffe, A.G., Maiden, N.A.M.: Analysing the novice analyst: cognitive models in software engineering. Int. J. Man Mach. Stud. **36**(5), 719–740 (1992). https://doi.org/10.1016/0020-7373(92)90038-M
18. Theodorakis, M., Analyti, A., Constantopoulos, P., Spyratos, N.: Contextualization as an abstraction mechanism for conceptual modelling. In: Akoka, J., Bouzeghoub, M., Comyn-Wattiau, I., Métais, E. (eds.) ER 1999. LNCS, vol. 1728, pp. 475–490. Springer, Heidelberg (1999). https://doi.org/10.1007/3-540-47866-3_32
19. Van Der Valk, T., Van Driel, J., De Vos, W.: Common characteristics of models in present-day scientific practice. Res. Sci. Educ. **37**(4), 469–488 (2007). https://doi.org/10.1007/s11165-006-9036-3
20. Wilmont, I., Hengeveld, S., Barendsen, E., Hoppenbrouwers, S.: Cognitive mechanisms of conceptual modelling: how do people do it? In: Ng, W., Storey, V.C., Trujillo, J.C. (eds.) ER 2013. LNCS, vol. 8217, pp. 74–87. Springer, Heidelberg (2013). https://doi.org/10.1007/978-3-642-41924-9_7
21. Wilmont, I., Hoppenbrouwers, S., Barendsen, E.: An observation method for behavioral analysis of collaborative modeling skills. In: Metzger, A., Persson, A. (eds.) CAiSE 2017. LNBIP, vol. 286, pp. 59–71. Springer, Cham (2017). https://doi.org/10.1007/978-3-319-60048-2_6

The Subjective Cost of Writing Reusable Code: The Case of Functions

Itamar Lachman[1], Irit Hadar[1(✉)], and Uri Hertz[2]

[1] Department of Information Systems, University of Haifa, Haifa, Israel
Itamar.lachman@gmail.com, hadari@is.haifa.ac.il
[2] Department of Cognitive Sciences, University of Haifa, Haifa, Israel
uhertz@is.haifa.ac.il

Abstract. Functions provide substantial benefits for software development, simplifying programming through decomposition, reusability and abstraction. In a previous study, our group identified a tendency of high-school students to not use functions, even in programming tasks where functions can be a good solution strategy. The current research extends this observation to university students and aims to provide an explanation for the factors underlying this tendency. We focus on the subjective cost of the cognitive effort required for writing functions. Our experiment examined how information systems students solved a set of programming tasks, which varied by the number of repetitive questions. The results showed that most of the students avoided using functions altogether. We further found that in the subgroup of students who used functions at least once, the likelihood of using functions was positively associated with (a) the number of repetitive questions in each task, and (b) the task order, i.e., the progress of the experiment. These results indicate that the subjective cost of writing functions is taken into account when making a decision on how to solve a task at hand and is compared with the cost of repetitive work without using function, and that the former cost is updated with experience.

Keywords: Programming · Functions · Code-reuse · Abstraction · Cognition · Dual-process theory · Subjective cost

1 Introduction

Software development requires the ability to design and write code using abstract constructs, such as functions and classes. This requires to think abstractly, a skill which is not easily mastered [5, 9]. For example, Hadar [4] showed that while developers possess the knowledge about the concepts and principles of object-oriented design (OOD), they demonstrate design errors, some of which stem from the need to think in abstract terms. The explanation offered for these errors is heuristics thinking [7], reflected in developers' intuition about objects in the real world, which in some cases conflicts with the formal principles of object-oriented design (OOD).

Omar at el. [12] found that when asked to write code for simple tasks, in which the use of functions is a good strategy, high-school students did not spontaneously use functions unless they were explicitly asked to do so, even when they had proven

© Springer Nature Switzerland AG 2019
H. A. Proper and J. Stirna (Eds.): CAiSE 2019 Workshops, LNBIP 349, pp. 29–39, 2019.
https://doi.org/10.1007/978-3-030-20948-3_3

knowledge and ability to use them successfully. A qualitative analysis of the reasons the students provided for their decision why they did not use functions, indicated three main reasons: (1) The principle of least effort [8, 18] – choosing the easiest solution available of the perceived options. (2) The principle of satisficing [14, 15] – choosing the first solution that comes to mind which seems good enough. (3) Comfort zone [1] – choosing familiar habits. All three identified reasons are closely related to habitual and intuitive thinking, as explained by the dual-process theory [7].

In this study, we extend the previous research [12] about how cognitive factors affect the decision whether to use functions when writing code. First, we extend the population of high-school students to university students. Second, we seek a more in-depth explanation as to how the process of deciding whether to use functions is affected by the effort required in the different tasks. More specifically, our objective is to understand which factors lead developers to migrate from the strategy of not using functions to that of using them. Finally, we examine whether learning occurs over the course of repetitive decisions as to the use functions, thus affecting future decisions.

Our approach combines an additional cognitive perspective – the value-based subjective cost of effort [16] – with the aforementioned explanation of the dual-process theory. According to this approach, when faced with a coding task, the developer contemplates different solutions and evaluates their subjective cost in terms of cognitive effort. For example, not using functions may incur little effort in non-repetitive tasks but will be very costly when the task is highly repetitive. This estimation is based on the developer's previous experience or assumptions and may change after additional experience is gained. The developer compares the different subjective values of the alternative coding solutions, e.g. using functions and not using functions, to decide on her course of action.

Guided by this approach, we address the following research questions:

RQ (1): How will the number of questions (repetitions) in each coding task influence the use of functions in solving these tasks?

RQ (2): Can we observe an order effect (experience) on the use of functions?

The remainder of this paper is organized as follows: Sect. 2 provides some theoretical background on the cognitive theories used in this research. Section 3 describes the research method and Sect. 4 presents its results. Section 5 discusses the results and threats to validity and Sect. 6 concludes.

2 Theoretical Background

2.1 The Dual-Process Theory

The phenomenon investigated in this paper, namely the selection of the a satisfactory solution to a problem even when inferior to an alternative solution, is related to Herbert Simon's study on bounded rationality and concept of satisficing [14]. Bounded rationality is the idea that decision makers' rationality is limited by the tractability of the decision problem, the cognitive limitations of their mind, and the time available to make the decision. As a result, they will seek a satisfactory, good enough, solution rather than an optimal one.

This idea was also examined in Kahneman's Nobel Prize lecture (2002), "Maps of bounded rationality: A perspective on intuitive judgment and choice," relying on the dual-process theory. According to this theory, two distinct systems operate in our minds: an intuition-based system (S1) and a reasoning-based system (S2). The first (S1) is characterized as fast, parallel, with automatic, effortless and associative slow-learning heuristics, whereas the other (S2) is characterized as a slow, serial, controlled, effortful, rule-governed and flexible.

The relation of this model to the idea of least cognitive effort is that the purpose of humans' S1 is to reduce the cognitive effort required by S2. When we need to do things that can be done automatically, mostly habitual tasks we have already acquired some knowledge of how to perform, we prefer to do them by using the S1-based intuitive thinking [7]. This preference of S1 over S2 results in some of the principles explained previously, for example, the availability heuristic, i.e. selecting the first answer that comes to mind, which also adds to its presumed correctness ("it feels right") [7]. Based on this theory, we predict that functions would be less used (unless the participant has previously used them habitually), because using functions requires abstract thinking involving S2, which in turn requires a more effortful thought process than that involved in S1 thinking of the dual-process model [7].

2.2 Subjective Cost of Cognitive Effort

The idea of subjectivity of an option's cost or value (i.e., subjective value) draws from studies in behavioral economics. Subjective values have been studied in the context of delayed reward [6], for example, where decision makers preferred smaller amounts of money delivered immediately over higher sums delivered in some future time. In the context of cognitive effort, participants were shown to prefer tasks which were less cognitive demanding but were associated with low rewards, over more cognitively demanding tasks which incurred high rewards [16]. In another study participants implicitly learned to choose between two decks of cards of task instructions, one of which included more cognitively demanding tasks than the other [8]. In these studies, the experimenters parametrically manipulated the reward associated with high cognitive load (or future delay) to track the participants' indifference point, e.g. how much reward should be associated with a demanding task to make the participant choose it over an easy task on 50% of the trials. This indifference value represented the participants' individual subjective cost associated with cognitive effort.

These results demonstrate the idea that people try to avoid cognitive effort, such that high cognitive effort is associated with higher subjective cost. This behavior may bear a resemblance to our investigation on the decision of using functions. If we harness the idea that the subjective cost will increase as the need for cognitive effort arises, then we can assume that because functions require abstract thinking, their subjective cost will be higher than using an alternative option that does not require this type of thinking (for example, writing loops). It is therefore reasonable to assume that when people choose between the two options of writing code, one using functions and the other using loops, they would prefer the option to which they allocate a lower subjective cost of effort.

Moreover, we assume that tasks that involve more work will be considered as having higher subjective cost of effort. At the same time, tasks that require abstract thinking will be considered as having higher subjective cost as well. However, while the subjective cost of using functions does not change when the number of repetitive questions change, the subjective cost of using loops is to be considered based upon the amount of work required, which is derived from the number of repetitions in the tasks. Accordingly, our aim is to identify the point in which the subjective cost of using loops becomes higher than that of using functions.

3   Method

3.1   Experiment Design

The experiment was designed to test the following hypotheses:

For **RQ (1):** How will the number of questions in each coding task influence the use of functions in solving these tasks?

H (0): There will be no correlation between the number of questions in each task and the frequency of use of functions.
H (1): The frequency of use of functions will be positively correlated with the number of questions in each task.

For **RQ (2):** Can we observe an order effect (experience) on the use of functions?

H (0): There will be no correlation between the task order and the frequency of the use of functions.
H (1): There will be a positive correlation between the task order and the frequency of the use of functions.

The experiment consisted of an introduction explaining the experiment to the participants, a precondition part aimed at ensuring that the participants have the knowledge needed for developing code using functions, and the main part of the experiment including a series of 15 coding tasks. Participants were asked to use a coding language of their choice, or pseudo code. Participants were able to use copy and paste within a task but copying text between tasks was restricted by the experiment, in order to isolate the effort invested in each task.

The precondition part included a single task in which the participants were asked to write a function that adds a value to an array of elements, in a coding language of their choice. While all our participants completed at least one academic programming course (C), this part allowed us to identify and exclude participants who nevertheless still struggle with the proper use of functions.

The functions part included 15 simple arithmetic tasks on arrays which included: adding, multiplying or subtracting each of the elements of multiple arrays, as follows:

- **Add:** consists commands to perform the operation of adding each time a different number to each of the elements of a new array.
- **Subtract:** consists commands to perform the operation of subtracting each time a different number from each of the elements of a different array.
- **Multiply:** consist commands to perform the operation of multiply each time a different number with each of the elements of a different array.

Each of the add, subtract and multiply operations were used in tasks which included 1, 3, 5, 8 or 15 questions (number of arrays), resulting in 15 tasks all together (3 operations × 5 number of questions). The order of the tasks was randomized for each participant. Table 1 demonstrates the type of actions and reoccurrence patterns of the tasks.

Table 1. Examples of tasks

Type	Examples of a 3 questions (repetitions) tasks
Add	1. Please add 24 to each element in array A
	2. Please add 11 to each element in array B
	3. Please add 35 to each element in array C
Subtract	1. Please subtract 24 out of each element in array A
	2. Please subtract 56 out of each element in array B
	3. Please subtract 7 out of each element in array C
Multiply	1. Please multiply each element in array A by 12
	2. Please multiply each element in array B by 44
	3. Please multiply each element in array C by 75

3.2 Participants

The experiment was executed at the University of Haifa, during the spring of semester of 2018, in an object-oriented programming course. The participants were 42 students in their 1st year of study in the department of Information Systems. The participants included 24 males and 18 females, of ages 19–29 with the average age of 21. The study was approved by the institutional ethics committee, and participants gave their informed consent to participate.

3.3 Procedure

The experiment took place in a computer lab classroom. Each of the participants was provided with a computer and a link to the experiment website, a general explanation about the experiment and the reward for completing it (extra credit in the course).

Upon entering the website, each participant filled a consent form and registered into the experiment, filling non-identifiable data only (e.g., age, course, gender and coding experience). Then the participants were presented with a short introduction including an explanation about the series of tasks of code writing they are about to receive. This

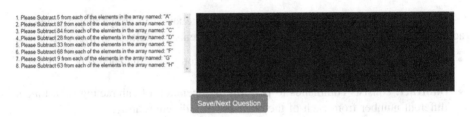

1. Please Subtract 5 from each of the elements in the array named: "A"
2. Please Subtract 87 from each of the elements in the array named: "B"
3. Please Subtract 84 from each of the elements in the array named: "C"
4. Please Subtract 28 from each of the elements in the array named: "D"
5. Please Subtract 33 from each of the elements in the array named: "E"
6. Please Subtract 68 from each of the elements in the array named: "F"
7. Please Subtract 9 from each of the elements in the array named: "G"
8. Please Subtract 63 from each of the elements in the array named: "H"

Save/Next Question

Fig. 1. Example of a coding task

was followed by the precondition task, and then by the series of tasks, as detailed above (see example in Fig. 1).

3.4   Data Analysis

The evaluation of function use in the participants' answers (code) in both the precondition and the main experimental tasks was performed according to the following criteria: for the code to be considered a proper function, it had to be surrounded by a block name and at least two parameters, and to be called from another block of code. Two external evaluators evaluated the use of functions in the answers of the participants. An additional criterion employed was that for a solution to be evaluated as a function, both evaluators' answers needed be positive.

First, a screening of the precondition task was performed, in order to exclude participants who failed in this task. Following the evaluation of this task, one participant was excluded, leaving 41 participants included in the dataset. Next, the evaluators evaluated the full set of the experiment tasks for the 41 participants. A Pearson correlation ($r = 0.85$, $n = 40$, $p = 0.02$) between the evaluators and Kappa Cohen Test ($k = 0.85$) for nominal scales were calculated, indicating high agreement level.

4   Results

Analyzing the answers elicited in the experiment, we first identified the following three main patterns:

1. "Always use functions" (3/41 participants) – in this behavior pattern, the participants chose to write a function in the first question that followed the precondition task and continued using functions in each of the tasks throughout the experiment. See an example solution with the use of function in Fig. 2.
2. "Never use functions" (22/41 participants) – in this behavior pattern, the participants did not use functions in any of the questions. See example solution without the use of function in Fig. 3.
3. "Sometimes use functions" (16/41 participants) – in this behavior pattern, the participants used functions from time to time during the experiment.

This pattern of results reveals that most of our participants (see Fig. 4) never used functions, even when the task included 15 repetitive questions. This finding supports

Question No. 9

1. Please Multiply each element in the array named: "A" by 52
2. Please Multiply each element in the array named: "B" by 45
3. Please Multiply each element in the array named: "C" by 10
4. Please Multiply each element in the array named: "D" by 62
5. Please Multiply each element in the array named: "E" by 64

```
addToArray(a[], number) {
    for(int i = 0; i<a[].size(); i++)
        a[i]=a[i]+number;
    }

addToArray(A,52);
addToArray(B,45);
addToArray(C,10);
addToArray(D,62);
addToArray(E,64);
```

Save/Next Question

Fig. 2. Example of a solution with the use of function

Question No. 7

1. Please Add 44 to each of the elements in the array named: "A"
2. Please Add 83 to each of the elements in the array named: "B"
3. Please Add 98 to each of the elements in the array named: "C"
4. Please Add 25 to each of the elements in the array named: "D"
5. Please Add 33 to each of the elements in the array named: "E"
6. Please Add 4 to each of the elements in the array named: "F"
7. Please Add 53 to each of the elements in the array named: "G"
8. Please Add 34 to each of the elements in the array named: "H"

```
for(int i ; i<A.length;i++)   A[i]+=44;
for(int i ; i<B.length;i++)   B[i]+=83;
for(int i ; i<C.length;i++)   C[i]+=98;
for(int i ; i<D.length;i++)   D[i]+=25;
for(int i ; i<E.length;i++)   E[i]+=33;
for(int i ; i<F.length;i++)   F[i]+=4;
for(int i ; i<G.length;i++)   G[i]+=53;
for(int i ; i<H.length;i++)   H[i]+=34;
```

Save/Next Question

Fig. 3. Example of a solution without the use of function

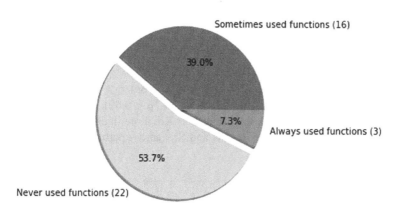

Fig. 4. Patterns of function usage

the findings of Omar et al. [12], and further generalizes them for increased repetitiveness and to the population of university students. We discuss these findings in Sect. 5.

We next focused on the subgroup of participants who used functions from time to time. We used a mixed-effect logistic regression [11] to evaluate the effects of the number of questions in a task and task order on their decisions to use functions.

We used the trial-by-trial decision to use functions using this decision (a binary parameter: 1 = function used, 0 = no function) as a dependent variable, and the number of questions (1, 3, 5, 8, 15) and task number (order in the experiment, 1–15) as fixed-effects independent variables, and the participants' ordinal number as a random effect independent variable. The model's AIC score was 373, and a null model's AIC score (a model with only the intercept random effect) was 453. The likelihoods of these two models were used to calculate the McFadden's pseudo-R squared for the fixed effects [10]: $R^2 = 0.19$.

We found that the number of questions had a positive effect on the decision to use functions (Estimate ± Standard Error (SE) = 0.22 ± 0.06, z = 3.29, p < 0.001). This effect confirms our hypothesis for RQ (1), H (1), as participants' frequency of using functions increased with the number of questions (Fig. 5 includes means and SEs across participants).

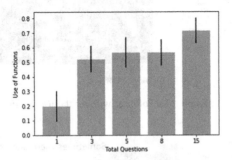

Fig. 5. Effect of number of questions in a task on the use of functions

Our analysis also revealed a positive effect of task order on the probability of using function (Estimate ± SE = 0.21 ± 0.05, z = 3.89, p < 0.001). This result confirms our hypothesis for RQ (2): H(1), as participants were more likely to use functions later in the experiment (Fig. 6 includes means and SEs across participants).

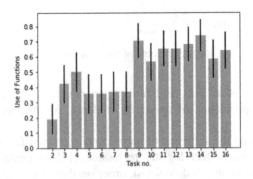

Fig. 6. Effect of order on using functions

5 Discussion

In this experiment, we aimed to evaluate the subjective cost of function use of participants performing simple coding tasks, in which functions are a good strategy. In order to evaluate the subjective cost of writing functions, we controlled the number of repetitive questions in each task.

Our main hypothesis was that by increasing the number of questions, the cost of avoiding functions will at some point meet and exceed the subjective cost of using functions, and participants will migrate from not using to using functions. This means that the likelihood of using functions will increase with the number of questions (repetitions) in a task. We based this hypothesis on the idea that in each of the tasks, unless the participants have already chosen to use functions, their default habitual solution will be to use loops. However, as the number of questions increases so will the number of loops required to complete the task, and thereby the subjective cost of this task. As a result, in some of the tasks, we assumed that the subjective cost of coding the loops will be high enough so that the participants will consider the alternative solution of using functions.

We also hypothesised that each decision that the participants will make in each of the tasks will contribute to their experience about the benefits of using functions instead of loops, and thus that there will be a temporal learning effect in which as the number of previous tasks increases, so does the likelihood of the participants to use functions.

Based on the results of the experiment presented above, we identified several interesting behavior patterns. First, we found that most participants did not use functions at all, even in tasks which included 15 repeated questions, and even after writing a similar function successfully in the precondition task. This pattern amplifies the effect found by Omar et al. [12], where high-school students avoided using functions in a one-shot design. This pattern of thinking resembles the heuristic-based decision of S1 in the dual-process theory [6], which supports habitual and automatic behavior, without deliberation and reasoning. These participants might be following a habit of using loops, which they may perceive as a good enough solution.

Another subset of our participants did use functions from time to time. These participants' decision to use functions was found to be dependent on the number of repetitive questions in a task and the task order in the experiment, in line with our hypotheses and the concept of subjective cost [3, 8, 13, 16, 17]. This pattern of results reflects a subjective cost pattern, in which the cost of function use is compared with the cost of not using functions on a trial-by-trial basis. When the task is highly repetitive, the cost of not using function exceeds the cost of using functions, and therefore the probability of using functions increases. The cost of using function decreases with experience, e.g. after using functions in previous tasks, making the use of functions a more compelling option. The effort of designing the function reduces after this solution has already been used. The mixed pattern, which we view as subjective learning, resembles more the thinking process that may occur in S2, in which there is an analytical comparison of the two options and the subjective cost of using functions is estimated and compared to the alternative of writing loops.

Lastly, we assume, but can currently not confirm, that the reason that some of the participants decided to use only functions and no loops, could be the result of an earlier epiphany effect caused by the precondition task of the experiment [2]. According to this assumption, when the participants were asked to perform the precondition task in which they were explicitly instructed to use a function, some of them may have grasped the benefit of using functions and used it from this point onwards.

5.1   Threats to Validity

Construct validity: Concerns the relationships between theory and observation. In this study, while some of the participants displayed a decision behavior of subjective cost, most of them (about 54%) chose to avoid using functions altogether. We can therefore not be confident with the subjective cost of effort being a sole explanation for our research question regarding the factors that affect the decision to use functions.

External validity: Concerns the generalization of the results. The main threats in this area stem from the fact that our multi-tasks experimental design permitted using simple tasks such as mathematical operations on arrays that do not match the real-life demands and complexity of the environment of the software development industry.

6   Conclusion

In this work we aimed to investigate the cognitive factors affecting writing reusable code, specifically in the case of functions. We found that a subset of the participants reflected a subjective cost pattern, namely a decision based on comparing the cognitive effort to be invested in each alternative, in line with the concept of subjective cost [3, 8, 13, 16, 17]. These results demonstrate the manifestation of the concept of subjective cost, originated from economic decision making [3, 17], in the domain of software engineering, focused here on programing decisions. Most of the participants chose to not use functions at all. We propose that this pattern is not based on the subjective cost of the tasks but rather on habits and heuristical thinking [7]. Taken together, these results shed light on the different cognitive factors and mechanisms underlying programmers' decision making.

Future work may investigate the factors that lead to the different behavior patterns observed in this study. An understanding of these factors may inform future efforts to design strategies that would lead students and developers to more frequently chose to program code in a reusable manner.

References

1. Brown, M.: Comfort Zone: model or metaphor? Aust. J. Outdoor Educ. **12**, 3–12 (2008)
2. Chen, W.J., Krajbich, I.: Computational modeling of epiphany learning. Proc. Natl. Acad. Sci. **114**, 4637–4642 (2017). https://doi.org/10.1073/pnas.1618161114
3. Green, L., Myerson, J.: A discounting framework for choice with delayed and probabilistic rewards. Psychol. Bull. **130**, 769–792 (2004). https://doi.org/10.1037/0033-2909.130.5.769

4. Hadar, I.: When intuition and logic clash: the case of the object-oriented paradigm. Sci. Comput. Program. **78**, 1407–1426 (2013). https://doi.org/10.1016/j.scico.2012.10.006
5. Hashim, K., Key, E.: A software maintainability attributes model. Malays. J. Comput. Sci. **9**, 92–97 (1996)
6. Kable, J.W., Glimcher, P.W.: The neural correlates of subjective value during intertemporal choice. Nat. Neurosci. **10**, 1625–1633 (2007). https://doi.org/10.1038/nn2007
7. Kahneman, D.: Maps of bounded rationality: a perspective on intuitive judgment and choice. Sveriges Riksbank Prize Econ. Sci. Mem. Alfred Nobel, 449–489 (2002). https://doi.org/10.1037/0003-066x.58.9.697
8. Kool, W., McGuire, J.T., Rosen, Z.B., Botvinick, M.M.: Decision making and the avoidance of cognitive demand. J. Exp. Psychol. Gen. **139**, 665–682 (2010). https://doi.org/10.1037/a0020198
9. Kramer, J.: Is abstraction the key to computing? Commun. ACM **50**, 36–42 (2007). https://doi.org/10.1145/1232743.1232745
10. Maddala, G.S.: Limited-Dependent and Qualitative Variables in Econometrics. Cambridge University Press, Cambridge (1986)
11. Manlove, K.: Introduction to Statistical Analysis using R commander, pp. 1–23 (2014)
12. Omar, A., Hadar, I., Leron, U.: Investigating the under-usage of code decomposition and reuse among high school students: the case of functions. In: Metzger, A., Persson, A. (eds.) CAiSE 2017. LNBIP, vol. 286, pp. 92–98. Springer, Cham (2017). https://doi.org/10.1007/978-3-319-60048-2_9
13. Patzelt, E.H., Kool, W., Millner, A.J., Gershman, S.J., Note, A., Patzelt, E.H.: Building N In press at Scientific Reports 4729
14. Simon, H.A.: Administrative behaviour. Aust. J. Public Adm. (1947). https://doi.org/10.1111/j.1467-8500.1950.tb01679.x
15. Stanovich, K.E.: What Intelligence Tests Miss: The Psychology of Rational Thought. Yale University Press, New Haven (2009)
16. Westbrook, A., Braver, T.S.: Cognitive effort: a neuroeconomic approach. Cogn. Affect Behav. Neurosci. **15**, 395–415 (2015). https://doi.org/10.3758/s13415-015-0334-y
17. Westbrook, A., Kester, D., Braver, T.S.: What is the subjective cost of cognitive effort? Load, trait, and aging effects revealed by economic preference. PLoS One **8**, 1–8 (2013). https://doi.org/10.1371/journal.pone.0068210
18. Zipf, G.K.: Human Behaviour and the Principle of Least Effort: An Introduction to Human Ecology, 588 pages. Addison-Wesley Press, Cambridge (1949)

Climb Your Way to the Model: Teaching UML to Software Engineering Students

Teaching Case

Naomi Unkelos-Shpigel[1,2(✉)], Julia Sheidin[1,2], and Moran Kupfer[2]

[1] Software Engineering Department, Ort Braude College, Karmiel, Israel
{naomius, julia, moran}@braude.ac.il
[2] Information Systems Department, University of Haifa, Haifa, Israel

Abstract. Unified Modeling Language (UML) courses are an essential part of software engineering curricula. There is increasing evidence that embedding active learning techniques in courses in general, and in UML courses in particular, increases students' motivation and performance. In this paper, we contribute to this body of work by presenting model for embedding active learning in an undergraduate UML course. The model was used throughout a course, providing interesting results, and promoting students' participation and motivation. We present our insights and plans for further inspection of the model.

Keywords: UML · Active learning · Motivation

1 Introduction

Software engineering and information systems students are required to take a software-modeling course, as part of their training as software designers. The course usually consists of learning several UML (Unified Modeling Language [7]) diagrams. In some cases, the course is taught before the students have practiced any object-oriented language (the design-first approach [2]).

The first UML course presents several challenges to both instructors and students [3]. First, for understanding and fully implementing diagrams, a lot of practice is needed. Students are usually required to submit 3–4 homework tasks per semester. As they need a lot of training in understanding and designing, simply performing the tasks is hardly enough training. Second, as the teaching method is traditionally frontal, the instructor cannot get a clear picture of students' perceptions, and in particular, their misconceptions. Third, as UML diagrams usually consists of a large number of details, and several modeling variants are available, solving questions with the students on the board is usually not enough to cover many solution options. Fourth, as the modeling requires a cognitive resource, students lack the motivation of performing the task [5].

Several teaching mechanisms and tools were offered in recent years to improve student's motivation and understanding. These methods all rely on active learning during the lecture and recitation. In example, the flipped classroom [5] is a learning method that includes both learning at home and performing practical activities in the

H. A. Proper and J. Stirna (Eds.): CAiSE 2019 Workshops, LNBIP 349, pp. 40–46, 2019.
https://doi.org/10.1007/978-3-030-20948-3_4

classroom. However, this method requires a great deal of time investment from both students and teachers. Additional teaching method are in order.

This paper presents the summary of a teaching case of a UML modeling course called "Climb Your Way to The Model". The teaching method drew inspiration from the onion model for collaborative learning [9], the 21st century skill movement [4] and motivation theories such as the Self Determination Theory (called SDT henceforth), [8], and the 4C's Model [6]. These motivation theories discuss how to motivate employees to take active part in the work, and to encourage them to strive for more productive behavior, mainly by encouraging intrinsic and extrinsic motivation [8], and by achieving a state where the worker is immersed into the task [8]. The Kahoot! Application[1] was used each lecture, to test students' knowledge from the previous lecture, and to present the results to all the class in a gamified manner. The Moodle environment[2] was used to perform additional collaborative exploratory assignment during class. Google forms were used for a reflection.

Leveraging on the principles of collaborative and gamified tools for education, our work fills this gap by asking the following research questions: (1) How can we promote software engineering students' achievements and participation in UML design courses? (2) What are the benefits of embedding active learning techniques in UML courses?

In the rest of paper, we first discuss the background for the teaching case. We then introduce the teaching method (Sect. 3). Section 4 presents students' responses to the teaching method. We conclude with a discussion of the findings and further work.

2   Scientific Background

2.1   Active Learning in UML Teaching

Trying to deal with the challenge of teaching an abstract model such as UML, different research works described tools and techniques for active learning. In example, Hansen et al. [4], used collaborative tools, involving instructors and students, to achieve a more usable and functional UML diagrams. However, their research claim that a previous knowledge in object-oriented programming is needed. Briggs [1] presents another case of an experiment for active learning in UML teaching, using simple tasks given to the students, with no special tools required.

Yet, these examples lack the aspect of students' reflection on the task, and a rigorous reasoning for the structure of the task, resulting in an increase of students' motivation and performance.

2.2   Cognitive Theories

Several cognitive theories address the topic of encouraging motivation for increasing the participation and motivation during the semester in learning tasks. Here we briefly present two of the most influential theories in this field.

---

[1] https://kahoot.com/.

[2] https://en.wikipedia.org/wiki/Moodle.

The 4 C's of 21st century skills [6] are some of the learning strategies in today's environment. They state that if students want to compete in today's global society, they must be proficient: (1) communicators, being able to identify the information needed and how to use or leverage it effectively; (2) creators: can create creative design and possess out of the box thinking ability; (3) critical thinkers: analyze mistakes and improve their thought processing, and (4) collaborators: work effectively with diverse teams, making necessary compromises to accomplish a common goal, and assuming shared responsibility for collaborative work.

The Self Determination Theory (SDT) [8] presents a continuum of motivation types, from intrinsic motivation that emerges from the employee, to extrinsic motivation created by rules and regulation in the workplace. Although intrinsic motivation is considered to be linked to positive human behavior, SDT suggests that proper use in extrinsic motivation can lead to motivated behavior. SDT suggests that there are three basic needs that need to be fulfilled in order to increase motivation: *Competence* - seek to control the outcome and experience mastery; *Relatedness* - will to interact, be connected to, and experience caring for others; *Autonomy* - desire to be causal agents of one's own life and act in harmony with one's integrated self.

The proposed solution is described in the next section.

3   The Course Structure

The course is a mandatory course given in one of the leading academic colleges in Israel, at the department of software engineering. We covered five main UML diagrams in our course (see Table 1).

Table 1. Subjects and activities during the course

	Subject	Active learning task
1	Requirement engineering methods	Lecture: Collaborative task - software that failed Recitation: Data collection practice - pairs
2	Use Case diagram	Lecture: Use case modeling - pairs Recitation: Use case modeling - pairs
3	Activity diagram	Lecture: Activity diagram - pairs Recitation: Activity modeling - pairs
4	Class diagram	Lecture: Use case modeling and Class - pairs Recitation: Class modeling - pairs
5	Sequence diagram	Lecture: Class and sequence diagram - pairs Recitation: Exam questions solving, and peer review - individuals
6	Statechart diagram	Lecture: Statechart diagram - pairs Recitation: Statechart modeling - pairs

We teach the course for three years, and gradually embedded various individual and group activities during the classes. The course is taught in the design-first approach [2], meaning – before the students learnt to program in an object-oriented language.

Building this model, we relied on the principles of the 4 C's model – students were treated as *creators* and *communicators*, responsible for dealing with new and complex problems by teamwork. They were also collaborators, as they changed teams each class. Finally, they were also *critical thinkers*, as we asked them to refer to other students' work from the previous lecture. We also provided them with conditions for the three basic needs of SDT – they worked on each exercise with little instruction (autonomy), worked in small teams and helped each other to understand the task (relatedness), and dealt with tasks that were more challenging than what they learn during the frontal class (competence).

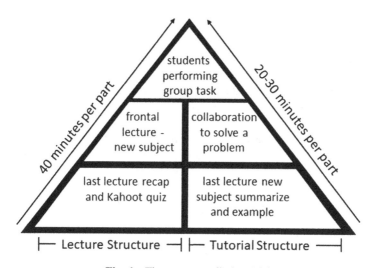

Fig. 1. The two-way climb model

This paper refers to a semester, which included 175 students, all in the second year of their studies. The course had a weekly three academic hours lecture, followed by a two academic hours tutorial (not at the same day) and consisted of three home works and a final exam. 8% of the grade are given for attending at least 80% of all class activities (in both lectures and recitations).

Each lecture consisted of three academic hours, which were divided, according to "Climb Your Way to The Model" model we designed, into three parts. Two parts were frontal, and the last one active learning (see Fig. 1). The first hour was devoted to recap of the last lecture, performing Kahoot quizzes, and reviewing students' models form the previous week; the second hour consisted of frontal teaching, presenting a new subject; the third hour was dedicated to active learning. Students worked in small groups, dealing with the new model they have just learned, and trying to produce a solution.

Each tutorial consisted of two academic hours, which were divided into three parts. One frontal, one collaboration and the last one active learning (see Fig. 1). The first 30 min were devoted to lecture summarize and exercise example of the new subject learned in the last lecture. The next 30 min consisted of collaboration to solve an exercise with discussion on different approaches to solution. The last 20 min included independent problem solving, where students worked in small groups, dealing with an exercise where they had to produce a solution on their own.

4 Insights and Students Perceptions Toward the Task

Several insights arose during the semester, which we categorized according to our research questions:

RQ1 – we noticed that indeed there was a significant increase in both student participation and solution quality:

- *Student attendance* – at the previous to our teaching method semester, where the teaching was frontal, many students stopped coming to class, usually at week seven. In this semester, we experienced a high rate of attendance throughout the semester.
- *Solutions complexity* – as students solved various problems during the classes, their solutions included interesting and even complex variants, even after a class or two on a subject. In example, they used constraints in class diagrams, inheritance in use case diagrams, and loops and multiple objects in sequence diagrams [6], in state chart [6], they used nested states and variables.
- *Students as thinkers, teachers as mentors* – in both lectures and recitations, during the active learning session, we served as mentors rather than teachers. In many cases, the students came up with interesting variants that were different from our solution, so we could encourage them to follow their line of thinking and construct an interesting new solution. In the following lecture, we shared these variants with the entire class. This method had two advantages: we exposed the entire class to multiple solutions and discussed the advantages and drawbacks of each solution.

RQ2– we asked the students to fill a survey, reflecting on the different activities they performed in the course. 52 students filled the survey. Here we had several interesting insights (see Table 2):

- *Activities cs. Kahoot* – Though Kahoot! Quizzes were very popular in previous semester, 70% of the students this semester thought they were redundant. 72% of the students said the class activities were helpful for their learning.
- *Promoters of iterative work and team work* – 55% of the students felt that the tasks they performed helped them to enrich their knowledge each week. 70% of the students felt that team work was better than solving the task on their own.

The quotes also comply with the cognitive theories we relied on. The students expressed in their feedback the characteristics of SDT – they expressed capability to perform the task (competence); they felt that they had solved the problems on their own

Table 2. Reflection (representative sample) on the activities from the student' perspective

Quote	SDT	4C's
The activities helped me to develop a technique for modeling	✓	✓
Reviewing my peers was useful, as I understood how much time to spend on a question, and how to plan the solution		✓
I learnt from both my correct and incorrect solutions	✓	
The class activities helped me realize that every student has his unique way to solve the problem	✓	✓
The class activities encouraged me to look at the problem from different perspectives		✓

(autonomy), and they felt related to the task and to their peers, understanding that there were different ways to solve the same problem (relatedness).

5 Conclusions and Future Work

We conducted a teaching case of a UML modeling course, inspired by existing cognitive theories. 175 students, all in the second year of their studies, took a part at this mandatory course given in one of the leading academic colleges in Israel, at the department of software engineering. Our observations indicate that there are benefits of embedding active learning techniques in UML courses in sense of improving students' achievements and increasing the participation and motivation during the semester.

Our findings support the students need for being more active during the semester in order to improve their learning skills. It adds to the growing evidence of the benefits of promoting students' work during class - solving problems, creating, communicating, collaborating and being a critical thinker. However, we further realized that the workload students face needs to be more balanced throughout the semester and personal feedback following each assignment is in order. We plan to further embed these activities in this course, providing students with continuous feedback for their performance. We also plan to adapt this model to additional courses, which require abstract thinking.

References

1. Briggs, T.: Techniques for active learning in CS courses. J. Comput. Sci. Coll. **21**(2), 156–165 (2005)
2. Cooper, S., Dann, W., Pausch, R.: Teaching objects-first in introductory computer science. ACM SIGCSE Bull. **35**(1), 191–195 (2003)
3. Chrysafiadi, K., Virvou, M.: Student modeling approaches: a literature review for the last decade. Expert Syst. Appl. **40**(11), 4715–4729 (2013)
4. Hansen, K.M., Ratzer, A.V.: Tool support for collaborative teaching and learning of object-oriented modeling. ACM SIGCSE Bull. **34**(3), 146–150 (2002)

5. Jensen, J.L., Kummer, T.A., Godoy, P.D.D.M.: Improvements from a flipped classroom may simply be the fruits of active learning. CBE—Life Sci. Educ. **14**(1), ar5 (2015)
6. National Education Association - Alexandria, VA.: Preparing 21st Century Students for a Global Society: An Educator's Guide to the "Four Cs". National Education Association (2012)
7. Pilone, D., Pitman, N.: UML 2.0 in a Nutshell. O'Reilly Media Inc., Sebastopol (2005)
8. Ryan, R.M., Deci, E.L.: Self-determination theory and the facilitation of intrinsic motivation, social development, and well-being. Am. Psychol. **55**(1), 68 (2000)
9. Unkelos-Shpigel, N.: Peel the onion: use of collaborative and gamified tools to enhance software engineering education. In: Krogstie, J., Mouratidis, H., Su, J. (eds.) CAiSE 2016. LNBIP, vol. 249, pp. 122–128. Springer, Cham (2016). https://doi.org/10.1007/978-3-319-39564-7_13

KET4DF 2019

The 1st International Workshop on Key Enabling Technologies for Digital Factories KET4DF 2019

Preface

The manufacturing industry is entering a new digital era in which ICT technologies and collaboration applications will be integrated with traditional manufacturing practices and processes to increase flexibility and sustainability in manufacturing, mass customization, increase automation, better quality and improve productivity.

A digital factory is defined as a multi-layered integration of the information related to various activities along the factory and product lifecycle manufacturing related resources. A central aspect of a digital factory is that of enabling the product lifecycle stakeholders to collaborate by software solutions. The digital factory thus expands outside the actual company boundaries and offers the opportunity for the business and its suppliers to collaborate on business processes that affect the supply chain.

This translates into strong technological evolution but also into an unprecedented extension of companies' information systems. Exploitation of data and services derived from disparate and distributed sources, development of scalable and efficient real-time systems, management of expert knowledge, advanced data analytics and optimized decision making are some of the key challenges which advanced information systems can address in an effort to reach the vision of Industry 4.0.

The goal of this workshop is to attract high quality research papers focusing on technologies for Industry 4.0, with specific reference to digital factories and smart manufacturing. The idea of the workshop was born to promote the research topics of some international projects, which has also become the supporters of the workshop: FIRST (H2020 grant # 734599), UPTIME (H2020 grant # 768634), Z-BRE4K (H2020 grant # 768869), COMPOSITION (H2020 grant # 723145).

The workshop received 18 submissions, and the Program Committee selected 9 high-quality papers for presentation at the workshop, which are included in the CAiSE 2019 Workshops proceedings volume.

We thank the Workshop Chairs of CAiSE 2019, Janis Stirna and Erik Proper, for their precious support. We also thank the members of the Program Committee and the external reviewers for their hard work in reviewing the submitted papers.

April 2019

Federica Mandreoli
Giacomo Cabri
Gregoris Mentzas
Karl Hribernik

KET4DF 2019 Organization

Organizing Committee

Federica Mandreoli	Università di Modena e Reggio Emilia, Italy
Giacomo Cabri	Università di Modena e Reggio Emilia, Italy
Gregoris Mentzas	ICCS, National Technical University of Athens, Greece
Karl Hribernik	Bremer Institut für Produktion und Logistik GmbH (BIBA), Germany

Program Committee

Marco Aiello	University of Stuttgart, Germany
Kosmas Alexopoulos	University of Patras, Greece
Dimitris Apostolou	University of Piraeus, Greece
Yuewei Bai	Shanghai Polytechnic University, China
Alexandros Bousdekis	Institute of Communication and Computer Systems, NTUA, Greece
Fabrício Junqueira	University of São Paulo, Brasil
Fenareti Lampathaki	Suite5, Cyprus
Alexander Lazovik	University of Groningen, The Netherlands
Marco Lewandowski	University of Bremen, Germany
Sotirios Makris	University of Patras, Greece
Ifigeneia Metaxa	Atlantis Engineering S.A., Greece
Michele Missikoff	IASI-CNR, Italy
Hervé Panetto	University of Lorraine, France
Pierluigi Petrali	Whirlpool Europe Srl, Italy
Marcos André Pisching	Federal Institute of Santa Catarina, Brasil
Pierluigi Plebani	Politechnico di Milano, Italy
Walter Terkaj	Politechnico di Milano, Italy
Lai Xu	Bournemouth University, UK
Paul de Vrieze	Bournemouth University, UK

A New Method for Manufacturing Process Autonomous Planning in Intelligent Manufacturing System

Shuangyu Wei[1(✉)], Yuewei Bai[1(✉)], Xiaogang Wang[1], Liu Kai[1],
Lai Xu[2], Paul de Vrieze[2], and John Paul Kasse[2]

[1] Shanghai Polytechnic University, Shanghai 201209, China
{sywei,ywbai}@sspu.edu.cn
[2] Bournemouth University, Bournemouth BH12 5BB, UK

Abstract. This paper presents a new method for autonomous computer aided process planning (A-CAPP) in intelligent manufacturing system, in which the related input and output of the system are discussed on the basis of comparative analysis of traditional CAPP. The crucial functional components of the A-CAPP system, such as event scheduling management, manufacturing process planning, operation process/step planning, numerical control machining program planning, process simulation and evaluation, are introduced; and the methods of process knowledge management, including process feature knowledge, manufacturing resource knowledge and process method knowledge, are discussed as well. A-CAPP applied for intelligent manufacturing system can effectively support the production line reconstruction dynamically; shorten the time of production line configuration modification in accordance with customers' requirement change or market requirement fluctuation, and further more to balance the production lines load.

Keywords: Process autonomous planning · Intelligent manufacturing system · Event scheduling · Manufacturing process knowledge management

1 Background

An intelligent manufacturing system is a complex system, which involves the technologies of industrial network, industrial software, artificial intelligence, information security and others. After Germany launched the "industry 4.0 standardization roadmap" in 2014, the United States, Japan, the United Kingdom and China have also formulated their national smart manufacturing strategies. Consequently, intelligent manufacturing technology has become a research hotspot of advanced manufacturing technology.

CAPP (Computer Aided Process Planning) is one kind of indispensable industrial software in intelligent manufacturing system. It plays an important role as bridge between design and manufacturing, which determines the manufacturing process, processing operation sequence, required resources etc. [1–6]. Resources refers to the equipment, machine tools, process equipment (e.g., cutter, fixture, gauge, auxiliary appliance etc.) needed in production. According to the requirements, CAPP scheme

© Springer Nature Switzerland AG 2019
H. A. Proper and J. Stirna (Eds.): CAiSE 2019 Workshops, LNBIP 349, pp. 51–63, 2019.
https://doi.org/10.1007/978-3-030-20948-3_5

needs to define (or match) the required manufacturing resources for each process operation, and then associate the relevant the technical documents with the resources, such as associate NC/CNC programs for the selected machine tools and programmed PLC programs for the automatic equipment (such as robots) etc.

In the traditional CAPP method, manufacturing experts used empirical knowledge to solve process planning problems and prepared process technical documents to guide downstream product manufacturing [7, 8]. The planning process for technical documents accounts for at least 40% to 60% of the time used in the entire production process. Currently, computer aided design (CAD), computer aided process planning (CAPP) and manufacturing (CAM) [1, 9] have become indispensable industrial software in the process of modern product design and manufacturing.

2   CAPP Development and Study Motivation

2.1   The State of the Art

At present, the R&D in process planning and production line reconstruction are mainly promoted by PTC, DASSAULT, SIEMENS and other leading companies. In addition, IBM, TOYOTA, FANUC and SAP also put forward some of relevant research and development plans recently. In terms of CAPP, various commercial CAPP systems have emerged one after another. This has laid a solid foundation for the integration of product design, process planning and production.

PTC has developed a platform, MPMLink [14]. Using the systems, enterprises can effectively support their manufacturing process management via the platform, i.e., product development, production process and manufacturing resource data of entire enterprises can all be unified managed through the system. DASSAULT has developed the DELMIA [15] digital manufacturing solution, which is based on open software architecture and provides a unified product design, process planning, and resource portfolio model (PPR) that companies can use to continuously compile and validate product processes throughout the product development process. Although this platform can closely combine the process planning and product design, it still is separated from the manufacturing resource management at the production end, and it does not fully realize the integrated management of product design, process planning and production. SIEMENS has developed Siemens PLM Software [16], which can cover product design, production planning, production engineering, production and service of five repeated iteration of industrial business process; then divide them into: Idea, Implementation and Application of three parts. The system is designed to help companies to solve the product idea generation and evolution of production and processing and optimize the three levels of change of the pattern in some extent. However, the technical preparation and production process integration still is not quite close, and it remains to be further optimized.

The popular domestic CAPP systems in China are KM CAPP, TIANHE CAPP and JINYE CAPP, among which KM CAPP is prominent and it has been successfully applied in more than 8,000 companies with hundreds of customized functional modules. However, the required input data of manufacturing resources by CAPP systems were static or historical. In other words, data has a large time delay and is still far away from real-time acquisition of production data. It may possibly be due to the fact that the planned process document is inapplicable for real production, especially when short production cycles are used. Presently, the research and development of autonomous CAPP system that can support enterprises to dynamically adjust production configuration, quickly make production decision in accordance with the market changes is almost non-existent.

2.2 Study Motivation

Process planning is the basic activity of transforming product design scheme (such as CAD model) into detailed technical documents to guide production, that is, how to establish the corresponding manufacturing process documents under the given conditions of manufacturing resources and put them into the operation site/workshop to instruct production. In this process, enterprises can shorten the delivery time to market by using effective CAPP schemes [10]. In addition, it can be used to solve basic problems such as part/component cost control, production planning and production efficiency. With the decrease of the number of experienced process engineers, the research of the advanced CAPP has gradually become a hot issue, and this situation has attracted more attention than ever before.

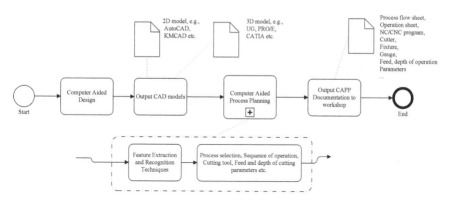

Fig. 1. The traditional CAPP planning workflow and its input

As shown in Fig. 1, the input of the CAPP mainly comes from CAD model and the manufacturing resources of workshop [4, 5]. It includes: (a) machining features; (b) geometric dimensions and tolerances of machining features (GD&T); (c) materials of the object to be processed; (d) surface roughness of machining features; and non-CAD model information, i.e. (e) the processing capacity of the workshop, such as number of machine tools, equipment, operators, etc. CAPP can help to output the process route according to process knowledge by accurately analyzing and evaluating the input information. The final output process plan includes: (a) the selected process route; (b) defining the processing operation steps and the contents of each operation step; (c) selection of cutting tools; (d) selection of machining parameters; (e) design tooling, fixture etc.; (f) plan the cutting path of the tool and calculate the machining cycle to be completed; (g) estimating the manufacturing time and cost of parts.

Although many studies have been carried out on automated CAPP, the current CAPP technology is still considered to be incomplete due to the multidisciplinary characteristics and complexity of process planning [1]. And most of the current research is focused on how computer assist in process document generation, rather than autonomous generation process scheme.

A significant feature of intelligent manufacturing is to support mass customization at an economic cost. When the production line resources are abnormal, or the market feedback demand changes, or the user request to change the orders, etc., the intelligent manufacturing system can start manufacturing process autonomously planning through MES (Manufacturing Execution System), and A-CAPP will feed back the results to MES, and then realize the RMS (Reconfiguration Manufacturing System). Therefore, A-CAPP is the driving force to realize the dynamic adjustment of the production line via configuration, and RMS is the concrete implementer to realize RMS [11–13]. A-CAPP and RMS crucial parts of the intelligent manufacturing system cooperate with MES to complete the intelligent adjustment of production line resources. This paper therefore contributes to the subject with the aim to explore method of A-CAPP system development based on the heritage industrial software, and then provide a feasible reference technical solution for the relevant research.

3   Key Technology to Build A-CAPP System

The traditional manufacturing process planning is separated from the real-time data of the production line due to the technologies' limitation. In the process planning scheme, the resources data of the production line, e.g., machine tools, equipment, cutting tools and measuring tools, were static or historical information, which may be inconsistent with the actual resource allocation of the production line. Once the process document is released to workshop, it will guide production as a programmatic document, and the workshop must comply with. When there is a contradiction between the process plan and the actual resource usage on operation site, e.g., the production line capacity is not balanced and the bottleneck resource is seriously blocked, it will affect the actual production. When it happens, the released process document needs to be re-planned by the process engineers by following a process change workflow. It not only takes time, but also may affect the process availability after the re-planning due to the dynamic changes of the actual utilization of production resources.

A-CAPP cannot only autonomously design new process plan, but also associate the real-time data of workshop production line resource use. Among the process handling, MES will feedback the useful information to A-CAPP, which greatly improves the usability of the process schemes. In addition, it takes advantages of manufacturing process knowledge library, A-CAPP can autonomously and effectively plan the process sequences, defines the process operation step tasks, configures the required tools, fixtures, gauges and other process equipment for each operation step. This way, it helps to generate practical process document in line with the actual situation of the workshop manufacturing resources and can optimize reconfiguration overheads. The data processing workflow of a practical A-CAPP is described in Fig. 2.

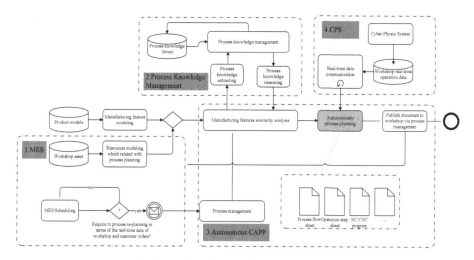

Fig. 2. Data processing workflow of A-CAPP system

3.1   Redefining Input for A-CAPP

Compared with the traditional CAPP, its input should be redefined properly. Ideally, it mainly comes from three sources as described in below.

(1) Firstly, it should come from MES (Manufacturing Execution System). MES can access the real-time data of production line resources, and know whether there has been a problem of uneven load of machine tools/equipment, and whether there are symptoms of task queue blocking of bottleneck resources through the CPS (cyber-physical System) and DNC (Distributed Numerical Control) System. Also MES can get the prediction information through the Business Intelligence Module through which it can predict possible adverse condition of the production line resources. When production line resources develop faults and the MES cannot adjust it via the internal job scheduling module (e.g., to balance the tasks among the machines with different NC/CNC system), a process engineer is required to modify the pre-planned process document with the real-time data of manufacturing resources, e.g., modify process sequence, change machine tool, re-design process equipment etc. When this happens, MES can automatically trigger request

and send message to A-CAPP; it will handle it autonomously. Because time is critical (every hour costs money) in a fault condition and autonomous manufacturing process re-planning makes it faster/cheaper.

(2) Second source input is the CPS. It collects the real-time operation data of the manufacturing resource, i.e., machine tools, equipment, robot etc., through sensor network. The data will be actively pushed to MES. MES will analyze/predict the possible abnormalities of production line resources use through the job scheduling module and manufacturing resource management module. At the same time, CPS also pushes the real-time resource data to the A-CAPP system, which is useful for relevant processes/operation steps modification. It helps to make feasible and rational modifications to the related process plans.

(3) A third source is the process knowledge management component. In the daily operation of A-CAPP, the extracted processing features, machining methods, cutting tools, fixtures, measuring tools etc., will be collected as process knowledge and stored in the process knowledge library by means of data analysis methods (e.g., clustering, classification etc.). In the late new process planning or modifying the released process plan/document, A-CAPP can deduce new process routes, operation steps, defining machine tools and equipment, tools, CNC machining programs and other information for each operation step in accordance with the processing features of the new specific mechanical part, where it will be supported in auxiliary decision-making manner by the process knowledge library. The proposed process plan set will contain multiple feasible schemes which need to be evaluated and one selected as the most feasible scheme to workshop by a process engineer. The notification can be in e-mail, SMS etc., manner sent to engineer by A-CAPP. For the changed NC/CNC machining program, manual intervention is required, and it can only be released after an offline simulation by the process engineer. After all the changed process routes, operation steps, NC/CNC program are evaluated, the workflow component of A-CAPP system will distributes the documents to MES system. The MES receives the new process scheme (process document, NC program, process equipment design model etc.) from A-CAPP; it will deliver and dispatch them automatically to the target machines (e.g., machine tools) by DNC and other related systems.

3.2   The Crucial Components of A-CAPP

The traditional CAPP mainly focused on providing tools for process document generation and design/planning of process equipment. In addition to integrating the CAPP functions, the proposed A-CAPP system needs to provide and improve some new crucial components, e.g., event manager and other components (as shown in Fig. 3), which are briefly discussed as below.

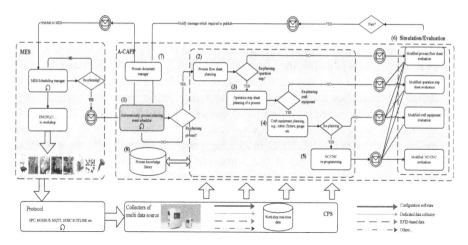

Fig. 3. The routine logic model and crucial components of A-CAPP

(1) Event manager (EM) component. It is the core component in A-CAPP imple-mentation for autonomous planning. It is responsible for sending the start process planning command (including planning new process and modifying the release process schemes), including terminating, completing commands. For example, when the A-CAPP receives the request message with a permanent event ID (e.g., ID_ReqNumber) from MES, the A-CAPP will trigger a processing flow for the process planning. It will verify firstly through component 7 and judge whether if the request is a valid new activity. If so, the A-CAPP will handle it immediately (otherwise ignores it). When the request is confirmed to be processing, it will send a request message to component 7, which generates a new task ID_TaskNumber in line with the ID_ReqNumber. And then A-CAPP marks the activity of ID_ReqNumber as locked. It can be unlocked until the job is completed or ter-minated. When the A-CAPP needs to release the process document to MES, EM will send an event message of transaction request to MES by component 7.

(2) Process flow sheet planning (PFSP) component. PFSP is a designed to make an outline scheme, which determines the process of machining, and the corre-sponding manufacturing resources (workstations, machine tools, equipment, type of work, etc.). It is from the overall view to describe the technical route of the part being processed. On one hand, PFSP recommends multiple process schemes based on CAD model of machining features and corresponding process knowl-edge; on the other hand, the proposed process schemes will comprehensively consider the factors of the real-time data of the production load, the available manufacturing resources and their processing capacity which provided by MES/DNC/CPS. In some situations, PFSP even can plan the outsourcing tasks of those the overload or overcapacity machining jobs ahead by means of the SPC data of the production lines, and then to adjust the proposed process schemes timely. As a result, the generated process document by PFSP contains a set of

schemes, which can provide multiple feasible alternatives to workshop through manufacturing resource configuring.

(3) Operation step sheet planning component. A-CAPP is similar to traditional CAPP in operation step planning (or operation step sheet), i.e., each operation step job should be refined after the main process route is determined. First of all, it will define the items for each step that includes machining sequences and contents (geometric surfaces etc.), cutting parameters (e.g., spindle speed, cutting depth, and feed of pre revolution), the required machine tool, cutting tool, jig, measuring tools, and developing NC/CNC machining program according to the extracted information from CAD model (i.e., processing dimensional, tolerance, surface roughness etc.). Then to design the related cutters for operation steps in terms of the operation step sheet file.

However, the difference with the traditional CAPP is that A-CAPP develops the operation step sheet using real-time data of the production line and manufacturing resources use, for example to guide optimal resource scheduling. In the intelligent manufacturing system, A-CAPP will autonomously start modification to the released process document when the workshop organizes production accordingly but may meet problems in manufacturing resources use. MES can help to find the potential problems in resources use via CPS and DNC. When it happens, MES will work with A-CAPP to handle it accordingly in the three main way as follows:

(a) Modifying the released machining program. MES will send a request of adjusting the released process document to A-CAPP when some abnormal in manufacturing resources use are met. If the request is limited in machine tools change with different NC/CNC (Numerical Control/Computer Numerical Control) system for a specific operation step, the related machining program (G codes) should be autonomously revised. For the modification part of machining program, it is mainly concerned with the pre-and-post processing codes due to the different requirement by varied NC/CNC systems. However, the main part of machining codes (e.g., cutting path etc.) do not need to be modified. This also is highly frequent adjustment case that occurs in job scheduling.

(b) Modifying the released process flow sheet document. When the MES cannot solve the resources use problem by simple change machine tools, it has to modify the machining sequence (machining process route) in terms of the real-time load data of production lines. In this case, the PFSP will be triggered by A-CAPP autonomously. The PFSP will respond and handle it when receives the change request event message from EM. This is a more complicated process that will affect the related operation step sheets file.

(c) Modifying the equipment, machine tools and the other resources. When workshop encounters abnormal situation in use of equipment defined by the released process document for execution the operation step found by the MES, e.g., the planned cutters, fixtures, gauges etc. are not available, A-CAPP will be involved to fix it in terms of the real-time data of the workshop's equipment provided by MES/CPS. It will provide a few recommended change schemes (e.g., a list of the specific process equipment) for the process engineer to decide which is most suitable by using the process equipment knowledge database.

(4) NC machining program planner component. The NC program is the control program stored in the numerical control system. It consists of numbers, words and symbols to form the machine/equipment motion control instructions, which include parameters such as cutting tool coordinate, angle and speed etc. The popular NC/CNC systems include Japanese products, e.g., FANUC (such as 16i/18i/21i), Mitsubishi (M700V, E68, etc.), MAZAK; German products, e.g., Siemens of Germany (SINUMERIK series), Heidenhain (iTNC 530), Bosch Rexroth, French Schneider (NUM1020/1040, etc.), Spanish FAGOR, Chinese Huazhong Numeral Control, etc. Different numerical control systems need different initial codes to pre-define the parameters of the systems, in order to meet the initial requirements of the coordinate system, cutting parameters and the others of the NC/CNC system. When the modified machining program only is made due to the change of NC/CNC system, the corresponding processing of the change (i.e., pre-and-post processing of NC/CNC program) can be automatically processed by dedicated software kit, and then published to workshop after engineer evaluation. The other functions of NC/CNC machine program planner component are in line with the current CAM software.

(5) Process simulation and validation component. It uses computer graphics technology and dynamic programming to predict if the planned cutting path is feasible, e.g., generation free collision moving path among the designed cutter, the fixtures to hold/clamp the machining part and the other related items; and also no undercutting/overcutting situations occurring in terms of the comparison between the original CAD and the simulation result in advance. Process simulation functions can be realized in A-CAPP by adopting Add-In or other programming methods to integrate the third parties products of CAM simulation/verification (e.g., UG, VERICUT, Pro/E, MasterCAM, CATIA, Cimatron, EdgeCAM, CAXA, etc.), or developing CAM simulation functions. The functions of process simulation and verification are important; it belongs to the final evaluation phase before the generated process documents are released to workshop. Thus, it needs the process engineers' verification. Depending on the devices, fully automatic deployment may not be safe

(6) Process document manager component. Theoretically, the functions of process document/file manager are the part of PDM (Product Data Management). It realizes the management routines of process files version, configuration scheme, workflow (such as the flows of evaluation/audit and technical document change etc.) by associating the process document/files through the design document. Since this is concerned with releasing process documents and involving the other important technical activities, the management of the manufacturing process documents requires the intervention of the process engineers, and the process is not fully automated. Regarding the specific functions development, it can be achieved by extending the traditional PDM (Product Data Management) system and integrating the core components of A-CAPP system, such as the Event Manger (EM) component and the process knowledge library components etc.

3.3   Knowledge Management Component of A-CAPP

A-CAPP can establish a reliable process knowledge library by using the knowledge of machining feature classification, manufacturing resources, machining methods (i.e., fusion of the manufacturing process and the resources). It will support autonomous planning of machining process, operation steps and developing the NC machining program, by which it can improve the overall performance of the manufacturing system, change the traditional CAPP use mode and realize the manufacturing process planning autonomously. The knowledge management component functions of A-CAPP consist of the followings.

(1) Machining feature knowledge management. This has a number of aspects. Firstly, machining feature knowledge management needs to define meta-machining features and combination methods; further more to map them with common machining features, and gradually establish the classification model of the machining features required by enterprises. Secondly, it needs to establish the mechanism of the manufacturing process information expression based on MBD (Model-based Definition), which is useful to build the association relation between the B-rep's (Boundary Representative) geometrical & topological information of the elementary geometric objects (i.e., point, line, face of the CAD Model) and the engineering properties of the CAD model such as dimensional, tolerance, surface roughness, and the other technical requirements. The mixed expression (e.g., object-oriented semi-structured XML data format files) can be used to express the correlation model which reflects the mapping relation between the geometric features and the manufacturing features. The geometric feature recognition and machining feature mapping of the part model can be completed automatically by using the established correlation model and the results can be used as the input information of the machining features for A-CAPP.

(2) Knowledge management of machining resources. It is mainly about the information of the production line (including machine tools, equipment, robot etc.) and process equipment (such as cutting tools, fixtures, measuring tools, etc.) in the workshop, which is managed by the model of process resources. The model should have the ability to describe the resources in both static and dynamic ways that can reflect the production line, machine tool, equipment etc., from the physical structure, geometric aspect, function, information and control system of the resources. Then A-CAPP will use the information to evaluate the manufacturability of products or judge the applicable scope of the production line or equipment. The process resource model can not only support intelligent reasoning in process planning, and judge the relevance among the objects such as process features, manufacturing resources and machining methods, but also can be used to support the effectiveness analysis of process procedures.

(3) Machining process knowledge management. The machining method selection of typical process features is to judge the similarity between the current processing object and the features in the feature database by searching the pre-defined feature database, and then extract the process knowledge items with high similarity as the basic process (or template) to establish the current part process in an automatic or

semi-automatic way. The similarity machining process analysis is realized by the clustering learning model. It needs to define the coding rules of the entire feature vector by establishing the mapping relationship between the machining process features and process plan, and then to use the learning algorithm based on the auxiliary domain data learning and fusion algorithm based on the matching model. In addition, it needs to access the quality assurance data of the machining products and the running data of the machine tools, equipment, robot etc., and the process parameters, which achieved by means of combining the actual information of the machining process features from MES with analysis result of the processing sequence, the clamping way, machining range constraint etc., plus introduction of the association rules in the learning process similarity model. Finally, it can improve the reliability of machining process similarity study performance and realize the continuous optimization for the machining parameters of the knowledge library.

(4) Process knowledge maintenance. The production process knowledge fusion model is established by means of projecting the basic information of the CAD model (e.g., geometric features, process features) and the processing resources, process parameters into the same semantic shared subspace; and then completing the data mining tasks such as association and clustering. The knowledge management component establish the relationship between the process parameters and the quality of products, equipment status data from MES, through the association data mining via the improved *a priori* big data association rules algorithm. Finally, it can continuously improve the effectiveness of the planned processes of parts in an autonomous way. In the process of knowledge mining, A-CAPP system need to safely share the related data across time, region, physical space and network space through the whole process of non-destructive transmission of important process data and its fusion information in encryption, compression, transmission, reception and analysis.

4 Conclusions

Traditional CAPP is applied in a relatively independent technical preparation phase. Although it can be integrated with collaborative design to some extent, it still occurs solely in the process of technical preparation phase and does not scale with the actual production phase. Furthermore, it used the outdated and unrealistic production data in static/historical manner, which lacks the improvement for the manufacturing process schemes and process parameters via the actual production quality data.

A-CAPP can solve or relieve it by extending and developing some crucial components, e.g., the event manager and process knowledge library and the others, based on the heritages. The autonomous process planning function can work in an integrated environment among PDM/MES/DNC/CPS in automatic and semi-automatic ways. For the important jobs of A-CAPP, e.g., valuation and review if a manufacturing process plan is feasible and whether if it can be released to workshop etc., engineer intervention is needed. The quality and the feasibility of the process schemes planned by A-CAPP will be higher than before.

In an ideal intelligent manufacturing system, A-CAPP is able to relieve bottleneck resources constraints, balance the loads of the production lines and improve the corresponding productivity of the whole manufacturing system by using the real-time production line data provided by MES. In addition, the relationship between product quality and process parameters can be established and the product quality can be continuously optimized. Therefore, the manufacturing system with autonomous process planning ability is able to meet the needs of small batch production and personalized mass customization; and it is also the direction of the development of intelligent manufacturing.

The future work for this project will mainly focus on two aspects: one is to use the proposed method of A-CAPP based on KMCAPP, developed by KMSoft and applied widely in China, to establish a prototype system which can realize the preliminary integration with MES; the other aspect is to carry out research on dynamic reconstruction technology of production line, integrate the prototype A-CAPP system with production line configuration management system, realize the integration of A-CAPP, DNC and other related systems to reach a closed-loop control of the whole manufacturing system.

Acknowledgement. This project is funded by the State Key Research and Development Program of China (2017YFE0118700); and received funding from the European Union's Horizon 2020 research and innovation programme under the Marie Skłodowska-Curie grant agreement No 734599.

References

1. Xu, X., Wang, L., Newman, S.T.: Computer-aided process planning—a critical review of recent developments and future trends. Int. J. Comput. Integr. Manuf. 24(1), 1–31 (2011)
2. Cay, F., Chassapis, C.: An IT view on perspectives of computer aided process planning research. Comput. Ind. 34(3), 307–337 (1997)
3. Marri, H.B., Gunasekaran, A., Grieve, R.J.: Computer-aided process planning: a state of art, 261–268(1998)
4. Kumar, M., Rajotia, S.: Integration of scheduling with computer aided process planning. J. Mater. Process. Technol. 138(1–3), 297–300 (2003)
5. Bard, J.F., Feo, T.A.: The cutting path and tool selection problem in computer aided process planning. J. Manuf. Syst. 8(1), 17–26 (1989)
6. Yusof, Y., Latif, K.: Survey on computer-aided process planning. Int. J. Adv. Manuf. Technol. 75(1–4), 77–89 (2014)
7. Halevi, G., Weill, R.D.: Computer-aided process planning (CAPP). In: Halevi, G. (ed.) Principles of Process Planning, pp. 317–332. Springer, Dordrecht (1995). https://doi.org/10.1007/978-94-011-1250-5_15
8. Ciurana, J., Ferrer, I., Gao, J.X.: Activity model and computer aided system for defining sheet metal process planning. J. Mater. Process. Technol. 173(2), 213–222 (2006)
9. Sarcar, M.M.M., Rao, K.M., Narayan, K.L.: Computer aided design and manufacturing. PHI Learning Pvt. Ltd 10. (2008)
10. Culler, D.E., Burd, W.: A framework for extending computer aided process planning to include business activities and computer aided design and manufacturing (CAD/CAM) data retrieval. Robot. Comput. Integr. Manuf. 23(3), 339–350 (2007)

11. Rösiö, C., Säfsten, K.: Reconfigurable production system design theoretical and practical challenges. J. Manuf. Technol. Manag. **24**(7), 998–1018 (2013)
12. Hasan, F., Jain, P.K., Kumar, D.: Optimum configuration selection in reconfigurable manufacturing system involving multiple part families. Opsearch **51**(2), 297–311 (2014)
13. Wang, G.X., Huang, S.H., Yan, Y., Du, J.J.: Reconfiguration schemes evaluation based on preference ranking of key characteristics of reconfigurable manufacturing systems. Int. J. Adv. Manuf. Technol. **89**, 2231–2249 (2017)
14. http://support.ptc.com/help/windchill/whc/whc_en/index.html#page/Windchill_Help_Center %2FExpMPM_Oview.html%23. Accessed 25 Feb 2019
15. https://www.3ds.com/products-services/delmia/products/. Accessed 25 Feb 2019
16. https://www.plm.automation.siemens.com/global/en/. Accessed 25 Feb 2019

Design of Meshing Assembly
Algorithms for Industrial Gears
Based on Image Recognition

Jinhua Jiang[✉], Qin Qin, Yuewei Bai, and Zhenyu Chen

School of Intelligent Manufacturing and Control Engineering,
Shanghai Polytechnic University, Shanghai 201209, China
jhjiang@sspu.edu.cn

Abstract. Aiming at the assembly efficiency of industrial gears, the meshing assembly algorithms of industrial gears based on image recognition were proposed to realize the assembly of industrial gears by industrial robots with the guide of machine vision. In this design, working area were photographed, and then the images were processed. The obtained coordinates of gear edge were converted with the curve fitting, and the initial phase of the curve was calculated. According to the properties of gears and the initial phase difference between two curves, the rotation angle of gears could be calculated. Using simulation method, the precision and error of meshing assembly according to the algorithms could be calculated, and a margin of error of the rotation angle by simulation could be fallen within 0.01°.

Keywords: Gear · Meshing assembly · Image processing ·
Coordinate conversion · Curve fitting

1 Introduction

With the advent of the Industry 4.0, China has also put forward the plan of "made in China 2025" for its own industry, and the progress of intelligent manufacturing has gradually penetrated into every corner of the manufacturing industry. The introduction of machine vision in intelligent manufacturing accelerates the pace of industrial development. Machine vision is mainly used in product sorting, vision measurement and artificial intelligence in current industrial manufacturing field [1–5]. In the production process of products, the requirements for the accuracy of products are increasingly higher and higher. The traditional measurement method brings the problems of low efficiency and substandard accuracy, and the introduction of machine vision greatly improves the accuracy and efficiency of measurement.

As a crucial element of industrial production, the gear is essential in the assembly of equipment, but most of them still use manual assembly. In order to realize and replace manual operation, machine vision is introduced into gear assembly operation. In the machine vision system, the application for gear is mainly used in the defect detection of gear and the detection of meshing degree after assembly, and the machine vision is not used in the gear assembly [6, 7]. From the perspective of the application of

© Springer Nature Switzerland AG 2019
H. A. Proper and J. Stirna (Eds.): CAiSE 2019 Workshops, LNBIP 349, pp. 64–72, 2019.
https://doi.org/10.1007/978-3-030-20948-3_6

machine vision in industrial production, the non-contact measurement of objects is mainly realized through camera calibration in the field of measurement. However, the relative position of gear teeth should be measured in the assembly of gears, and the main problem is the angle difference between gears in the assembly process. By determining the attitude and position of each gear, the rotation angle of the gear can be calculated, and the meshing assembly of the gears can be realized through rotation in the assembly process. By means of the gear assembly guided by machine vision, the manual operation in gear assembly can be replaced by machine. In this paper, design the corresponding algorithm for machine vision to realize the assembly of gears in simple cases, which fills the automatic assembly of gears in industrial assembly, and provides a design method for the automatic assembly of gears in complex cases in industrial production, thus the efficiency and safety in the production process can be improved.

2 Working Principle and Structure of Visual System

The hardware of the machine vision system mainly consisted of camera and light source, the camera came mainly from ALLIED Industrial Camera and light source used white-light surface one. The whole design was mainly to complete the recognition and overall positioning of the two industrial gears in the field of view, as well as the positioning of the outer teeth of the gears, and then to calculate the rotation angle of the two gears to be rotated in advance during the translational assembly process of the two gears by means of image processing. The system software engineering mainly included camera calibration, image acquisition, image filtering, binarization, edge processing, and image processing, etc. The detailed design procedures were shown in Fig. 1.

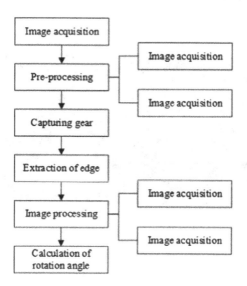

Fig. 1. Flow chart of the system

3 Design of the Image Processing Software

In the design of the image processing, at first it is necessary to determine the field of view that the camera was able to take, and then the light source of the device. The choice of light source determined if the images could achieve the desired effect for post-processing. The objects to be photographed in this design were white industrial gears, so in the selection of the shooting environment, and the white surface light source was selected to be placed above the object to be photographed. Black matte iron plate was selected as the background which was sharp contrast and non-reflective.

3.1 Image Filtering

There may be some impurities in the field of view taken by the camera, which may form noise points in the captured images. At this time, the captured images need to be filtered first. The commonly used filtering includes median filtering, mean filtering, maximum filtering, minimum filtering, Gaussian filtering, etc. [8]. The Gaussian filtering is superior to the mean filtering in edge protection and can meet the requirement of the edge information higher in the design.

3.2 Binarization

The photos taken by the camera in this design were color ones, which will result in slow of computing speed due to the large amount of data in the later image processing. What's more, the binarization of the original image was adopted, which greatly reduced the memory occupied by each pixel. It was not only reduced the size of the image data, but also made the image edge of the image more clearly. In this design, threshold transformation method was used to realize the conversion of image binarization, as shown in Fig. 2.

(a) Original image   (b) Binarization image

Fig. 2. Pre-processing image

3.3 Image Capture

In the process of image processing, the gears in the image need to be processed separately, so the gears in the image need to be recognized and captured before the image processing. The capturing of images was to find the centroid of each gear and the dimension of gear in the images.

Here, we used the property of centroid in regionprops() function to get the centroid position of the gear in the image, while its boundingbox property was also used to get the position and dimension information of each gear in the image. The Boundingbox property was the minimum matrix containing the region. The property could be used to get the coordinates of the upper left corner of the minimum matrix and the length and width values of the minimum matrix.

The two properties of the regionprops() function could be used to capture the location and dimension information of each gear in the binarization image. In order to obtain the better edge features for the subsequent gears, additional tenpixel points were captured at the edge of the gear image when the image was captured. The final captured images of gears were shown in Fig. 3.

Fig. 3. Binarization images of gears captured

3.4 Extraction of Edge Features of Image

Extraction of edge features is the processing of image profile and the edge is the set of points where image pixel value has step change [9, 10]. Since the image had been converted to a binarization image in the previous step, the profile information of gear could be only obtained by four-domain analysis during the extraction of edge features.

There were two kinds of edge information of the gear in the captured image, the outer profile could be used for data post-processing, and the inner hole of the gear were treated as interference information, which used for extraction of profile after filling treatment. And the infill() function was used to fill the empty area in the binarization image. In this way, the area with black part in the gear was filled with white, and then the edge feature of the image was extracted. The final extracted gear profile diagram was shown in Fig. 4.

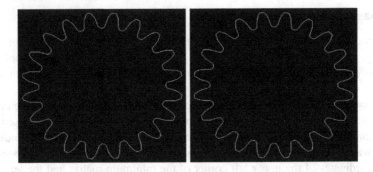

Fig. 4. Outer profile diagram of gear

3.5　Image Processing

The main function of image processing was to obtain the attitude information of each gear under the current state. Firstly, the center position of the gear in the profile diagram should be found, and the origin of the original coordinate system of the image could be shifted to the center position of the gear, so as to realize the uniform distribution of the gear profile coordinates in the four quadrants. The coordinates of the gear profile in the new coordinate system were calculated again, and then the coordinates in the rectangular coordinate system were converted to ones in the polar coordinate system. Therefore, the set of polar coordinates of the gear profile could be obtained.

$$C = \{(r1, \theta1), (r2, \theta2), \ldots\ldots, (ri, \theta i)\}, \ (i, \ \text{Number of coordinate points}) \quad (1)$$

With the conversion of the coordinate system, a set of two polar coordinates were obtained, and then they could be arranged in order from small to large according to the θ value in each set. The obtained new coordinate set was plotted to obtain the profile polar coordinate diagram, was shown in Fig. 5.

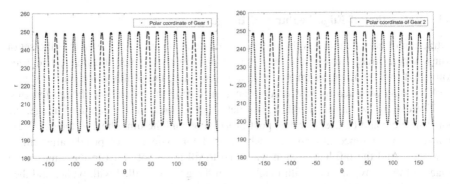

(a) Polar coordinate diagram of Gear 1 profile　(b) Polar coordinate diagram of Gear 2 profile

Fig. 5. Polar coordinate diagram of gear profile

Observed from Fig. 5, the distribution of polar coordinates of the gear profile presented a sinusoidal wave trend, and the curve fitting performed with the points of the coordinate system. The mathematical model of the fitting formula was following:

$$f(\theta) = A \cdot \sin(\omega\theta + \varphi) \tag{2}$$

where the A and ω represented the amplitude of the fitting curve and angular frequency, respectively. Since the gear had 20 teeth, the angular frequency was fixed at 20. φ was the initial phase. In order to reduce the computing burden of the computer, the amplitude A of the curve in the formula obtained by the mean value on the vertical axis of the coordinate.

$$A = \frac{1}{i} \cdot \sum_{j=1}^{i} r_j \tag{3}$$

The fitting curve was shown in Fig. 6.

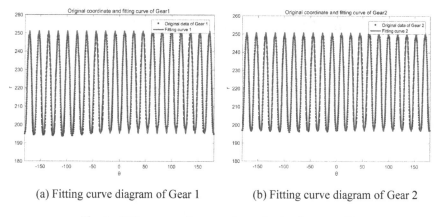

(a) Fitting curve diagram of Gear 1   (b) Fitting curve diagram of Gear 2

Fig. 6. Fitting curve diagram of coordinate of gear profile

According to the fitting curve of the polar coordinates of the two gear profiles, the initial phase of the two fitting curves could be get, which included the angles between the connecting line of top end on each gear tooth with the center of the gear. And the horizontal axis was determined by the initial phase. In order to realize the meshing of gears in the assembly process, the meshing between the gear teeth and the tooth slots was needed, which means that the peak and trough of the two gears in the fitting curve had same θ value. The two gears had 20 teeth each, and the curve period was $\pi/10$. To achieve meshing of gears, only difference between the initial phase of two fitting curves was required to be integer times of $\pi/20$ through calculation.

$$\text{rotate} = \frac{\pi}{20} \cdot k - |\varphi_1 - \varphi_2| (k = \pm1, \pm2, \pm3, \ldots\ldots) \tag{4}$$

Through the above calculation, the angle value of gear 2 rotated was obtained when gear 1. In general, the value of k should not be too large. After rotating the gear, the resulting image was shown in Fig. 7.

Fig. 7. Image of gear after rotating

4 Conclusion and Analysis of Experiments

It could be observed which the two gears were engaged rotating the gear under translation for the rotated image. In order to better verify the stability and accuracy of the design, several experiments were carried out to test the system performance under the same condition. The measured data under different placement conditions were shown in Table 1.

Table 1. Measurements of gears after rotation under different placement conditions

No.	Gear 1 $\varphi_1/°$	Gear 2 $\varphi_2/°$	Rotation angle/°	Gear 2 after rotating $\varphi_2'/°$	Absolute error/°	Relative error/°
1	8.5593	9.3162	8.2431	−0.4416	0.0009	1.1085×10^{-2}
2	−6.9245	4.7061	−2.6306	2.0740	0.0015	1.6483×10^{-2}
3	4.1687	8.6378	4.5309	−4.8334	0.0021	2.3010×10^{-2}
4	1.9595	−0.9513	−6.0892	−7.0403	0.0021	2.3010×10^{-2}
5	−1.1131	−7.2178	−2.8953	7.8900	0.0031	3.4068×10^{-2}
6	−6.4141	2.8153	0.2294	2.5871	0.0012	1.3333×10^{-2}

By analyzing the data in Table 1, it could be found that the gears were placed by different ways in the same environment, while no error occurred during recognition of image of gears. After processing the image of gear, the initial phase of each gear was obtained. With the initial phase difference of the two gears, the rotation angle of the gears to be assembled were calculated. After rotating the image of the gears to be rotated with the corresponding angle, the rotated image was processed to obtain the curve fitted by the rotated gear edge, and the initial phase of the rotated gear was calculated, as well as the inherent error of the algorithm. The results of gear assembly in the real operation process were thereby simulated. It could be seen from the results that the error of the simulation result obtained by rotating the image after outputting the rotation angle was fallen within the range of 0.01°. As many errors might be introduced in the field operation while the error range of the output result given in the image processing was negligible, which reduced the systematic error caused by followed robot in the assembly process.

5 Summarization

After filtering image, binarization, processing image and taking edge features for the two gears randomly placed in the field of view, computing the initial phase of each gear, and the rotation angle of the gears to be rotated, the meshing of the translation gears could be thus realized. Through the realization of gear meshing assembly guided by machine vision, it filled the gap that industrial gear manual assembly in the process of industrial production and manufacturing could be replaced by machine.

In this paper, the experimental was demonstrated. In the results that the image processing algorithm could realize the recognition of the plane gear and the rotation angle value of the gear to be assembled. And the accuracy of the theoretical rotation angle measured by the experiment within the range of 0.01°. The high-precision output reduced the system error for the field assembly of the subsequent robot.

The idea provided by the algorithm could not only be used to the assembly of flat gears in the industrial production and manufacturing process, but also be extended to the assembly between different types of gears.

Acknowledgments. This research had been partially sponsored by National Key R & D Program of China (2017YEE0118700), EUH2020 FIRST project (Grant No. 734599, FIRST: vF Interoperation supporting business innovation), National Natural Science Foundation of China under Grant (No. U1537110 and 51605273), Shanghai Polytechnic University Key Discipline Construction (Mechanical Engineering, XXKZD1603), and Shanghai Polytechnic University School Fund (EGD19XQD06).

References

1. Xie, B.: Industrial robot positioning and grasping technology based on machine vision. Intern. Combust. Engine Accessories **21**, 216–218 (2018). https://doi.org/10.19475/j.cnki.issn1674-957x.2018.21.107

2. Shi, L.: A defect detection method for packaging and printing based on machine vision and image processing. Chin. Sci. Technol. Bull. **10**, 105–108 (2008). https://doi.org/10.13774/j.cnki.kjtb.2018.10.017

3. Yuan, W., Xue, D.: Review of algorithms for crack detection of tunnel lining based on machine vision. J. Instrum. **38**(12), 3100–3111 (2017)

4. Zhu, Y., Yin, D., Zou, S., Wang, H., Zhou, W.: Development and application of machine vision in the automotive industry. Automot. Pract. Technol. **22**, 8–11 (2017). https://doi.org/10.16638/j.cnki.1671-7988.2017.22.004

5. Liu, X., Liu, H., Haibo, W., Zhang, L.: Simulation realization of industrial robot sorting workstation based on vision. Sci. Technol. Innov. **33**, 11–12 (2017). https://doi.org/10.3969/j.issn.1673-1328.2017.33.006
6. Niu, J., Shen, J., Xing, M.: Measurement method of tooth shape parameter of gear based on vision. Mach. Tool Hydraul. **45**(22), 148–153 (2017). https://doi.org/10.3969/j.issn.1001-3881.2017.22.038
7. Zhou, X.: Rapid detection of small modulus gear. Autom. Technol. Appl. **36**(10), 104–107 +127 (2017). https://doi.org/10.3969/j.issn.1003-7241.2017.10.025
8. Guan, X.: Research on Matlab image filtering processing technology. J. Anyang Normal Univ. **05**, 37–39+94 (2018). https://doi.org/10.16140/j.cnki.1671-5330.2018.05.010
9. Shu, J., Chenghong, X., Yang, L., Jiang, H., Li, Z., Ke, W.: Extraction of 3-D image edge feature based on machine vision. Inf. Commun. **12**, 22–23 (2017). https://doi.org/10.3969/j.issn.1673-1131.2017.12.008
10. Duan, Z., Shan, Z., Zhao, W., Yang, X.: Research on algorithm of fast extraction of digital image edge. Modular Mach. Tool Autom. Process. Technol. **12**, 12–14+20 (2017). https://doi.org/10.13462/j.cnki.mmtamt.2017.12.003

Detecting Anomalous Behavior Towards Predictive Maintenance

Athanasios Naskos[1(✉)], Anastasios Gounaris[2], Ifigeneia Metaxa[1],
and Daniel Köchling[3]

[1] ATLANTIS Engineering Ltd., Thessaloniki, Greece
{naskos,metaxa}@abe.gr
[2] Aristotle University of Thessaloniki, Thessaloniki, Greece
gounaria@csd.auth.gr
[3] BENTELER GmbH, Paderborn, Germany
daniel.koechling@benteler.com

Abstract. A key Industry 4.0 element is predictive maintenance, which leverages machine learning, IoT and big data applications to ensure that the required equipment is fully functional at all times. In this work, we present a case study of smart maintenance in a real-world setting. The rationale is to depart from model-based and simple rule-based techniques and adopt an approach, which detects anomalous events in an unsupervised manner. Further, we explore how incorporation of domain knowledge can assist the unsupervised anomaly detection process and we discuss practical issues.

Keywords: Anomaly detection · Predictive maintenance · Industry 4.0

1 Introduction

Predictive Maintenance (PdM) is considered a key task in Industry 4.0 with a view to decreasing, if not eliminating, machinery downtime and operational costs [1]. Modern PdM heavily relies on machine learning, e.g., [10,11,13], where the key concept is to intensively process event logs and then train models to identify failure patterns well in advance.

In this work, we advocate a complementary approach, where we employ unsupervised machine learning, and more specifically anomaly detection [2]. We show that, in addition to devising predictive models, we can continuously monitor the incoming data and apply state-of-the-art algorithms for streaming outlier detection. The outliers reported by such a process can be safely regarded as early signs of failure and thus become part of an advanced PdM solution. The key strength of our approach is that it does not rely on representative event logs and model training.

© Springer Nature Switzerland AG 2019
H. A. Proper and J. Stirna (Eds.): CAiSE 2019 Workshops, LNBIP 349, pp. 73–82, 2019.
https://doi.org/10.1007/978-3-030-20948-3_7

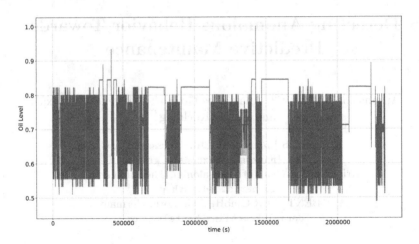

Fig. 1. Oil level.

1.1 Our Case Study

The case study is motivated by a typical maintenance activity in industrial plants, such as those of BENTELER Automotive. BENTELER produces and distributes safety-relevant products, serving customers in automotive technology, the energy sector and mechanical engineering. The production of such plants employs to a large extent machinery with several mechanical and hydraulic systems, which entail frequent and/or periodic maintenance such as lubrication oil replacement and refill, given that oil leakages are a common and expected phenomenon.

More specifically, our study focuses on early detection of oil leakage occurrences. Despite the fact that, typically, oil is mostly stored in large tanks equipped with oil level sensors, oil leakage detection is a challenging problem due to the continuous movement of oil across the machinery equipment parts. Such movement results in frequent increases and decreases of oil level, as depicted in Fig. 1. Therefore, and somehow counter-intuitively, simply monitoring the oil level is not adequate to provide concrete evidence about oil leakage.

To detect incidents, the main metric needs to be combined with two other types of information. Firstly, to process the oil level in relation to the concurrent IoT measurements of other aspects of the same equipment, such as temperature, current, mechanical part position and movement sensors, accelerometers, pressure sensors and so on. This allows oil level to be regarded in a specific context but has the drawback that not all other measurements are relevant. Secondly, to employ domain specific knowledge, which can assist the data analyst to understand whether the system is in idle state, as the oil level will be stabilized. The most straightforward way is to infer the time periods in which operation intermission takes place, when such information is not explicitly provided. For example, in such periods, some mechanical parts are often in a position in which they can never be during normal operation. Or, specific measurements of some other parts are below some threshold. The challenge here is to automatically detect the data rules that define the operation status of the machinery before applying anomaly detection.

Overall, the goal is to provide a detection tool to the maintenance engineers, which can monitor and analyse at runtime key measurements of the system, in order to detect and report oil leakages at early stages. We consider that the measurement collection and fault reporting mechanisms are already provided, as the description of their development is out of the scope of this paper.

1.2 Summary and Paper Structure

In summary, in our case study, the aim is to detect oil leakage through combining oil level sensor measurements with other IoT device readings and inferring through data pre-processing the stabilized time periods. From the machine learning point of view, the goal is to devise unsupervised learning solutions that do not rely on a well-defined training set of past problematic states. The techniques are described in Sect. 2 and evaluated in Sect. 3. We conclude in Sect. 4. Non-essential technical details regarding our solutions are deferred to the Appendix.

2 Timely Failure Detection Approaches

2.1 Rule-Based Approach

Traditionally, thresholds are set to sensor measurements to trigger alerts on their violation. In the evaluation, a rule-based mechanism is used as a baseline approach. The simplicity of such a reactive approach is both an advantage and a disadvantage, as it is simple enough to be easily understood, developed and deployed, but rather naive to detect more complex events, which potentially encapsulate valuable information and to adapt in unstable environments, producing lots of false positive reports. As already explained in the use case presentation, due to the movement of the oil inside the machinery and the storage tank, the definition of a static rule for the detection of an oil leakage is a challenging task and if the requirement of an early detection is considered, more advanced solutions are required as explained hereby.

2.2 Outlier Detection Approach

Outlier detection is a vivid research field that has developed broad and multifaceted algorithmic solutions. Through a variety of unsupervised learning solutions, ranging from basic clustering techniques like k-means [6], to Neural Network solutions like self-organised maps [8], we have selected an efficient and effective algorithm proposed in [9], namely the Micro-cluster Continuous Outlier Detection (MCOD) technique. For the challenging task of detecting outliers in data streams, MCOD provides low memory and processing footprint and its results are easily understandable, compared to the other solutions.

As the comparative study [12] suggests, the MCOD algorithm is considered as a state-of-the-art solution in the streaming data processing for distance-based outlier detection. Utilizing the MCOD algorithm in our case study, we can detect sudden changes (i) in the oil level or (ii) in other measurements related to the oil level, or (iii) combinations of measurements related to each other and to the oil level. The detected sudden changes may or may not be an indication of a fault.

MCOD on Raw Data. In this scenario, we apply the MCOD algorithm to the (normalized) raw measurements, without applying any filtering to the incoming data of a hot forming line. Maintenance experts have defined a short list of measurements (8 out of ~1000) that might be correlated to the oil leakage use case. In the evaluation section we presents results from the application of the MCOD algorithm to a subset of these measurements. This setup increases the flexibility of the monitoring tool since it can be easily transferred to other use cases without the need of any prior knowledge of the production cycle.

MCOD Combined with Prior Domain Knowledge. Domain knowledge is important to interpret the machinery functionality and provide more specialized solutions, which can potentially give an edge over any other application agnostic proposal. In this scenario we have utilized domain expert knowledge to identify the status of the machinery (healthy/unhealthy) and obtain more stable results considering the oil level. Oil level is stabilized within 10 s after the machinery functionality is halted. Analyzing the incoming measurements considering the position of specific moving parts of the machinery, as in Fig. 2 (red line), we are able to define when the machinery is halted, and after a 10 s interval (green area of the Figure), apply the MCOD algorithm.

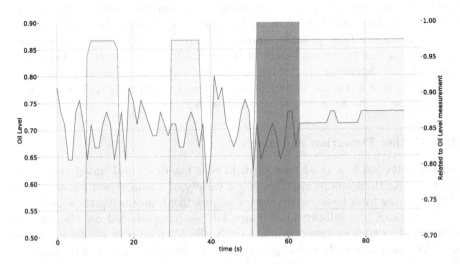

Fig. 2. Mechanical part movement in relation to oil level (Color figure online)

Algorithm 1. Outlier Reporting Filtering

$minOutlierLife$ is a user defined parameter
po represents the last reported outlier
while $true$ **do**
    $sensor\_meas \leftarrow$ fetch_measurements()
    $outliers \leftarrow$ detect_outliers($sensor\_meas$)
    for all o in $outliers$ **do**
        if $o.life < minOutlierLife$ **then**
            if $o.time > po.time + 5mins$ **then**
                report_outlier()
                $po \leftarrow o$

Practical Considerations. In distance-based outliers, a data point that has less than k neighbours inside a radius R, is an anomaly (see more details in the Appendix).

MCOD applies on data streams using a sliding window, hence there are user-defined parameters considering both the actual functionality of the algorithm and the streaming approach. There are four main parameters: (1) the window size W, which to either the time duration of the amount of the most recent data points considered; (2) the slide size S, which defines how fast/far the window moves in each algorithm step; (3) the threshold k on the number of neighbors in order a point to be labeled either as an inlier or an outlier in each step; and (4) the radius R that defines the radius of the neighborhood.

In continuous outlier detection, the detected outliers between all the active points are reported for every slide. If the slide size is lower than the window size (which is the usual case), then outliers will be reported multiple times. In a real case scenario of deployment of the algorithm in the production line, multiple reports of outliers can lead to frustration of the maintenance engineers. In addition, it is not practical to report all the outliers spotted in a short time range, as the maintenance engineers can physically investigate the machinery upon the first report of an outlier and usually the investigation requires more than some seconds or even minutes.

Hence, as it is presented in Algorithm 1, to provide a solution that is practically usable, we have defined a period of time (i.e. 5 min) after the first report of an outlier, where no other detected outlier is reported. We have also specified a parameter ($minOutlierLife$), which defines the amount of time (expressed in percentage of total number of slides inside a window) an outlier should be active before been reported.

3   Evaluation

The evaluation is based on real data obtained from the machinery of interest, working in the actual production line. The available data extend through 7 months. We have divided the available data into 2 datasets, which are examined separately. The first dataset, includes the first 4 months and its sampling

Table 1. Parameters for the first experiment

Parameter	Techniques			
	RL	MCOD	MCOD_DK	MCOD_M
meas.	oilLevel	oilLevel	oilLevel	oilLevel meas_1
W	-	3600	3600	3600
S	-	360	360	360
R	-	0.17	0.11	0.2
k	-	70	550	45
outlierLife	-	1	1	1
rule	<8800	-	-	-

rate is unstable but ground truth data exist. The ground truth reveals that in 13 days, maintenance tasks either explicitly or implicitly related to oil leakage have been reported. The second dataset includes the last month of the available data, where the measurements sampling rate is stabilized but there is no ground truth.

3.1   Proof of Concept Experimentation

In the initial set of experiments, we have used the first dataset and we have applied four variants: (i) rule-based (RL), (ii) MCOD on raw data (MCOD), (iii) MCOD with domain knowledge (MCOD_DK), and (iv) MCOD on multiple fields (MCOD_M).

The parametrization for each technique variant is presented in Table 1. The difference is in the R and k values. For the MCOD_DK approach, k is set to a higher value, while R to a lower than the other approaches, as the oil level measurement is much more stable, hence it is "safe" to set more strict thresholds to the algorithm (i.e. it will not produce too many outlier detection reports). Considering the R value, when more than one measurements are used for monitoring (i.e. the MCOD_M case), the R value should be increased, as the Euclidean distance is computed between pairs of points, not single points; otherwise, multiple false positives outlier reports will be created. For the RL approach the minimum acceptable value is 8300, however this threshold was never reached by the measurements of the date range of the experiment. Hence, we set the threshold to 8800, to maintain the number of the reported violations to an acceptable level, while detecting as much maintenance incidents as possible.

Table 2, presents the results for each one of the four experiments. In the Table, an X is placed if there is an outlier reported in the correct shift[1], a dash if there is no outlier reported and an $e[1|2]$, if an outlier is reported on an earlier shift (e1: one shift earlier, e2: two shifts earlier) than when it should be

---

[1] For D3 there are two maintenance tasks, hence we have used two places for an X divided by a slash.

Table 2. Results of the first experiment.

Dates	Techniques			
	RL	MCOD	MCOD_DK	MCOD_M
Day1	X	X	X	X
Day2	-	X	X	-
Day3	-	-/X	X/X	X/X
Day4	X	e1	e1	X
Day5	X	X	X	X
Day6	X	-	X	X
Day7	X	-	e1	X
Day8	X	-	e2	X
Day9	-	X	X	X
Day10	-	e1	X	e2
Day11	-	X	X	X
Day12	-	X	X	-
Day13	X	X	e1	-
FPD	3	15	10	12
#R	2790	56	32	39

reported based on the maintenance task logs. In the last two rows of Table 2, we present the number of false positive dates (FPD). FPD represents the number of days that the approaches reported at least one outlier unnecessarily. #R represents the total number of reported outliers. The lower the values of these two measurements, the better the possibility of acceptance of the approach by the maintenance engineers.

As it is observed, MCOD_DK achieves more balanced results, being able to detect all the incidents reported in the maintenance logs, with an exception of D4, D7, D8 and D12 where there was an outlier reported on an earlier shift. If this is considered a correct proactive warning, then the recall of the technique becomes optimal (i.e., 100%). MCOD also achieved remarkable results, if we take into consideration the unstable environment that it was applied on. Monitoring two measurements (i.e. MCOD_M) lowered both the number of FPDs and #R, detecting 5 more maintenance incidents and missing 2 compared to the MCOD approach. The RL approach produced the least number of FPDs, however it created too many violation reports (i.e. highest #R), missing the most maintenance incidents. The precision of MCOD_DK in terms of days remains above 50%.

3.2   Sensitivity Analysis

To demonstrate the sensitivity due to the R and k parameters, we present an experiment using the second dataset and the MCOD_DK technique. The used parametrization is presented in Table 3. The results are presented in Table 4,

Table 3. Sensitivity analysis parameters.

Parameters	Techniques		
	MCOD_DK1	MCOD_DK2	MCOD_DK3
meas.	oilLevel	oilLevel	oilLevel
W	3600	3600	3600
S	360	360	360
R	0.19	0.1	0.19
k	180	180	360
outlierLife	1	1	1

Table 4. Sensitivity analysis results.

Parameters	Techniques		
	MCOD_DK1	MCOD_DK2	MCOD_DK3
DA	9	19	14
#R	12	75	47

in terms of total number of days with alerts (DA) and total number of detected outliers (#R). The first parameterization is one achieved through combining fine-tuning and visual inspection of the raw data logs. This experiment reveals the most important weak point of an unsupervised learning approach, such as MCOD, namely its sensitivity to the input parameters: decreasing the R or increasing the k parameter (i.e. providing more strict parameters to the MCOD algorithm) creates more outlier reports.

4 Discussion

In this work, we considered a real industrial case study, where the main aim has been to detect oil leakages in a manner that (i) is automated; and (ii) can be used as an early notice for maintenance, in line with the PdM vision. In our techniques, we employed a state-of-the-art streaming outlier detection algorithm and we combined it with (i) domain knowledge and (ii) filtering mechanisms in order not to produce spurious or repeating results. The experimental results are particularly encouraging, given that we managed to report outliers for all or the immediate preceding shifts, where a maintenance task was reported.

The most important lesson learnt is that pure unsupervised learning techniques are inadequate to provide effective solutions. Domain knowledge, even in a simple form, can play a key role in devising techniques with very high accuracy and capability in detecting events in a timely manner. We have further verified this fact by repeating the experiments using another type of domain knowledge, where the machinery was in full operation and the results were similarly encouraging.

This work can be extended in several ways. For example, it can be combined with a machine learning-based predictor that can report on the estimated time of future failure. This direction calls for more holistic solutions based on an ensemble of techniques with complementary strengths. Also, further work is needed to render the technique less sensitive to its parameters capitalizing on existing work in the field of multi-parameter outlier detection, e.g., [4].

Acknowledgement. This research work is funded by the BOOST4.0 project funded by European Union's Horizon 2020 research and innovation program under grant agreement No 780732.

Appendix

Distance-Based Outlier Definition. A data point that has less than k neighbours inside a radius R, is called a distance-based outlier [7]. Figure 3 shows an example of a dataset that has two outliers with k = 4. The points *o1* and *o2* are outliers since they have 3 and 1 neighbours, respectively inside the R radius. In a data stream, we assume that we keep in a sliding window the most recent points, and the challenge is to continuously report all the outliers among the objects in that window. Apart from the technique in [9], additional streaming solutions are proposed in proposals, such as [3,5].

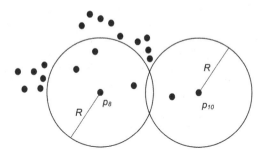

Fig. 3. Outliers example.

MCOD Algorithm. Finding the neighbours of each alive data object in a streaming scenario is a particularly computation-intensive process. The MCOD algorithm uses micro-clusters, as depicted in Fig. 4 (i.e. MC1. MC2, MC3) of radius $R/2$, inside which all the data points are inliers. Hence it alleviates the need of (re-)computing distances between all the data points on every window movement. The rationale is that, normally, most data points fall into one of such clusters and thus need not be further processed. Therefore, only a small portion of all objects needs to be examined. More details about the algorithm's functionality are provided in [9].

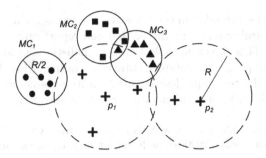

Fig. 4. MCOD - Micro-clusters.

References

1. Lu, Y.: Industry 4.0: a survey on technologies, applications and open research issues. J. Ind. Inf. Integr. **6**, 1–10 (2017)
2. Aggarwal, C.C.: Outlier Analysis. Springer, New York (2013). https://doi.org/10. 1007/978-1-4614-6396-2
3. Angiulli, F., Fassetti, F.: Detecting distance-based outliers in streams of data. In: CIKM, pp. 811–820 (2007)
4. Cao, L., Wang, J., Rundensteiner, E.A.: Sharing-aware outlier analytics over high-volume data streams. In: Proceedings of SIGMOD, pp. 527–540 (2016)
5. Cao, L., Yang, D., Wang, Q., Yu, Y., Wang, J., Rundensteiner, E.A.: Scalable distance-based outlier detection over high-volume data streams. In: ICDE, pp. 76–87 (2014)
6. Hartigan, J.A., Wong, M.A.: Algorithm as 136: a k-means clustering algorithm. J. Roy. Stat. Soc. Ser. C (Appl. Stat.) **28**(1), 100–108 (1979)
7. Knorr, E., Ng, R., Tucakov, V.: Distance-based outliers: algorithms and applications. VLDB J. **8**(3–4), 237–253 (2000)
8. Kohonen, T.: Self-organizing Maps, vol. 30. Springer, Heidelberg (2012)
9. Kontaki, M., Gounaris, A., Papadopoulos, A.N., Tsichlas, K., Manolopoulos, Y.: Efficient and flexible algorithms for monitoring distance-based outliers over data streams. Inf. Syst. **55**, 37–53 (2016)
10. Korvesis, P., Besseau, S., Vazirgiannis, M.: Predictive maintenance in aviation: failure prediction from post flight reports. In: 2018 IEEE 34th International Conference on Data Engineering (ICDE), pp. 1414–1422. IEEE (2018)
11. Sipos, R., Fradkin, D., Moerchen, F., Wang, Z.: Log-based predictive maintenance. In: Proceedings of the 20th ACM SIGKDD International Conference on Knowledge Discovery and Data Mining, pp. 1867–1876. ACM (2014)
12. Tran, L., Fan, L., Shahabi, C.: Distance-based outlier detection in data streams. PVLDB **9**(12), 1089–1100 (2016)
13. Wang, J., Li, C., Han, S., Sarkar, S., Zhou, X.: Predictive maintenance based on event-log analysis: a case study. IBM J. Res. Dev. **61**(1), 11–121 (2017)

Data Analytics Towards Predictive Maintenance for Industrial Ovens

A Case Study Based on Data Analysis of Various Sensors Data

Vaia Rousopoulou[1]([⊠]), Alexandros Nizamis[1], Luigi Giugliano[2], Peter Haigh[3], Luis Martins[4], Dimosthenis Ioannidis[1], and Dimitrios Tzovaras[1]

[1] Centre for Research and Technology Hellas-Information Technologies Institute (CERTH/ITI), 57001 Thessaloniki, Greece
`vrousop@iti.gr`
[2] MLW, Links Foundation, Turin, Italy
[3] Tyndall National Institute, Lee Maltings, Cork T12 R5CP, Ireland
[4] Boston Scientific Limited, Clonmel E91 T862, Ireland

Abstract. In Industry 4.0, predictive maintenance aims to improve both production and maintenance efficiency. The interconnected machines and IoT devices produce a variety of data that enable the early detection of anomalies and failures by predictive analytic algorithms. Predictive analytics can also reduce the machines downtimes and decrease the production of faulty products. This paper introduces predictive analytics for industrial ovens and their application in a real-world's oven used by a leading medical devices manufacturer. Two distinct approaches are presented in this work. A technique based on existing sensors for oven failure prediction based on monitoring and log data; and a technique based on deployed sensors for fault diagnosis based on acoustic data. Deep learning techniques have been applied on existing sensor and event log data, especially temperature monitoring, whereas an outlier detection analysis were implemented on acoustic sensor measurements. Both analytics methods create a complete solution able to detect early oven failures from their root.

Keywords: Industry 4.0 · Predictive maintenance · Deep learning · Outlier detection · Acoustic sensors

1 Introduction

In Industry 4.0, the interconnectivity of machines and systems, the installation of IoT devices and the development of novel predictive algorithms enable predictive maintenance processes. In particular, in the case of printed circuit boards' (PCB) production, data from built-in sensors from ovens can be used alongside with data from externally installed sensors. These data sources enable the creation of a variety of big datasets that can be used by data analytics tools in order to boost predictive maintenance processes and enhance the decision-making in the shop-floor.

© Springer Nature Switzerland AG 2019
H. A. Proper and J. Stirna (Eds.): CAiSE 2019 Workshops, LNBIP 349, pp. 83–94, 2019.
https://doi.org/10.1007/978-3-030-20948-3_8

In this case study, the predictive maintenance procedures are focused on PCBs production line and the ovens that were used on Boston Scientific facilities in Clonmel (BSL). Boston Scientific is one of the largest medical device companies in the world. It manufactures implantable electronics that use printed circuit boards (PCB) to connect and physically support all the necessary electronic components, in which solder paste is used to temporarily attach these components to the electric contact pads onto the PCB into a final circuit assembly (PCBA). Once that assembly is complete, and in order to make this attachment permanent, this assembly is then passed through a reflow oven[1], an equipment that uses heat to transform the solder paste into a permanent joint and obtain a PCBA ready for the next steps of manufacture. To achieve an even heat distribution as well as maintain the interior temperature bellow a safety threshold, reflow ovens also include several blower fans on the inside.

In the manufacturing environment of BSL, it is normal and expected for small malfunctions with the blower fans to occur from time to time. However, their continuous operation at suboptimal conditions gradually leads to instability inside the oven. If this fact remains unnoticed, the machine deteriorates over time, thus leading to failures. Higher than normal or uneven temperatures can cause malfunctions and breakdowns on the machines. Also, a malfunction inside the oven leads to poorly built PCBAs that will then be classified as non-compliant (NC) and considered scrap to be thrown away. As the products built at BSL have a very high cost, it is extremely important to prevent as many NC's as possible, as well as to understand what causes them. This helps resolving systemic faults along the process steps which can lead to huge savings in manufacturing cost. For every actual failure (motor/blower fan failure) the company loses thousands of euros and some millions of them in yearly basis.

In the reflow ovens, several parameters like temperature, pressure and power consumption are constantly being monitored and logged. However, due to their daily experience with the equipment, the operators are able to realize, even before the NC's start to appear, when a reflow oven is close to having a malfunction due to fan failure. When these fans begin to fail, their motors often start making high pitched noises. Based on this, acoustic data was therefore defined as useful data to collect and use in combination with the data the oven itself already outputs.

Prediction of the blower fan failures in these ovens is therefore extremely important to BSL both from quality and cost perspectives. In order to achieve this, a combination of the data outputted from those reflow ovens with additional acoustic data outputted from installed acoustic sensors will be used by a variety of analytic tools. These tools will apply different algorithms and methodologies for prediction of failures and detection of abnormalities and outliers on real time. The analytics output would be used by decision support systems that offer monitoring, display abnormalities and generally provide a status update to the maintenance manager in a near real-time manner. The analytics output is also

---

[1] http://www.hellerindustries.com/pdf/1809EXL_SPEC_SHEET.pdf.

possible to support the maintenance team's decision about when and what to replace before failure occurs, helping them to determine the optimal time of replacement for each blower fan.

In this paper, a complete solution for predictive maintenance for the afore-mentioned ovens based on the analysis of acoustic sensors data and data from ovens' built-in sensors is presented. By providing the analysis outcomes to a company's decision support system, time and costs are saved in maintenance procedures since failures can be predicted and the maintenance plan adjusted accordingly, thus boosting an overall equipment efficiency, preventing unnecessary NC product and decreasing the overall scrap costs.

The paper is structured as follows. Following the Introduction, a related review is presented. The deployed acoustic sensors and the analysis of the fans acoustic data are presented on Sect. 3. Section 4 contains a thorough analysis of ovens' events based on deep learning techniques. Finally, the conclusions and are drawn at Sect. 5.

2   Related Work

While various approaches have been put forward to address the issue of predictive maintenance through fault diagnosis in industrial machines, in the following we will focus on a selection of literature that investigate condition based maintenance depended on log event monitoring in addition to non-invasive maintenance techniques. The work of [1] is a review of developments in condition based maintenance field, emphasizing on three key steps: data acquisition, data pre-processing and decision-making step. The writers expound on the combination of analyzing event data and condition monitoring data together in time and frequency domain and point out the advantages of multi-sensorial data fusion for accurate condition monitoring, fault diagnosis and prognosis. In the same regard, the work of [2] presents a data-driven approach based on multiple-instance learning for predicting equipment failures by mining equipment event logs. The proposed method of [2] utilizes state-of-the-art machine learning techniques to build predictive models from log data.

Additionally, a comprehensive state-of-the-art analysis of predictive maintenance techniques is conducted in the work of [3], indicating the need of dealing with random failures of industrial equipment. This research defines three major types of predictive maintenance technologies, based on their data sources: the existing sensor-based maintenance technique, the test-sensor-based maintenance technique and the test signal based maintenance technique. The first two categories that concern our research consist of methods that use data from existing process sensors that measure variables like temperature, pressure, level, and flow and methods that use data from test sensors such as accelerometers for measuring vibration and acoustic sensors for detecting leaks, respectively.

A pertinent work, carried out recently is [4], presenting an acoustic sensing system for industrial fans fault detection. The writers highlight the ability of the acoustic sensors to give a better high-frequency response to the system.

The system uses the combination of fan rotation speed and its corresponding sound and conduct filtering and abnormal feature analysis, resulting in an effective, real-time early fault detection and prediction system.

Last but not least, a systematic study on fault diagnosis was carried out by Glowacz [5–7]. His preliminary work in the field is [5], where fault diagnosis of electric motors through acoustic signals is presented, implementing feature extraction from acoustic signals of faulty and faultless motors and pattern recognition methods to detect imminent flaws. More recent works are [6] and [7], which focus on fault diagnostic techniques based on acoustic signals for induction motors. In both works, the method pipeline consists of the three signal processing steps: pre-processing, feature extraction, classification. The acoustic signal is recorded, transformed into smaller audio files and processed by implementing amplitude normalization and Fast Fourier transform. Then characteristic features are extracted from the acoustic signals and classification is performed with Nearest Neighbour and other classifiers, resulting in a system capable of detecting unexpected failures.

3   Acoustic Data Analysis Techniques

In order to take the prediction level in an earlier phase, we deployed acoustic sensors in the ovens. We selected the use of acoustic test sensors intrigued by the advantages of them: the easy accommodation, the low-cost equipment and the accessible data information that they provide.

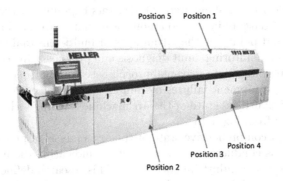

Fig. 1. Positions of deployed acoustic sensors on the oven.

3.1   Acoustic Sensors Deployment

Typical solder reflow ovens of the type deployed at Boston Scientific have over 30 fans within them. The key objective of the condition monitoring system is;

- To alert the operating technician that there is a high potential of failure about to occur.

– To notify the maintenance technician which area (zone) within the oven the faulty fan is located.

The acoustic sensing deployment consists of five sensors placed within specific zones that is within hearing distance of all 30 fans as shown in Fig. 1. The zonal approach to sensing failures also reduces system cost and complexity.

The design approach of the sensing system was to use standard equipment as well as open standards based protocols and formats. This enables greater flexibility in the tools to process the data and provides for ease of use to future development of the system. Closed bespoke systems can be difficult to maintain as well as harder to adopt more broadly outside the initial deployment.

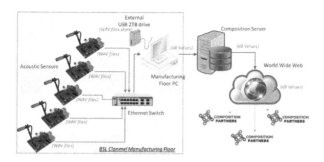

Fig. 2. Hardware architecture overview.

Figure 2 gives an overview of the hardware architecture. The acoustic sensors are constructed with a Raspberry Pi integrated with a SPH0645LM4H microphone via an I2C interface. The sensors record 20 s of sound every 5 min in a standard PCM format. This data is sent in an uncompressed WAV format to the Manufacturing floor PC via Ethernet. The WAV files are processed on the PC where each 20 s recording is converted into a single amplitude value. The WAV file is stored locally on a USB drive and the single amplitude value is stored on a server remote from the factory.

In this work, the algorithms require a single amplitude value in dBSPL. This value is calculated by taking the mean of the peak envelope filtered data and then converting to a dBSPL value. Raspberry Pi sensors record 20 s of sound every 5 min via a shell-script that runs in a continuous loop. The data is timestamped and saved locally in a WAV file format. Thereafter, a local PC is used where a continuous running script collects the newest WAV files from each of the five Raspberry Pi, and then a MATLAB script that passes the data through a peak envelope filter and then takes the mean value to produce a single dB amplitude value. For each set of 5 measurements a single CSV file is generated that stores the 5 values from each sensor. The timestamp in the filename is identical to that of the WAV files and so cross correlation is possible at a later date if required. Then, this data is copied to the server in order to be accessible from analytics tools.

3.2   Acoustic Outlier Analysis for Failure Detection

A method for predictive maintenance in industrial ovens is presented hereby. The proposed method is based on outlier detection out of acoustic measurements. The dB amplitude values derived from the deployed acoustic sensors, as described in Sect. 3.1, formulate the required dataset. This dataset suffers from a pitfall: the industrial oven cannot fail intentionally for the purpose of the specific research, thus the acoustic measurements entail only healthy information. In order to address the challenge of absence of faulty acoustic measurements, we propose an outlier analysis of the imbalanced dataset followed by implementation of well-known classification techniques. The scope of the proposed method is to detect observations in the audio data measurements which deviate so much from the other samples as to indicate that there might exist a possible failure in the ovens. An operational period can be considered as an outlier and indicate an upcoming abnormality. The calculated outliers will constitute the false class of the upcoming classification and prediction process.

Outlier Detection. Three outlier detection algorithms where implemented and compared in this respect: Mean Absolute Deviation (MAD), Local Outlier Factor (LOF) [8] and Density-Based Spatial Clustering of Applications with Noise (DBSCAN) [9]. The MAD value of a signal is calculated over a rolling window with a fixed number of data points of the sample. The rejection criterion of the MAD value is defined based on [10], meaning that the values that lie between specific limits are considered outliers. Next, LOF algorithm is implemented to compute the local density deviation of an acoustic data sample with respect to its neighbors. It considers as outliers the samples that have a substantially lower density than their neighbors. The last outlier detection algorithm used is DBSCAN. The data are fitted to DBSCAN, clusters are created and each acoustic sample is assigned to a cluster. The number of clusters is estimated automatically and outliers (noise) are assigned to the −1 cluster. The parameters of DBSCAN are selected after a few trials.

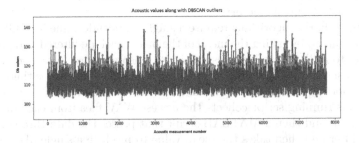

Fig. 3. The outliers detected by DBSCAN.

The three algorithms search for samples that deviate from the majority. The lack of faulty data lead to a quite small number of detected outliers, though DBSCAN identified the most outlier points, 1149 out of 7767 samples, which are noted as the faulty class for the classification process (Fig. 3).

SVM Classification. The previously described algorithms are used for indicating noisy points in the acoustic samples. The outliers are characterized as faulty data in order to create a binary class problem. However, the faulty data are only 14% of the overall data points, forming an imbalanced dataset. A classifier fed with this dataset will be more sensitive to identify the majority class of non-faulted fans and the classification will be biased always predicting the positive class. In order to address the issue of imbalanced dataset, an oversample of the minority class is performed. Synthetic Minority Oversampling Technique (SMOTE) is used to resample and synthesize new elements for the minority class, based on those that already exist [11]. A minority class point is chosen randomly and the k-neighbours of it are calculated. The synthetic data are placed between the picked point and the calculated neighbours. SMOTE technique diminishes the issue of overfitting as the new synthetic data are created rather than reproducing samples and corrupting information. The oversampling of the detected outliers (red points) is illustrated below.

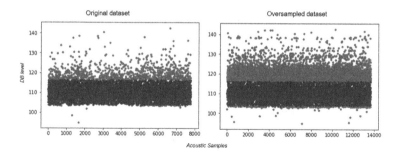

Fig. 4. The dataset oversampling with SMOTE.

The original dataset in shown in the left sub-figure of Fig. 4, where the positive class consists of the 86% of the dataset and the negative class is the 14% respectively. After implementing SMOTE for oversampling the two classes contain 50% of the samples each (right sub-figure of Fig. 4). An SVM classifier is used for training the new dataset. The two possible label classes are faulted acoustic sample (=1) and non-faulted acoustic sample (=0). A training dataset is created including the 70% of the overall dataset and the rest 30% is used for the testing dataset. The SVM model is trained with the following parameters: cost = 0.5 and kernel = Radial basis function kernel (RBF).

In order to evaluate the trained model the testing dataset is used to predict the class of the points based on their decibel values. Figure 5 is the illustration of the confusion matrix, to evaluate the quality of the output of the SVM classifier on the acoustic data set. The diagonal elements represent the number of points for which the predicted label is equal to the true label, while off-diagonal elements are those that are mislabelled by the classifier. The diagonal values of the confusion matrix are quite high, indicating many correct predictions of the faulted and not-faulted acoustic data.

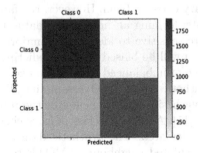

Fig. 5. The confusion matrix of the SVM classifier on the acoustic dataset.

The evaluation metrics are accuracy, precision, recall and F1 score. Accuracy is the ratio of correctly predicted observation to the total observations. Precision is the ratio of correctly predicted positive observations to the total predicted positive observations. Recall is the ratio of correctly predicted positive observations to the all observations in actual positive class. The F1 score is a weighted average of the precision and recall.

Table 1. SVM model evaluation metrics.

Metrics	Result
Accuracy	0.85
Precision	0.76
Recall	1.0
F1-score	0.86

The evaluation metrics were calculated and the results indicate that the model is capable of detecting faulted measurements (Table 1). All of the metrics are over 75%. Note that the recall metric reaches 1.0 because of the fact that the non-faulted data are generated and do not exist in the initial dataset. New measurements can be given to the SVM prediction model, optimally live data, that can predict if there exist a possible failure in the reflow ovens with 85% accuracy.

SVM Prediction Model. For each audio sensor, an SVM prediction model is extracted according to the aforementioned classification analysis. The purpose of the proposed method is to be applied in live audio measurements and detect possible failures in reflow ovens. The SVM model of each sensor receives as input the result value of the audio measurement, namely a timestamped decibel level. The model decides whether the decibel measurement belongs to the faulted or non-faulted class. In case that the model detects the faulty class for five consecutive measurements, the system informs that there is a possible abnormal function in the oven.

4   Existing Oven Sensor and Log Data Analysis Techniques

This section describes a deep learning method for predictive maintenance of industrial ovens based on log data and events. The log data are collected as part of the operational routine for monitoring the system performance. The proposed method indicates that the value of these data can be exploited to serve as indicators of a system' s health condition.

Data Acquisition. BSL provided sensor data files containing the temperature set by the user, the measured temperature and the output power at the solid state relay of the reflow, and event files containing a list of failure events related to the oven. The dataset has been created by merging the data files and the event files using the timestamp value as key. The event with the closest timestamp is assigned to each data entry in the data file, duplicating the available events. The process follows the creation of each single entry and the matching of events for each data entry. The selection of this approach was based on two facts: (a) there are more data entries than event entries for each file; there is the assumption that if an event occurs at the time t, (b) there is a high probability that the same event "was occurring" or about to occur at the time $t - 1$ or $t + 1$ since the sampling time is short.

Next is the replacement of the feature of constant temperature value, for each zone of the oven, with the difference between the constant and the present temperature value. The feature of constant temperature value defines the value of temperature set by the operator of the oven and it is constant within a time interval. Lastly, there were identified 11 classes of events which are of the most interest to our scope and they were assigned to a numerical value from 1 to 11:

1. Flux Heater High Warning
2. Hi Warning
3. Lo Warning
4. Hi Deviation
5. PPM Level within limit
6. PPM Level has exceeded the amount set
7. High Water Temp Alarm Cool Down Loaded

8. Low Exhaust Alarm
9. Exhaust is insufficient
10. Heat Fan Fault
11. Blower Failure (Fan Fault).

On the ground that each sensor output and each event can be seen as a discrete variable that changes through time, the selected deep learning technique is the Recurrent Neural Network (RNN). The data are fed to the network in consecutive time series of length 32 and the network will predict the next (starting from the last point of the time series) 5 future events (25 min of events). Figure 6 is a depiction of the data format and it is worth to mention that events of both input and output will be specified in one-hot encoding format.

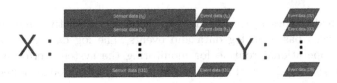

Fig. 6. Training data format.

Network Architecture. The network consists of an encoder and a decoder linked to each other. The encoder consists of the first Long Short Term Memory (LSTM) network with 256 units while the decoder is the last LSTM with 64 units. The first layer takes as input 32 time steps for the 73 features and returns only 64 vectors representing the "encoding" version of the input data. The data encoding step is repeated 5 times (the number of time step in the future we want to predict) by the Repeat Vector layer creating a new time series of $[5 \times 256]$. This newly created time series is given as input to the decoder, the second LSTM. The decoder returns the new five values along with their "sequence": this can be seen as a time series (of $[5 \times 64]$) too that passes through a Dense Layer in a "time distributed fashion". The last layer uses the softmax activation.

Results. The findings of the evaluation of the proposed method suggest that the models is able to predict future log events based on the previous ones and existing sensor data. The evaluation was made for each of the five events. The first event represents the "less in the future" class while the fifth event represents the "more in the future" class. Indicatively, in Fig. 7, the confusion matrix of the first and fifth event are depicted. The Confusion Matrix in Fig. 7 suggests that almost all the classes are predicted correctly. Note that class 4 is the most difficult to classify due to its small dimension and there are only six occurrences in the test set. Nevertheless, knowing the meaning of the class at prior the misclassification error from class 4 to class 2 is a minor error compared to the misclassification from class 4 to class 0. It is necessary to highlight the fact that the most important class is the last one, class 10, as it is the one denoting

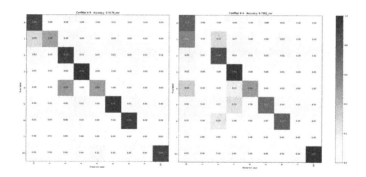

Fig. 7. Confusion matrices for event t1 (left) and event t5 (right).

that the oven is in a fault state. Having 89% percent of correct prediction it is a considerable result taking in account the qualitative and quantitative complexity of the class.

The results of the test set are very promising, although the accuracy metric will not be taking into account due to the highly imbalanced dataset. Based on the nature of the problem, the most attention is focused on the amount of false negative results, thus, recall and f1-score are the main focus metrics and Matthews correlation coefficient is just reported. The evaluation metrics were calculated for each of the five events. The first event reached the higher evaluation score while the fifth event achieved the lowest overall score. The next table contains the proposed model results (Table 2):

Table 2. RNN evaluation metrics results.

	Recall	F1-score	MCC
Event t1	0.917	0.920	0.876
Event t2	0.876	0.882	0.818
Event t3	0.837	0.846	0.763
Event t4	0.811	0.822	0.724
Event t5	0.790	0.803	0.691

The most substantial event, the fifth one, is 25 min in the future. The evaluation results are really promising and despite the long prediction time, the performance of the classifier on the event 5 is still acceptable.

5   Conclusions

Taken together, our research has come to a conclusion towards a complete solution for sensor-based data analysis in a case-study of an industrial oven. The study was divided in two parts: the analysis of deployed acoustic sensor data and the analysis of existing sensor data and log events. The aim of this work was to exploit operational routine for monitoring of the system performance using the already integrated sensors of the oven and then deploy extra test sensors (acoustic ones) in order to serve as indicators of a systems health condition. Both the analytic techniques achieve a failure prediction of the oven machine with high accuracy. Despite the fact that there are limitations due to the imbalanced dataset, we formed a competent technique, capable of detecting anomalies and failures on a primitive phase aiming to improve both production and maintenance efficiency. The predictive maintenance approach we presented can constitute an assisting tool for the decision support system of industries towards the prevention of potential failure and secure of safe operations of machineries.

Acknowledgements. This project has received funding from the European Union's Horizon 2020 research and innovation programme under grant agreement No 723145 - COMPOSITION. This paper reflects only the authors' views and the Commission is not responsible for any use that may be made of the information it contains.

References

1. Jardine, A.K., Lin, D., Banjevic, D.: A review on machinery diagnostics and prognostics implementing condition-based maintenance. Mech. Syst. Sig. Process. **20**(7), 1483–1510 (2006)
2. Sipos, R., Fradkin, D., Moerchen, F., Wang, Z.: Log-based predictive maintenance. In: Proceedings of the 20th ACM SIGKDD International Conference on Knowledge Discovery and Data Mining, pp. 1867–1876. ACM (2014)
3. Hashemian, H.M., Bean, W.C.: State-of-the-art predictive maintenance techniques*. IEEE Trans. Instrum. Meas. **60**(10), 3480–3492 (2011). https://doi.org/10.1109/TIM.2009.2036347
4. Gong, C.S.A., et al.: Design and implementation of acoustic sensing system for online early fault detection in industrial fans. J. Sens. **2018** (2018)
5. Glowacz, A.: Diagnostics of DC and induction motors based on the analysis of acoustic signals. Meas. Sci. Rev. **14**, 257–262 (2014). https://doi.org/10.2478/msr-2014-0035
6. Glowacz, A., Glowacz, W., Glowacz, Z., Kozik, J.: Early fault diagnosis of bearing and stator faults of the single-phase induction motor using acoustic signals. Measurement **113**, 1–9 (2018)
7. Glowacz, A.: Acoustic based fault diagnosis of three-phase induction motor. Appl. Acoust. **137**, 82–89 (2018)
8. Breunig, M.M., Kriegel, H.P., Ng, R.T., Sander, J.: LOF: identifying density-based local outliers. In: ACM SIGMOD Record, vol. 29, pp. 93–104. ACM (2000)
9. Ester, M., Kriegel, H.P., Sander, J., Xu, X., et al.: A density-based algorithm for discovering clusters in large spatial databases with noise. In: KDD 1996, pp. 226–231 (1996)
10. Miller, J.: Reaction time analysis with outlier exclusion: bias varies with sample size. Q. J. Exp. Psychol. **43**(4), 907–912 (1991)
11. Chawla, N.V., Bowyer, K.W., Hall, L.O., Kegelmeyer, W.P.: SMOTE: synthetic minority over-sampling technique. J. Artif. Intell. Res. **16**, 321–357 (2002)

A RAMI 4.0 View of Predictive Maintenance: Software Architecture, Platform and Case Study in Steel Industry

Alexandros Bousdekis[1(✉)], Katerina Lepenioti[1],
Dimitrios Ntalaperas[2], Danai Vergeti[2], Dimitris Apostolou[1,3],
and Vasilis Boursinos[4]

[1] Information Management Unit (IMU), Institute of Communication
and Computer Systems (ICCS), National Technical University of Athens
(NTUA), 9 Iroon Polytechniou Street, 157 80 Zografou, Athens, Greece
{albous,klepenioti}@mail.ntua.gr, dapost@unipi.gr
[2] UBITECH Ltd., 8 Thessalias Street, 15231 Chalandri, Athens, Greece
{dntalaperas,vergetid}@ubitech.eu
[3] Department of Informatics, University of Piraeus,
80 Karaoli & Dimitriou Street, 185 34 Piraeus, Greece
[4] M.J. MAILLIS S.A., Inofyta, Viotia, Greece
vasilis.boursinos@maillis.com

Abstract. The fourth industrial revolution is characterized by the introduction of the Internet of Things (IoT) into manufacturing, which enables smart factories with vertically and horizontally integrated production systems. The key issue of any design and system development in the context of Industry 4.0 is the proper implementation of Reference Architectural Model Industrie (RAMI) 4.0 in various manufacturing operations and the definition of appropriate sub-models for individual aspects and processes according to the technical background of Industry 4.0. Since maintenance is increasingly considered a strategic business function which contributes to overall reliability and profitability, predictive maintenance, as a novel lever of maintenance management, has been evolved. Predictive maintenance is a significant enabler towards Industry 4.0. In this paper, we design a predictive maintenance architecture according to RAMI 4.0. On this basis, we develop a unified predictive maintenance platform and we apply it to a real manufacturing scenario from the steel industry.

Keywords: Industry 4.0 · Predictive maintenance ·
Industrial Internet of Things · Steel industry

1 Introduction

The fourth industrial revolution is characterized by the introduction of the Internet of Things (IoT) into manufacturing, which enables smart factories with vertically and horizontally integrated production systems [1]. The physical and virtual worlds grow together and objects including machines are equipped with sensors and actuators [1]. The key issue of any design and system development in the context of Industry 4.0 is

© Springer Nature Switzerland AG 2019
H. A. Proper and J. Stirna (Eds.): CAiSE 2019 Workshops, LNBIP 349, pp. 95–106, 2019.
https://doi.org/10.1007/978-3-030-20948-3_9

the proper implementation of Reference Architectural Model Industrie (RAMI) 4.0 in various manufacturing operations and the definition of appropriate sub-models for individual aspects and processes according to the technical background of Industry 4.0 [2, 3]. To do this, several aspects should be taken into consideration, such as interoperability of devices and software components, cloud computing technologies, big data analytics and artificial intelligence [4].

Predictive maintenance has gathered a lot of attention by manufacturing firms and thus, several industrial and research works have focused on its implementation with sensory technologies, software systems and appropriate systematic methodologies. However, the scarcity of pilot cases in predictive maintenance, capable of proving its benefits, has led to the lack of implementation of predictive maintenance initiatives extensively in industry [5]. The systematic representation of a predictive maintenance solution enables the reusability and knowledge transfer, an aspect of outmost importance in Industry 4.0 platforms [6]. In this paper, we examine how RAMI 4.0 can be applied in the design of a software architecture for predictive maintenance. Moreover, we illustrate how the architecture can be used to develop a platform which covers all the aspects of predictive maintenance. The predictive maintenance platform is applied to a case from steel industry.

The rest of the paper is organized as follows: Sect. 2 presents a literature review about Industry 4.0 and predictive maintenance. Section 3 describes a predictive maintenance architecture as an instantiation of RAMI 4.0, while Sect. 4 presents its implementation to a platform. Section 5 describes an application of the predictive maintenance platform in a case from the steel industry. Section 6 concludes the paper and presents our plans for future work.

2   Literature Review

2.1   Industry 4.0

Industry 4.0 is defined as "the flexibility that exists in value-creating networks is increased by the application of Cyber Physical Systems (CPS). This enables machines and plants to adapt their behavior to changing orders and operating conditions through self-optimization and reconfiguration" [7]. Moreover, perceiving information and extracting business insights from the huge amounts of heterogeneous data is a key technological challenge in Industry 4.0 [6, 8, 9]. Industry 4.0 brings changes in the architecture of the classical control pyramid of production complexes as well as technological processes. The RAMI 4.0 is a three-dimensional model representing different interconnected features of the technical – economical properties and showing how to approach the issue of Industry 4.0 in a structured manner. It consists of three axes: (i) the hierarchy levels; (ii) the architecture layers; and, (iii) the lifecycle value stream.

Hierarchy Levels. The Industry 4.0 architecture at hierarchical level shows a functional assignment of components [3]. This axis within an enterprise or factory follows the IEC 62264 and IEC 61512 standards. The level over and below the IEC standards area represents steps further and describes also groups of factories, collaboration within external engineering firms, component suppliers and customers. Therefore, the hierarchy levels are: product, field device, control device, station, work center, enterprise, and connected world.

Architecture Layers. The architecture layers include the following: Asset Layer, Integration Layer, Communication Layer, Information Layer, Functional Layer, Business Layer. They enable the development of Industry 4.0 software solutions in a consistent way so that different and mutually dependent manufacturing operations are interconnected taking into account the physical and the digital world.

Lifecycle Value Stream. The lifecycle value stream axis is divided to Type and Instance. The Type is divided to Development and Maintenance/Usage, while the Instance is divided to Production and Maintenance/Usage [7]. A type represents the initial idea, while each manufactured product represents an instance of that type [7]. The value stream in the totally digitized production can be viewed in conjunction with value-adding processes, since it enables linking of purchasing, production planning, logistics, quality, customers and suppliers [7].

2.2 Predictive Maintenance

Manufacturing companies are increasingly considering turning to predictive maintenance by utilizing the capabilities of condition monitoring. The emergence of the Internet of Things (IoT) paves the way for enhancing the monitoring capabilities of enterprises by means of extensive use of physical and virtual sensors enabling them to decide and act ahead of time [10], i.e., to resolve problems before they appear (e.g. to avoid or mitigate the impact of a future failure). To this end, predictive maintenance has been evolved as a novel lever of maintenance management. However, predictive maintenance and associated information systems have received several criticisms due to their complexity and to their challenges for practical implementation [5], since they handle massive information, changing on time, and with complex relationships among them. For example, structuring the information sustainably and interrelating properly the consisting software services is a significant challenge in the complex and dynamic manufacturing environment [5, 11].

Several conceptual frameworks for predictive maintenance have been proposed in the literature [5, 11–15]. The most recent approach proposes a unified predictive maintenance framework covering the whole information processing lifecycle [15]: Signal Processing, Feature Extraction, Diagnosis, Prognosis, Decision Making & Actions Planning. These (near) real-time steps are fed by the Failure Mode, Effects and Criticality Analysis (FMECA) model and Historical Data Analytics, while the user interaction is facilitated with configuration and visualization capabilities.

3 A RAMI 4.0 View of Predictive Maintenance

The motivation for using RAMI 4.0 to scope and design a predictive maintenance architecture is the need to frame developed concepts and technologies in a common model that leverages further collaboration and integration with other industrial architectures and systems in the frame of Industry 4.0. This is a challenging task since the Industry 4.0 paradigm is still evolving with limited past experience of successful implementations. Our approach focuses on instantiating RAMI 4.0 to maintenance operations and examining how a unified predictive maintenance platform can be developed based on RAMI 4.0 – compliant architecture. Designing a unified predictive maintenance conceptual architecture in the context of RAMI 4.0 enables the integration of the maintenance process with the other operations and processes of the manufacturing enterprise based upon the Industry 4.0 paradigm. The following sub-sections describe the three axes of RAMI 4.0 in the context of predictive maintenance.

3.1 Hierarchy Levels

The predictive maintenance architecture in the frame of RAMI 4.0 is applicable at component, machine or production process level. In this sense, it can be implemented in flexible smart systems and machines capable of interacting and communicating across the hierarchy levels through a network. The implementation of the architecture in a "Connected World" (i.e. connected factories with integrated predictive maintenance processes) would require its use by all of them in order to create synergies (e.g. between a factory and its supplier of maintenance spare parts).

3.2 Architecture Layers

Figure 1 shows the predictive maintenance architecture in the frame of the RAMI 4.0 architecture layers. The individual layers and their interrelationships are described below.

Asset Layer: Since this layer represents the reality ("physical things in the real world"), production equipment and users are part of it. Predictive maintenance is implemented on the *Production Equipment* with the involvement of the platform *Users*. The production equipment can be further analyzed to "System", "Equipment Unit" and "Maintainable Item" according to the Industry Standard Solution for Plant Maintenance (ISPM)[1], which is based upon and extends the ISO 15926-2 [16] and the ISO 14224:2006 taxonomy [17].

Integration Layer: This layer makes provision of information on the assets in a form which is available for computer processing by connecting elements as well as people with IT. The integration of the information sources is critical for ensuring the reliability of the information and controlling the performance of the monitoring system [18]. This layer involves the equipment-installed *Sensors* and the *Legacy Systems* (MES, ERP, etc.). It also includes the *Human Machine Interfaces* of the legacy data systems (e.g. ERP GUI) and of the predictive maintenance platform (GUI for configuration) through which the users insert data.

Communication Layer: Since this layer provides standardization of communication by means of uniform data format and deals with the physical support of information processing (mainly according to the ISO 13374 standard [19] as implemented by

---

[1] https://reliabilitydynamics.com/Industry-Standard-Solution-for-Plant-Maintenance.

MIMOSA OSA-CBM [20]), it includes the *IoT Gateway*, the *Legacy Data Uplifting* and the *Event Broker*. In this way, a predictive maintenance platform gathers the data from the information sources for further processing in the subsequent Information Layer.

Information Layer: This layer provides pre-processing of events and execution of event-related rules by enabling their formal description for the interpretation of the information. It also manages data persistence, ensures consistent data integrity and transformation for feeding into the Functional Layer. Therefore, it includes sensor and legacy data pre-processing while feeding into the *Stream Processing* and the *Batch Processing* environment respectively. To this end, this layer also includes the *predictive maintenance platform's DB* and the *Time-Series DB* for the real-time sensor measurements. In this way, the required data are extracted and combined accordingly in order to be available by the functions of the next layer. This process is also in accordance to Data Acquisition and Data Manipulation of the ISO 13374 standard as implemented by MIMOSA OSA-CBM.

Functional Layer: This layer enables the formal description of functions and creates the platform for horizontal integration of various functions. It contains the run time and modelling environment for services supporting the business processes and a run time environment for applications and technical functionalities. In this layer, the following functions, which are executed on the basis of data integrity of the previous layer, take place:

- *System Definition*: The definition of all aspects regarding the manufacturing system including failure causes, failure modes and effects along with appropriate reactive and proactive actions, as well as the specification of the failure concepts and instances that affect the monitored systems. It is derived from FMECA.
- *Risk Assessment*: The criticality of the manufacturing system's assets and the indication of the most critical ones. The outcome is a risk matrix which highlights the most critical parts of the system. This is also derived from FMECA.
- *Batch Data Analytics*: Advanced data analytics algorithms based on legacy and operational data related to the maintenance activity. It generates offline models and rules that are used by Stream Data Analytics and Decision Making functions.
- *Stream Data Analytics*: Descriptive and predictive analytics on the basis of data streams generated by sensors. Descriptive analytics includes algorithms for real-time anomaly detection (diagnosis), while predictive analytics includes algorithms for real-time failure predictions (prognosis) for various failure modes according to the system definition. These functionalities are in accordance with ISO 13374 as implemented by MIMOSA OSA-CBM (in the sense that diagnosis refers to State Detection and Health Assessment, while prognosis refers to Prognostics Assessment) as well as with ISO 13379 [21], ISO 17359 [22] and EN 13306 [23].
- *Decision Making*: Prescriptive analytics on the basis of real-time failure predictions. It includes algorithms for proactive decision making (e.g. about the optimal actions and their optimal times) and the formulation of the maintenance plan including both preventive and proactive actions, upon user approval. This functionality is in accordance with ISO 13374, as implemented by MIMOSA OSA-CBM in the sense that it refers to Advisory Generation, as well as with EN 17007 [24].

Business Layer: This layer ensures the integrity of functions in the value stream and enables mapping business models and the outcomes of the overall process. It takes into account the policies, rules and constraints according to which the system operates through the interrelationships of predictive maintenance to other manufacturing operations. It also creates a link among different business processes, i.e. other interrelated *Manufacturing Operations* (e.g. logistics management, quality management, production planning), through the exposure of appropriate information to the user. In this sense, this layer involves the *User Interaction* with the predictive maintenance platform (e.g. configuration, feedback, etc.), the *Real-time Monitoring* and the *Visualization* functionalities.

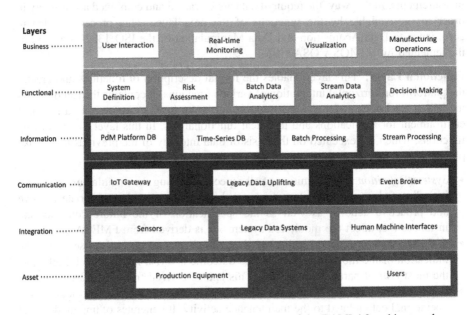

Fig. 1. Predictive maintenance architecture in the context of the RAMI 4.0 architecture layers.

3.3 Lifecycle Value Stream

The lifecycle value stream of predictive maintenance has both managerial and technical implications. As far as the managerial perspective is concerned, the type includes the idea as well as the development and validation of a predictive maintenance strategy. After successful validation, the new consulting service is released. Each instantiation of the predictive maintenance strategy to a specific production process or industry represents an instance of that type. As far as the technical perspective is concerned, the type includes the idea as well as the development and testing of a unified information system for predictive maintenance which sets the basis for serial production. Each instantiation of the predictive maintenance information system to a specific equipment, production process or industry, and to a specific legacy data system or installed sensor represents an instance of that type.

4   The UPTIME Software Architecture and Platform

The predictive maintenance architecture in the frame of RAMI 4.0 was implemented as an e-maintenance platform in the context of the EU H2020 Unified PredicTIve MaintenancE (UPTIME) project. Figure 2 depicts the technical architecture of the UPTIME e-maintenance platform (in accordance with RAMI 4.0) which shows the main interactions among the components through the definition of end-to-end integration and communication processes. The technical architecture consists of three tiers: Presentation Tier, Logic Tier, and Data Tier.

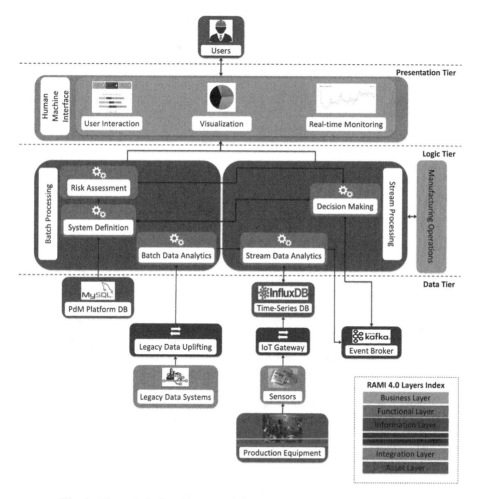

Fig. 2. The technical architecture of the UPTIME e-maintenance platform.

Presentation Tier: The Presentation Tier is implemented through a Graphical User Interface (GUI) which includes a menu consisting of the following items: Overview, Stream Data Analytics, Batch Data Analytics, Decision Making, Risk Assessment, System Definition. The main screen is shown in Fig. 3. Each one of these items is used for configuration, real-time monitoring and visualization of the results. Figure 3 provides an indicative depiction of the Overview screen of the UPTIME GUI. It includes aggregated information, easily accessible by the user, by incorporating advanced visualization capabilities with the use of Elasticsearch[2].

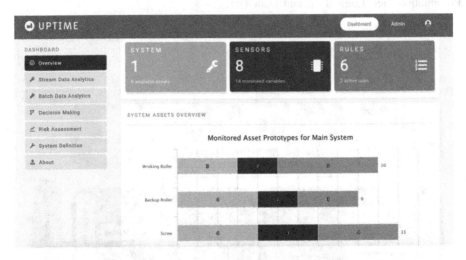

Fig. 3. The Overview screen of the UPTIME platform.

Logic Tier: The Logic Tier is implemented by integrating the core functionalities for predictive maintenance in Industry 4.0 (i.e. from the Functional Layer of RAMI 4.0). The System Definition and the Risk Assessment is initialized based on expert's input, while the Batch Data Analytics is fed by the legacy data. The sensor data are interlinked with those persisted in the UPTIME database in order to ensure the proper mapping among the sensor data and the instances that derived from the system definition. Kafka[3] orchestrates the whole end-to-end integration process. For the Stream Data Analytics and Decision Making functionalities, Kafka is the actual message broker where components can subscribe to, in order to consume data that are produced asynchronously and delegated among the various components.

Data Tier: The Data Tier of the UPTIME platform consists of two main parts: On the one hand, the UPTIME solution provides data harmonization in terms of manipulating streaming data from sensors. On this basis, the InfluxDB time-series database has been installed. On the other hand, the common UPTIME database, which is represented by a

---

[2] https://www.elastic.co/.

[3] https://kafka.apache.org/.

MySQL database handling the operations of the UPTIME platform, ensures consistency during the lifecycle of the platform. The UPTIME platform uses also the data that are stored in the legacy systems.

5 Application in the Steel Industry: The M. J. Maillis S.A. Case

The steel sector has been getting pressure from all sides in recent years as raw materials have become more expensive or difficult to source and growth has slowed to a crawl. The steel industry is strategic in the EU economy. With an average production of 170 million tons of steel per year at more than 500 steel production sites across 24 EU member states and with its close integration to Europe's manufacturing and construction industries, the steel sector is crucial for development, growth and employment in Europe [25]. Steel-making is a complex industrial process and defects introduced in early stages have an economic impact in posterior transformation.

The case under examination is the cold rolling process of M. J. Maillis S.A. Cold rolling is a process of reduction of the cross-sectional area or shaping a metal piece through the deformation caused by a pair of rotating in opposite directions metal rolls. Cold rolling occurs with the metal below its recrystallization temperature. In cold rolling mill production lines, M. J. Maillis S.A. uses cold rolling mills to produce rolling products with the closest possible thickness tolerances and an excellent surface finish. Given an entry steel coil of 4 tons weight and thickness of 2 mm, it produces steel strips over the whole thickness spectrum until 0.4 mm. The most important components of the milling station are summarized below:

- **The work rollers.** This pair of rollers is responsible for the actual milling; the material is passed through the gap between them and in a sequence of passes is milled to the desired width.
- **The backup rollers.** This pair of rollers (one backup roller for each working roller) transmits motion to the working roller.
- **The motor unit**, which is responsible for rotating the backup rollers.

Figure 4a depicts the milling station; Fig. 4b represents the manufacturing process of the milling station; while Fig. 4c shows the work and the backup rollers and sensors' positions. During the operation, the whole contents are enclosed and all the rollers are continuously being sprayed by soap oil in order to reduce heat and friction.

The main sensor infrastructure setup, which is used for data acquisition, is depicted in Fig. 5. All sensors are collected in an MVX which are then transmitted via Modbus TCP to a Siemens S7-1500 PLC. The values are exposed from the PLC to the DB port and can thus be collected external modules that have access to the PLC via network. An adapter samples the DB Port every 5 ms–5 s. The sampling rate can be configured and they generally depend on the variable. The data are then processed via a Storm-Kafka pipeline. This pipeline is responsible for performing normalization procedures. Normalization is also configurable and can be adjusted by attaching new Storm Bolts. 10 Accelerometers collect data relevant to vibrations, while one tachometer measures the speed of the motor and one current sensor measures the current of the motor. Accelerometers measure a set of four variables for vibration-related data (overall acceleration, overall velocity, sock finder and overall bearing defect), tachometer measures in rpm units, while the current sensor measures in Ampere.

The UPTIME platform is connected to the sensor infrastructure so that the generated data along with the data collected from the legacy and operational systems are processed accordingly. Below, we describe an illustrative predictive maintenance scenario covered by the UPTIME platform for the M. J. Maillis S.A. milling station.

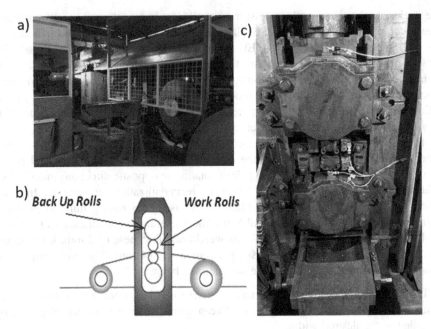

Fig. 4. The M. J. Maillis S.A. milling station: (a) an overview; (b) a representation of the manufacturing process; (c) the rollers when the main casing is open.

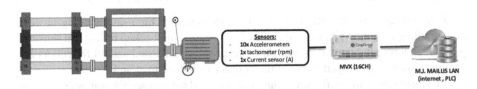

Fig. 5. Infrastructure setup for sensor data collection.

At <u>design time</u>, the user configures the platform through the *System Definition* and the initial *Risk Assessment* according to the assets, the failure causes, the failure modes and effects, i.e. taking into account the FMECA modelling of the manufacturing system. Other parameters, such as the costs of failure modes, the costs of maintenance actions, the failure thresholds, etc., are retrieved from legacy data uplifting and are updated dynamically, on a batch mode, as soon as new data is added. The latter is executed through *Batch Data Analytics* which implements machine learning and data mining algorithms such as Self-Organizing Maps (SOMs), k-means clustering, decision trees and association rule mining.

At <u>runtime</u>, the UPTIME platform provides real-time monitoring of the measured parameters (e.g. vibration) and ensures that the gathered data at the on-site PLC are transmitted through the communication channel. The acquired data feed into the *Stream Data Analytics* functionalities which subsequently perform feature extraction and anomalies detection (diagnosis), with algorithms such as Long Short-Term Memory (LSTM), as well as failure predictions (prognosis) (e.g. Remaining Useful Life, time-to-failure or failure Probability Density Function), with algorithms such as curve fitting, neural networks and Hidden Markov Models (HMM). The prediction about the roll break feeds into the *Decision Making* functionality which recommends the optimal proactive actions (e.g. lower the speed, increase the soap oil flow or perform full maintenance) along with their optimal times. To do this, it implements decision methods such as Markov Decision Process (MDP). Upon user approval through the GUI, the recommended actions are inserted in the maintenance plan. The models used in Stream Data Analytics and Decision Making functionalities are updated on the basis of the Batch Data Analytics outcomes as soon as new data is collected.

6   Conclusions and Future Work

A key issue of any design and system development in the context of Industry 4.0 is the proper implementation of RAMI 4.0 and the definition of appropriate sub-models for individual manufacturing operations [2, 3]. Predictive maintenance is a significant enabler towards Industry 4.0. However, up to now, it has not been considered in the frame of RAMI 4.0 in order to result in a unified predictive maintenance platform. In this paper, we designed a predictive maintenance software architecture according to RAMI 4.0. On this basis, we developed the UPTIME platform and we applied it to a real manufacturing scenario from the steel industry. Regarding future work, we aim to further develop advanced algorithms for all the aforementioned steps of predictive maintenance. Moreover, we will evaluate the results in three manufacturing scenarios from the steel industry, the home appliances industry and the aviation industry.

Acknowledgements. This work is partly funded by the European Commission project H2020 UPTIME "Unified Predictive Maintenance System" (768634).

References

1. Thoben, K.D., Wiesner, S., Wuest, T.: "Industrie 4.0" and smart manufacturing-a review of research issues and application examples. Int. J. Autom. Technol. **11**(1), 4–16 (2017)
2. Hankel, M., Rexroth, B.: The Reference Architectural Model Industrie 4.0 (RAMI 4.0). ZVEI (2015)
3. Zezulka, F., Marcon, P., Vesely, I., Sajdl, O.: Industry 4.0–an introduction in the phenomenon. IFAC-PapersOnLine **49**(25), 8–12 (2016)
4. Zhong, R.Y., Xu, X., Klotz, E., Newman, S.T.: Intelligent manufacturing in the context of industry 4.0: a review. Engineering **3**(5), 616–630 (2017)

5. Guillén, A.J., Crespo, A., Gómez, J.F., Sanz, M.D.: A framework for effective management of condition based maintenance programs in the context of industrial development of E-Maintenance strategies. Comput. Ind. **82**, 170–185 (2016)
6. Gröger, C.: Building an Industry 4.0 analytics platform. Datenbank-Spektrum **18**, 1–10 (2018)
7. Platform Industrie 4.0. https://www.plattform-i40.de/I40/Navigation/EN/Home/home.html. Accessed 26 Feb 2019
8. Gölzer, P., Cato, P., Amberg, M.: Data processing requirements of industry 4.0 – use cases for big data applications. In: Proceedings of the 23th European Conference on Information Systems (ECIS) (2015)
9. Roy, R., Stark, R., Tracht, K., Takata, S., Mori, M.: Continuous maintenance and the future– Foundations and technological challenges. CIRP Ann. **65**(2), 667–688 (2016)
10. Engel, Y., Etzion, O., Feldman, Z.: A basic model for proactive event-driven computing. In: Proceedings of the 6th ACM International Conference on Distributed Event-Based Systems (DEBS), pp. 107–118. ACM (2012)
11. Bousdekis, A., Magoutas, B., Apostolou, D., Mentzas, G.: A proactive decision making framework for condition-based maintenance. Ind. Manag. Data Syst. **115**(7), 1225–1250 (2015)
12. Peng, Y., Dong, M., Zuo, M.J.: Current status of machine prognostics in condition-based maintenance: a review. Int. J. Adv. Manuf. Technol. **50**(1–4), 297–313 (2010)
13. Voisin, A., Levrat, E., Cocheteux, P., Iung, B.: Generic prognosis model for proactive maintenance decision support: application to pre-industrial e-maintenance test bed. J. Intell. Manuf. **21**(2), 177–193 (2010)
14. Wang, J., Zhang, L., Duan, L., Gao, R.X.: A new paradigm of cloud-based predictive maintenance for intelligent manufacturing. J. Intell. Manuf. **28**(5), 1125–1137 (2017)
15. Hribernik, K., von Stietencron, M., Bousdekis, A., Bredehorst, B., Mentzas, G., Thoben, K.D.: Towards a unified predictive maintenance system-a use case in production logistics in aeronautics. Procedia Manuf. **16**, 131–138 (2018)
16. ISO 15926-2:2003: Industrial automation systems and integration—Integration of life-cycle data for process plants including oil and gas production facilities—Part 2: Data model (2003)
17. ISO 14224:2006: Petroleum, petrochemical and natural gas industries—Collection and exchange of reliability and maintenance data for equipment (2006)
18. Vachtsevanos, G.J., Lewis, F., Hess, A., Wu, B.: Intelligent Fault Diagnosis and Prognosis for Engineering Systems, pp. 185–186. Wiley, Hoboken (2006)
19. ISO 13 374:2012: Condition monitoring and diagnostics of machines—Data processing, communication and presentation (2012)
20. MIMOSA OSA-CBM 3.3.1. http://www.mimosa.org/mimosa-osa-cbm/. Accessed 26 Feb 2019
21. ISO 13379-1:2012: Condition monitoring and diagnosis of machines—Data interpretation and diagnosis techniques—Part 1: General guidelines (2012)
22. ISO 17359:2011: Condition monitoring and diagnosis of machines—General guidelines (2011)
23. BS EN 13306:2017: Maintenance—Maintenance terminology. BSI Standards Publication (2017)
24. BS EN 17007:2017: Maintenance process and associated indicators. BSI Standards Publication (2017)
25. EUROFER (European Steel Association): European Steel in Figures. http://www.eurofer.org/News%26Events/PublicationsLinksList/201806-SteelFigures.pdf. Accessed 26 Feb 2019

Different Perspectives of a Factory of the Future: An Overview

Giulio Salierno[1][✉], Giacomo Cabri[2][✉], and Letizia Leonardi[1][✉]

[1] Department of Engineering "Enzo Ferrari",
University of Modena and Reggio Emilia, Modena, Italy
{giulio.salierno,letizia.leonardi}@unimore.it
[2] Department of Physics, Informatics and Mathematics,
University of Modena and Reggio Emilia, Modena, Italy
giacomo.cabri@unimore.it

Abstract. *Digital factory*, and *Cloud Manufacturing* are two approaches that aim at addressing the Factory of the Future, i.e., to provide digital support to manufacturing factories. They find their roots in two different geographical areas, respectively Europe and China, and therefore presents some differences as well as the same goal of building the factory of the future. In this paper, we present both the digital factory and the cloud manufacturing approaches and discuss their differences.

Keywords: Digital factory · Cloud manufacturing · Industry 4.0

1 Introduction

European industrialists identify the radical change in the traditional manufacturing production process as the rise of Industry 4.0 [9]. Conversely, China mainland has launched his strategic plan named China 2025, to promote intelligent manufacturing as its primary direction. Both programs share the same goal about the realization of a Factory of the Future towards the development of an ICT-enabled intelligent manufacturing [14,25]. This need poses new research objectives which result in the development of new paradigms known as *Virtual Factories* for European factories, *Digital Factories* and *Smart Factories* with a widespread in both countries and *Cloud Manufacturing* finding its roots in China. Although both countries share the same goal, the context of implementation is different. This work aims to investigate the different perspectives in the realization of a Factory of the Future providing an overview of the major trends in the implementation and applications of cloud manufacturing in China, through a comparison with the European concept of Digital Factory. The paper is organized as follows. We start introducing the characteristics of *digital factories* discussing their extensibility as virtual factories (Sect. 2), then we describe the

This work was supported by the EU H2020 program under Grant No. 734599 - FIRST project.

H. A. Proper and J. Stirna (Eds.): CAiSE 2019 Workshops, LNBIP 349, pp. 107–119, 2019.
https://doi.org/10.1007/978-3-030-20948-3_10

cloud manufacturing providing an example of its application (Sect. 3). Starting from the above descriptions, in Sect. 4 we propose a comparison between virtual factories and cloud manufacturing. Finally, Sect. 5 concludes the paper and sketches some future works.

2   Characteristics of Digital Factory

A *digital factory* refers to a new type of manufacturing production organization that simulates, evaluates and optimizes the production process and systems. Digital factories are not confined only to the production stage; instead, they extend to address the entire factory lifecycle.

The production process in a digital factory takes place from the early stage of product design down to the lowest stage of product planning and realization. As key features of the design stage, we can mention digital design, modeling, and simulations which contributes to shortening the time for designing and manufacturing products [32]. Moreover, modeling and simulation capabilities are extended to all tangible and intangible assets of the factory. 3D-motion simulation can be applied in virtual models on various stages to improve the product and process planning on all levels [11]. The digital factory represents a bridge for the existing gap between product design and manufacturing [10]. Thus, the digital factory covers the entire product lifecycle at different manufacturing levels with a focus on the virtual representation of manufacturing assets of the factory, virtual plant visualization, intelligent control and optimization of the product lifecycle through model simulation. To this end, the digital twin model is based on different models representing physical manufacturing assets (i.e., 3D-model, discrete event model), virtual simulation technology to simulate and predicts the performance of virtual models, as well as an integration platform to realize two-way connectivity between digital and real factory [23]. Moreover, in a digital factory the product design shifts from traditional 2D drawings, to a collaborative 3D model design based on CAD [31]. In this context, there are some important aspects to be outlined: (i) product performances (i.e., manufacturability, cost) are predicted by model simulations; thus the entire manufacturing process is optimized; (ii) product design is collaborative, meaning that multiple design departments (within the company boundaries) take part to the product design.

2.1   From Digital to Smart Factory

The design of an intelligent shop floor layer of a *digital factory* is related to the emerging concept of *smart factory*. A *Smart factory* connects the main actors of the supply chain (people, products, and materials) to realize seamless communication and integration (man-and-machine) for the smart manufacturing realization. The adoption of high-end manufacturing equipment (i.e., smart devices, industrial robots, and robotic arms) as well as the integration of well-established equipment with IoT devices and sensors, allows collecting real-time data and information from the factory floor. Smart factory adds decision-making capabilities to the shop floor as well as data collected from equipment is analyzed to improve the production process of the lowest manufacturing layer.

The digital factory represents a necessary prerequisite for the enabling of a *smart factory* which in turn is necessary for the development of the next generation of smart manufacturing. A smart factory enhances the capabilities of the digital factory improving the simulation results by providing real-time data of the shop floor as well as simplify the construction of faithful 3D models typical of a digital factory. A typical application collects data from the shop floor to realize realistic models thus improving the simulation results, see Fig. 1.

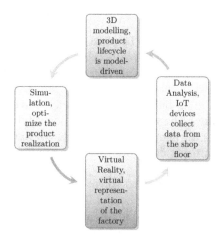

Fig. 1. Digital factory lifecycle. Smart factory enables the data collection

2.2 Digital Factory Applications

One of the key concepts of a digital factory is the representation of the physical objects composing the shop floor in a virtual space. The connection between the physical and the virtual world of a factory is realized through M2M OPC-UA protocol. 3D-Virtual Reality (VR) technologies replicate the shop floor in a virtual space and simulation results optimize the design process without the need for sample manufacturing. That is, through three-dimensional modeling, virtual simulation technology, the design layer predicts the performance of the production, and improves and optimizes the product lifecycle based on simulation results.

The core of the digital factory is represented by the integration of existing manufacturing systems at different operational layers as well as the adoption of 3D modeling technologies, virtual simulation and Virtual Reality/Augmented Reality technologies. The digital factory promotes technological support for the entire product life cycle by the creation of a digital twin model.

To this end, Authors of [17] propose a framework that enables the development of a feasible semantic model that supports easy creation of digital twins for physical assets of a factory. The virtualization of the shop floor hardware encompasses a data model that encapsulates the technical specification of the machines composing the factory floor.

Conversely, at the control layer, the virtual simulation plays a central role in modern manufacturing companies which adopt virtual reality for the design and verification of production systems as machines simulation, process verification, and factory layout planning and simulation. Simulation of virtual resources is made available through a variety of commercial tools such as Arena [28], DELMIA [4], Flexsim [7]. As an example, South Korea's Samsung Heavy Industries use DELMIA software to build a 3D layout of the factory floor and simulate processes in a virtual environment.

The model-based simulation also helps to identify bottlenecks in the production line whose identification in the real world would have required a long-term verification with high costs (i.e., to maximize the production by reducing the number of failures caused by poor processes and failures of mechanical parts). As an example, authors in [2] built a Flexsim model starting from real data of a packaging production line. The model helped in identifying machine failures of the hardware composing the shop floor. Therefore, continuously updating simulation models with monitoring data, improves the accuracy and precision of the predictions [19].

Augmented Reality is adopted to solve problems common to the current manufacturing plant. The increasing cost of labor and the loss of knowledge due to the retirement of highly skilled employees are minimized through the adoption of Augmented Reality technology. As an example, AR is used to train newcomers by providing visual training on mastering manufacturing equipment. Information is displayed directly on the eye screen through the use of standard AR glasses. This approach not only reduces the cost of training newcomers but also enables to instruct employees to handle hardware failures by displaying procedures to recovery from failures, thus improving the production.

2.3   Relationship Between Digital Factory and Virtual Factory

The European concept of *Virtual Factory* is a major expansion upon virtual enterprises in the context of manufacturing. The virtual organization approach integrates collaborative business processes from different enterprises to simulate, model and test different design options to evaluate performance, thus to save time-to-production [5].

Both *digital* factory and *virtual* factory share common reference models for the realization of a Factory of the Future. In a digital factory, decision-making technologies play a key role in real plant simulation and optimization.

Similarly, 3D virtual environments and discrete event simulation models are proposed for modeling, simulating and evaluating manufacturing assets [5] in a virtual factory. On the contrast, while a digital factory is likely to define their operational boundaries inside the company, a virtual factory extends the factories capabilities across multiple organizations to provide a unified virtual environment to test, model and simulates factory layouts and processes.

Similar applications are found in a digital factory where its application extend design and production processes across multiple departments within the company boundaries. This trend emerges in companies which implement a digital factory to support a collaborative process among departments. As an example, the China Aerospace Science and Technology 211 company, adopt a full step-by-step design process ranging from 3D-to-process to 3D-to-site and 3D-to-factory. It can be outlined that process collaboration is driven by the adoption of 3D models through the entire development process. Therefore, three-dimensional modeling is a key enabler of a collaborative process promoting the sharing of product data flexibly within the digital factory boundaries.

Ultimately, there is a strong overlap between digital factory and virtual factory. While the digital factory provides cooperation within departments, the virtual factory extends this cooperation among multiple enterprises. Therefore, for the rest of the paper, we will refer to a virtual factory, as an extension upon the digital factory. The concept of collaborative manufacturing is also an important characteristic of cloud manufacturing described in the next section.

3   Characteristic of Cloud Manufacturing

Cloud manufacturing is an emerging trend in China, which takes benefit from cloud computing and information technology, to achieve resources sharing across small and medium-sized enterprises (SMEs). It has become a national trend due to rapid industrialization and advancement of information technology. Cloud Manufacturing can be defined as *a model for enabling ubiquitous, convenient, on-demand network access to a shared pool of configurable manufacturing resources (e.g., manufacturing software tools, manufacturing equipment, and manufacturing capabilities) that can be rapidly provisioned and released with minimal management effort or service provider interaction* [30]. Therefore, on-demand services, resources virtualization and decentralized services of centralized resources promote new forms of networked manufacturing to respond quickly to unpredictable demands of the market. Cloud Manufacturing inherits the concept of "everything is a service" from cloud computing and proposes a new paradigm of *Manufacturing as a Service* (MaaS), which encapsulates manufacturing assets (software tools, production systems, capabilities) into cloud services providing on-demand access to consumers. Further, cloud manufacturing promotes a new collaborative manufacturing business model represented in Fig. 2. The collaborative cloud manufacturing promotes the active role of the customers during the production process. Customers interact with manufacturers via a cloud platform by specifying their product requirements. Mass customization of products is enhanced by the creation of a network of enterprises (DMS) having different roles in the production process.

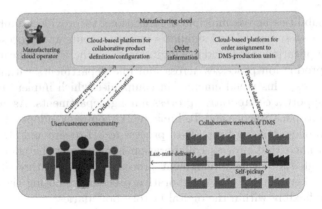

Fig. 2. Collaborative cloud manufacturing model taken from [6].

3.1 Type of Services

The nature of services provided in the cloud is extremely variegated due to the necessity to cover the entire product lifecycle of the traditional manufacturing process. According to [16], service delivery models (SDM) are typical of Cloud Computing, and they can be divided into: *Infrastructure-as-Service (IaaS)*, *Platform-as-Service (PaaS)* and *Software-as-Service (SaaS)*. In contrast to traditional cloud computing, services are provided both by cloud computing resources as well as manufacturing resources (smart robots, production systems, equipment). Services provided by the cloud can range from pure manufacturing services (i.e., equipment for product realization) to manufacturing software services (provided through a cloud computing resource). Cloud delivery models fit accordingly to the different manufacturing steps. As an example, considering the product lifecycle, the following delivery models are suitable for the different production stages:

- Product Design, Product Simulation and Product Management delivered as *SaaS*
- Product Planning delivered as *PaaS*
- Product Realization (requiring the use of physical equipment composing the factory floor) delivered as *IaaS*

In addition to the standard cloud manufacturing *services* mode, cloud manufacturing promotes a new form of enterprises collaboration through the on-demand access of virtualized and decentralized resources via a cloud platform. For example, virtual enterprises set up a collaborative network which supports a different form of coupling such as *loose* and *tight* coupling. According to the diverse enterprise needs, loose coupling is selected for occasional use of manufacturing assets while a tight coupling is chosen whenever a global manufacturing process relies on services offered by multiple enterprises. Therefore, a cloud architecture promotes enterprise collaboration through the enabling of multiple forms of alliances according to the diverse needs. Through the unified management of resources/capabilities, cloud manufacturing promotes the sharing of decentralized resources of manufacturing resources/capabilities highlighted by the manufacturing grid and also includes the integration and sharing of hard manufacturing resources.

3.2   Collaborative Deployment Models

Cloud manufacturing has four typical deployment modes inherited from cloud computing [30] (*public* cloud, *private* cloud, *hybrid* cloud, and *community* cloud).

– In the *public* cloud, service provider subscribes and publishes their services in a multi-tenant environment. A cloud platform provides on-demand use of services to an open community of customers.
– *Private* cloud restricts the operational mode within enterprises boundaries. In a private cloud, all actors belong to the same organization.
– *Hybrid* cloud mixes the previous mode to integrate different types of cloud (e.g., public, private or community). Forming a bridge, between different clouds, requires cloud owners to select proper resources sharing models. Authors in [18] proposed a framework for the development of hybrid cloud bridging multiple cloud platforms.
– A *community* cloud is shared among companies of the same community.

3.3   Some Examples of Cloud Manufacturing

The success case of cloud manufacturing in China mainly includes small- and medium-sized enterprises that have established their information systems [15]. Despite the cloud manufacturing aims to cover the entire manufacturing product lifecycle ranging from collaborative product design down to services integration and virtualization and sharing of manufacturing resources, at present, the development of a full-featured cloud manufacturing application case is still under development [16]. Nevertheless, many industries start to experiment with the development of a cloud manufacturing platform at a different level of awareness. The collaborative cloud platform proposed in [12] aims to balance uneven resources distribution and fragmentation in the integration of different services in the mold industry. The cloud platform acts as a trading platform where enterprises publish and trade their manufacturing assets. The main functionalities offered by the platform include enterprises registration as a service provider or customer, manufacturing assets registration, service discovery, service selection, service evaluation, transaction management.

Similarly, the features of the platform are extended [13] to enable integration at the process level as well as tight coupling of different manufacturing management systems (i.e., MES, ERP). The collaboration mode between enterprises is based on a social network model that guarantees interaction among partners in a relatively stable network environment. According to the diverse business requirements, enterprises seek new partners through the public market page,

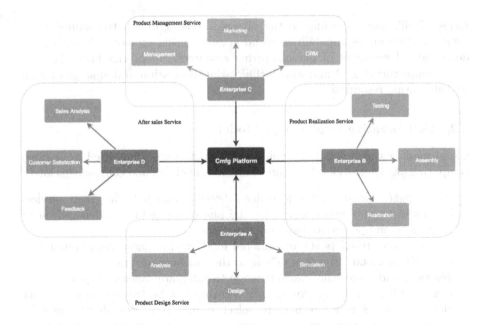

Fig. 3. An example of a collaborative network established via a cloud platform.

remove partners from an alliance or join multiple networks at the same time. The platform Tianzhi Net[1] enables enterprises business collaboration of local industrial chains [13]. The example reported in Fig. 3 shows a network alliance based on a social network model enabled by a cloud platform.

4   Comparison Between Cmfg and vF

In this Section, we compare the two approaches considering some aspects. Firstly we introduce the operational boundaries to examine the degree of interoperability across factories. Moreover, we examine different approaches to provide interoperability at each architectural layer. Then, we describe the main actors of a virtual factory and cloud manufacturing. Finally, we briefly introduce potential applications for simulating and optimizing a factory. Table 1 summarizes the comparison.

Operational Boundaries. While one of the goals of a virtual factory is the enabling of a wide collaboration to expand the business outside company boundaries, the cloud manufacturing encompasses resources virtualization, decentralized services, and collaborative deployment models to achieve enterprises collaboration. The concept of cloud manufacturing also includes dynamic resources

---

[1] www.cosimcloud.com.

allocation and different pricing models (i.e., pay-per-use, subscription, pay-for-resources) which not only open up powerful forms of collaborations but also promotes a networked production process to support the emerging trend of the mass-customization.

Data Interoperability. One of the major challenges in a virtual factory is enabling interoperability among SMEs. To this end, different works have been proposed in the literature to support interoperability. The cloud-based storage architecture proposed by [8] promotes the sharing of data across virtual factories activities through a Storage as a Service cloud model. The storage is based on the concept of buckets, which are specific isolated storage spaces managing data for the different data type. These buckets manage different types of data in multiple databases. In the European research project, Virtual Factory Framework (VFF) [29] the proposed Virtual Factory Data Model (VFDM) provides a unified common definition of data shared among the software tools connected to the framework, using a shared meta-language. Similar challenges arise in the cloud manufacturing where the goal is to enable interoperability in heterogeneous environments composed by multiple cloud services. Authors in [29] propose to deal with data interoperability issues in cloud manufacturing with an architecture based on Virtual Function Block (VFB). Data manipulation is driven by the function block which guarantees the data, related to the manufacturing process, to be consistent among heterogeneous cloud environments. To this end, a cloud manufacturing architecture [24] utilizes the OWL language to model Cloud resources, as well as other approaches, are proposed to provide a unified data modeling such: ontology-based models, cloud resources and services description based on XML language [29].

Service Interoperability. In a virtual factory, a collaborative process includes composition and integration of existing manufacturing services supported by technologies from the service-oriented computing (SOA) [22]. In cloud manufacturing, each manufacturing asset is virtualized via a virtual resource layer

Table 1. Key features of vF and Cmfg

	vF	Cmfg
Operational boundaries	Inter-factories	Expand to multiple heterogeneous cloud environments
Data interoperability	Common reference model for unified data representation (VDM)	Based on: OWL models, XML description language, Ontology-based models
Services interoperability	Service-oriented architecture	
Operational roles	Distinguish between resources consumer/provider and vF owner	Inherited from cloud computing
Simulation and optimization	As an IT platform provide optimization by simulations of the real plant of the factory	SaaS applications to monitor and controls the production process

and deployed as a service through a service-oriented layer, composing the cloud manufacturing (CMfg) architecture. For example, for virtual enterprises and collaborative networks, cloud manufacturing supports different forms of collaboration, such as loose coupling and tight coupling, and builds different forms of alliances through its highly flexible cloud architecture, as mentioned before. Cloud manufacturing enables the integration of decentralized social manufacturing assets to achieve high levels of sharing and collaboration. In cloud manufacturing, enterprises perform service development and provide manufacturing services to each other. It can be seen that the concept of cloud manufacturing and service-oriented manufacturing is completely consistent. Therefore, integration of cloud manufacturing services relies on the adoption of service-oriented architecture as in a virtual factory. As an example, we report the work of [27] in which authors propose a service-oriented architecture based on a service broker, to orchestrate services of multiple heterogeneous clouds.

Operational Roles. Finally, the Cmfg paradigm differentiates operational roles such as resources consumer, resources providers, and cloud operators. Although these roles are immutable in a standard cloud environment, as pointed out in the previous paragraph, the cloud manufacturing opens up new forms of collaborative models in which operational roles, as well as sharing policies, are interchangeable. Therefore, the roles of the actors in a multiple cloud collaborative environment need to be further studied to support a dynamic form of collaborations, flexible sharing policies, as well as diverse pricing models for each manufacturing asset. At the same time, the human role is taking into consideration during the design of a virtual factory [1]; in particular, the parties involved in a service-oriented virtual factory are defined as [22]: service provider, service consumer and service broker. These roles respectively identify the parties which offer physical services, the consumer of these services, and the owner who controls and governs the virtual factory. Therefore, although the virtual factory roles are coherent with the ones defined in the Cmfg, as proposed in the cloud, deployment models, as well as pricing models, need to be further examined to enable a flexible collaboration between virtual factories.

Simulation and Optimization. From a virtual factory as an IT platform perspective, the potential is extended to plan, simulate, control the shop floor to assess the future impact of production and maintenance planning decisions [26]. Similarly, in a cloud environment, cloud-based services monitor the production planning and control the discrete manufacturing environment (i.e., machine availability monitoring and collaborative and adaptive process planning [21], simultaneous shop scheduling, and material planning [20]).

5   Conclusions

Both *digital factory* and *cloud manufacturing* adopts different concepts for the realization of a Factory of the Future.

Despite sharing the same goal, the chosen directions differ under different points of view. From a common digital factory perspective, the aim is to automate and digitalize the intra-factory level with the help of new technological advancements such: virtual reality, augmented reality, and simulations to optimize the production of the shop floor. While from an inter-factories collaboration perspective, the most promising paradigms are the Chinese paradigm of cloud manufacturing and the European concept of virtual factory.

While the cloud manufacturing derives its roots from the widely accepted concept of cloud computing, the virtual factory forms its basis in the manufacturing environment. In this paper, we have introduced both the approaches, and we have proposed a comparison based on the main features of the two concepts.

Additionally, to further expand business between European and Chinese factories is necessary to examine interoperability issues between digital factories and cloud manufacturing better. With regard to future work, we are studying how to enable interoperability in digital factories [3].

References

1. Azevedo, A., Francisco, R., Bastos, J., Almeida, A.: Virtual factory framework: an innovative approach to support the planning and optimization of the next generation factories. IFAC Proc. **43**(17), 320–325 (2010)
2. Bartkowiak, T., Pawlewski, P.: Reducing negative impact of machine failures on performance of filling and packaging production line - a simulative study. In: 2016 Winter Simulation Conference (WSC), December 2016
3. Bicocchi, N., Cabri, G., Mandreoli, F., Mecella, M.: Dealing with data and software interoperability issues in digital factories. In: Proceedings of the 25th International Conference on Transdisciplinary Engineering (TE2018), pp. 13–22. IOS Press (2018)
4. Bzymek, Z., Nunez, M., Li, M., Powers, S.: Simulation of a machining sequence using delmia/quest software. Comput. Aided Des. Appl. **5**, 401–411 (2013)
5. Debevec, M., Simic, M., Herakovic, N.: Virtual factory as an advanced approach for production process optimization. Int. J. Simul. Modell. **13**, 66–78 (2014)
6. Erwin Rauch, P.D., Seidenstricker, S., Hämmerl, R.: Collaborative cloud manufacturing: design of business model innovations enabled by cyberphysical systems in distributed manufacturing systems. J. Eng. **2016**, 1–12 (2016)
7. Gelenbe, E., Guennouni, H.: Flexsim: a flexible manufacturing system simulator. Eur. J. Oper. Res. **53**(2), 149–165 (1991)
8. Hao, Y., Karbowski, R., Shamsuzzoha, A., Helo, P.: Designing of cloud-based virtual factory information system. In: Azevedo, A. (ed.) Advances in Sustainable and Competitive Manufacturing Systems. LNME, pp. 415–426. Springer, Heidelberg (2013). https://doi.org/10.1007/978-3-319-00557-7_34
9. Hozdić, E.: Smart factory for industry 4.0: a review. Int. J. Modern Manuf. Technol. **7**, 28–35 (2015)
10. Jianzhong, T.: Application status and prospects of digital factory. Innov. Technol. **5**, 35–37 (2017)
11. Kuhn, W.: Digital factory - simulation enhancing the product and production engineering process. In: Proceedings of the 2006 Winter Simulation Conference, pp. 1899–1906, December 2006

12. Li, B., Zhang, G.-J., Shi, S.-X.: Mould industry cloud manufacturing platform supporting cooperation and its key technologies. Comput. Integr. Manuf. Syst. **18**, 1620–1626 (2012)
13. Li, B., et al.: Research and applications of cloud manufacturing in China. In: Schaefer, D. (ed.) Cloud-Based Design and Manufacturing (CBDM), pp. 89–126. Springer, Cham (2014). https://doi.org/10.1007/978-3-319-07398-9_4. A Service-Oriented Product Development Paradigm for the 21st Century
14. Li, L.: China's manufacturing locus in 2025: with a comparison of "made-in-china 2025" and "industry 4.0". Technol. Forecast. Soc. Chang. **135**, 66–74 (2018)
15. Lin, Q., Xia, K., Wang, L., Gao, L.: Cloud manufacturing in China: a literature survey. Int. J. Manuf. Res. **9**, 369–388 (2014)
16. Liu, Y., Wang, L., Wang, W., Xu, X.: Discussion on cloud manufacturing. Chin. Mech. Eng. **18**, 2226–2237 (2018). (in Chinese)
17. Lu, Y., Xu, X.: Resource virtualization: a core technology for developing cyber-physical production systems. J. Manuf. Syst. **47**, 128–140 (2018)
18. Lu, Y., Xu, X., Xu, J.: Development of a hybrid manufacturing cloud. J. Manuf. Syst. **33**(4), 551–566 (2014)
19. Modoni, G.E., Caldarola, E.G., Sacco, M., Terkaj, W.: Synchronizing physical and digital factory: benefits and technical challenges. In: 12th CIRP Conference on Intelligent Computation in Manufacturing Engineering, Procedia CIRP, vol. 79, pp. 472 – 477, 18–20 July 2018, Gulf of Naples, Italy (2019)
20. Mourtzis, D., Doukas, M., Lalas, C., Papakostas, N.: Cloud-based integrated shop-floor planning and control of manufacturing operations for mass customisation. In: Procedia CIRP, 9th CIRP Conference on Intelligent Computation in Manufacturing Engineering - CIRP ICME 2014, vol. 33, pp. 9–16 (2015)
21. Mourtzis, D., Doukas, M., Vlachou, A., Xanthopoulos, N.: Machine availability monitoring for adaptive holistic scheduling: a conceptual framework for mass customization. In: 8th International Conference on Digital Enterprise Technology - DET 2014 Disruptive Innovation in Manufacturing Engineering towards the 4th Industrial Revolution, Procedia CIRP, vol. 25, 406–413 (2014)
22. Schulte, S., Schuller, D., Steinmetz, R., Abels, S.: Plug-and-play virtual factories. IEEE Internet Comput. **16**(5), 78–82 (2012)
23. Shoudian, L.: Discussion on digital factory construction plan. Manuf. Autom. **40**, 109–114 (2018)
24. Tao, F., Cheng, Y., Xu, L.D., Zhang, L., Li, B.H.: CCIoT-CMfg: cloud computing and internet of things-based cloud manufacturing service system. IEEE Trans. Industr. Inform. **10**(2), 1435–1442 (2014)
25. Terkaj, W., Tolio, T.: The Italian Flagship Project: Factories of the Future. In: Tolio, T., Copani, G., Terkaj, W. (eds.) Factories of the Future, pp. 3–35. Springer, Cham (2019). https://doi.org/10.1007/978-3-319-94358-9_1
26. Terkaj, W., Tolio, T., Urgo, M.: A virtual factory approach for in situ simulation to support production and maintenance planning. CIRP Ann. **64**(1), 451–454 (2015)
27. Parameswaran, A.V., Chaddha, A.: Cloud interoperability and standardization. SETLabs Briefings **7**, 01 (2009)
28. Vieira, G.E.: Ideas for modeling and simulation of supply chains with arena. In: Proceedings of the 2004 Winter Simulation Conference 2004, vol. 2, pp. 1418–1427 (2004)
29. Wang, X.V., Wang, L., Gördes, R.: Interoperability in cloud manufacturing: a case study on private cloud structure for SMES. Int. J. Comput. Integr. Manuf. **31**(7), 653–663 (2018)

30. Xu, X.: From cloud computing to cloud manufacturing. Robot. Comput. Integr. Manuf. **28**(1), 75–86 (2012)
31. Zhang Guojun, H.G.: Digital factory: its application situation and trend. Aeronaut. Manuf. Technol. **40**, 34–37 (2013)
32. Zhou, J., Li, P., Zhou, Y., Wang, B., Zang, J., Meng, L.: Toward new-generation intelligent manufacturing. Engineering **4**(1), 11–20 (2018)

Predictive Maintenance in a Digital Factory Shop-Floor: Data Mining on Historical and Operational Data Coming from Manufacturers' Information Systems

Minas Pertselakis[1(✉)], Fenareti Lampathaki[1], and Pierluigi Petrali[2]

[1] Suite5 Data Intelligence Solutions Limited, Limassol, Cyprus
minas@suite5.eu
[2] Whirlpool EMEA, Benton Harbor, USA

Abstract. Predictive maintenance is regarded by many as a key factor in Industrial Internet of Things (IIoT) and the development of "smart" factories. With the growing use of sensors and embedded computing systems, the term predictive maintenance is most often understood as a strategy that relies on collecting streaming sensor data and performing condition monitoring. Thus, the majority of academic papers base their research work solely on sensorial sources coming from the shop floor machinery, neglecting the knowledge already existing in legacy systems and maintenance historical logs. The UPTIME project aims to develop a unified predictive maintenance framework that incorporates information from heterogeneous data sources, both from sensor devices and legacy/operational systems. In this contribution, we share our first insights on legacy data analytics in the predictive maintenance context, and outline the tools and approaches we developed in the course of the project. Experimental work has been conducted using real world datasets deriving from an actual manufacturing facility in the White Goods/Home Appliances sector. The results provide significant knowledge about the manufacturing processes and show the potential of the proposed methodology.

Keywords: Predictive maintenance · Data mining · Manufacturing · Knowledge discovery · Machine learning · Digital factory

1 Introduction

Predictive maintenance, in general, describes strategies and actions to prevent breakdowns of technical equipment by predicting just in-time wear-out or failure situations. Such strategies usually imply the continuous processing of sensor data in order to derive information on possible abnormalities and prospective failures, which in turn, can lead to predictions on future states, trends and remaining useful life (RUL) of the observed equipment. In simple terms, the first objective of a predictive maintenance strategy is to identify abnormal behaviour of technical equipment by continuously

H. A. Proper and J. Stirna (Eds.): CAiSE 2019 Workshops, LNBIP 349, pp. 120–131, 2019.
https://doi.org/10.1007/978-3-030-20948-3_11

observing sensor data streams. The second objective is to analyse the data streams using prediction algorithms, already trained with historical sensor data, in order to provide a solid guess of a future undesired condition or failure. The latter is accompanied by an obvious challenge: such an analysis would require a large amount of sensor data that already have experienced failures of -ideally- all possible causes. And that, in the real world, could take many years to acquire and would require an enormous storage capacity. Additionally, in most cases, the sensor data involve only a few of the components of a production line, or a small number of aspects of each component (e.g. only temperature, or pressure), which means that a prediction system based on these sensors can rarely capture the whole picture of the factory shop floor and the possible correlations among all machines.

Legacy systems, on the other hand, refer to operational information already collected in databases that cover many aspects of the shop floor and manufacturing activities. Legacy datasets may contain historical values related to the daily production line operation (e.g. products created per day, wastes created per day, pause times of production line, etc.), or to maintenance events, failures and causalities, in the form of a log file (e.g. On date d, machine x stopped for n mins in order to be sufficiently lubricated). They can even include shift schedules, environmental conditions or logistics. All these factors indicate the need for intelligent and automated data analysis methodologies, which aim to discover useful knowledge from data. Data mining has emerged as a prominent tool for knowledge acquisition from the manufacturing databases with many examples in the academic research area [1, 2]. The knowledge extracted can come in various forms (predictions, optimized values, rules, etc.) and may be propagated to or/and combined with condition monitoring systems.

The combination of legacy systems' extracted knowledge with real-time data streams has been investigated in the past in few research studies [3–5]. The main outcome of all these studies is more or less identical; the combined power of data analytics can lead to more accurate predictive maintenance results and can cover a broader spectrum of manufacturing processes and operations. If we take into consideration that these approaches are over a decade old, and that machine learning has evolved significantly since then, we are confident that a data mining approach based on today's tools (software and hardware) can certainly advance predictive maintenance a step forward.

The next section outlines the methodology and architecture proposed in this paper, while Sect. 3 presents a real-world case study from the manufacturing domain of white goods. Section 4 is devoted to experimental results and Sect. 5 concludes the paper with useful insights and future challenges.

2 Methodology and Architecture

The UPTIME project introduces methodological and technological innovations to address the challenges of a predictive maintenance unified system. One of those innovations is a Data Analytics engine driven by the manufacturers' need to leverage legacy and operational data related to the broader overview of the shop floor performance and maintenance, as well as to extract and correlate relevant knowledge.

Variables in manufacturing databases that would be useful for analysis, could be classified into the following groups [6]:

1. Manufacturing process variables: machining, casting, forgings, extrusions, stampings, assembling, cleaning, etc.
2. Machining variables: cutting speeds, temperature, pressure, lubricants, coolants, voltage, current, etc.
3. Resource variables: product materials and numbers, machines, fixtures, etc.
4. Environment variables: humidity, temperature, etc.
5. Working condition variables: duration, shift, injuries and accidents, etc.
6. Target variables: quality, yield, productivity, performance index, etc.
7. Maintenance events variables: duration of downtime, duration of maintenance, reasons, causes, solutions, etc.

In the case study that follows, we use variables of the last 2 groups, but any combinations are possible depending on the availability and type of the data collected.

The proposed Data Analytics system allows a manufacturer to upload different datasets that have been extracted from the legacy and operational systems. In order to ensure that the datasets provided fall within the scope of predictive maintenance, they are mapped to a pre-defined predictive maintenance Data Model which is based on the MIMOSA international standard (OSA-CBM v3.3.1 and OSA-EAI v3.2.3a)[1]. In case a dataset has no correlation with the data model, it cannot be further processed; otherwise, its semantic and syntactic mapping is performed and the data are stored. From this phase on, two parallel processes start:

I. The data analyst has at his disposal the datasets and may experiment with the different machine learning algorithms already provided in the Data Analytics engine in the dedicated data analyst interface. Such an interface is built on a popular open-source notebook and allows for further customization of the features of the algorithms and comparison of their performance (accuracy, variance, etc.).

II. Through the business interface, the business user can obtain a quick understanding of the data uplifted, including: (a) the distribution of the values across the features/fields of the dataset to detect missing or unexpected values, min and max values, as well as stats like mean, median, and standard deviation, (b) the relationships detected within the data provided through interactive exploration of different data facets across multiple dimensions, and (c) the outcomes of the more "statistical" analysis that is automatically computed, e.g. timelines of the interruptions vis-à-vis the failures, the actual versus the planned downtime per day, and the different types of interruption per machine.

As soon as the analysis performed on any dataset is completed, it is appropriately exported from the data analyst interface and imported into the business user interface. In this way, the business users have the outcomes of the machine learning analysis at their disposal and may also browse and examine the different views and reports in an intuitive manner using their own interface.

---

[1] [online] http://www.mimosa.org/.

The high-level architecture and the workflow of this component can be viewed in Fig. 1. The data analytics engine practically consists of five layers:

1. The Data Uplifting Layer which handles the dataset upload process in the component, by receiving batch data extracts from legacy software platforms of earlier technology, as well as from operational systems on the shop floor with events collected by the workers Due to the nature of the data analysis to be performed, the uplifting may take place once a week or once per month or even once per year, so that we have sufficient data to work on.

2. The Data Curation, Matching and Transformation Layer which is responsible for mapping the data model of the dataset to the pre-defined predictive maintenance data model.

3. The Data Storage Layer that handles the storage of the data contained in one or more given datasets.

4. The Data Mining and Analytics Layer practically delivers the intelligence of the component by defining, training, executing and experimenting with different machine learning algorithms.

5. The Analytics Results Visualization, Patterns & Rules Extraction acts as the user interface to the business user, visualizing and interpreting the results of the Data Mining & Analytics Layer and extracting rules and patterns that are exposed (together with specific data extracts and results) through APIs to the integrated UPTIME platform.

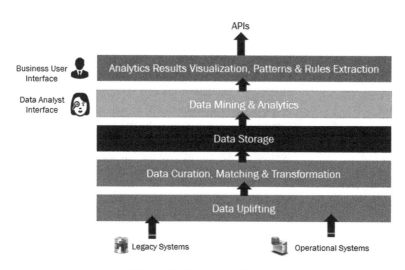

Fig. 1. High level architecture

The functionality of the proposed data analytics engine is evaluated over a real business case from the manufacturing domain of white goods and home appliances and is presented, along with the experimental results, in the following sections.

3 White Goods Case Study

The presented research study is supported by an industrial partner, that produces white goods and home appliances worldwide. It is a preliminary study that focuses on a single production line that produces drums for dryers. The product is basically a carbon steel cylinder used to keep and rotate clothes during drying stage. Currently only preventive and reactive maintenance are implemented in the shop floor and thus there is a requirement to expand the list of maintenance activities performed by effectively modifying their strategy to include predictive maintenance processes. In the UPTIME context, a set of sensors will be installed on important assets of the shop floor and data analysis will be performed covering two different viewpoints: data coming from sensors and data from legacy/operational systems.

This paper presents the second viewpoint's preliminary analysis. Along with useful insights, the results of this process can be used as an initialisation procedure for the first viewpoint, until sufficient amount of sensorial data has been collected and analysed. For this purpose, the industrial partner provided us with two different datasets with data collected through a whole year. They are both pretty common in manufacturing processes and can be extracted from typical software programs found in factory premises. The first dataset (OEE dataset) is related to the production line performance indicators and the way the OEE (Overall Equipment Effectiveness) is computed on a daily basis. Therefore, the most useful information in this dataset includes the number of items produced, the true operational time, the time of interruptions and pauses, the number and duration of breakdown events, etc. as depicted in Table 1.

Table 1. Description of main attributes from OEE dataset

	Attribute	Data type	Description
1	Day	Date	The date of the year
2	OEE	Number	Overall Equipment Effectiveness (%)
3	Total Mins of Interruption	Number	Amount of time the line was stopped due to some interruption (in mins)
4	Mins of Preventive Maintenance	Number	Amount of time the line was stopped due to scheduled preventive maintenance (in mins)
5	Mins of Alarms	Number	Amount of time the line was stopped due to some alarm firing (in mins)
6	Required Production	Number	The number of items the line is requested to produce
7	Actual Production	Number	Real gross production of items (waste included)
8	Wastes	Number	Defective items produced
9	Mins of Real Operation	Number	Amount of time the line operated with no interruption (in mins)
10	Number of Breakdowns	Number	How many times the line stopped due to a breakdown

The second dataset (M-log dataset) is a log file of maintenance events that occurred during a full year, and consists of brief textual descriptions of observed faults and interruptions per day and per asset, and the actions taken to correct these faults. Each instance in this dataset therefore, represents a single fault on a single machine at a particular date. It is worth noting that a single machine may have multiple interruptions during the same day, and a single fault, usually a breakdown, may persist for more than one day (Table 2).

Table 2. Description of main attributes from M-log dataset

Attribute	Data type	Description
Day	Date	The date of the year
Machine Id	String	An alphanumeric string that uniquely identifies a machine
Duration of Interruption	Number	Amount of time (in mins)
Interruption Category	String	Category of interruption
Type of Interruption	String	Type of interruption
Cause of Interruption	String	Detailed cause
Action Taken	String	Intervention of a human so as to fix the issue

These datasets can be analysed separately, but also as a joint set using the Day feature as a common key. The analysis presented in this paper is performed on each dataset separately. In the lines to follow, we first explore the dataset using descriptive analytics before applying a set of classification algorithms to make predictions about future failures.

3.1 Descriptive Analytics

Descriptive analytics is an initial stage of data processing in an attempt to visualize the available information, extract some initial useful insights and prepare the data for further analysis. To this end, several statistical approaches can be employed. Nevertheless, this paper will focus on data mining techniques for descriptive results with Self-Organising Maps being our first choice.

A self-organising map (SOM) is a tool for the analysis and visualization of high-dimensional data. It is based on the principles of vector quantisation and belongs to a set of unsupervised classifiers trained by competitive learning [6]. SOMs' ability of grouping patterns based on similarity make them ideal first technique for the descriptive analysis of complex datasets and for this reason it has been used extensively in industrial processes [8].

The SOM algorithm was applied to OEE dataset and the resulted visualization of the dataspace is depicted in Fig. 2. In simple terms, the blue squares show nodes of data with great similarity, while the reddish squares have nodes of data with much less similarity. Adjacent squares of approximately the same colour, can form larger groups which we call clusters. Therefore, one can observe clusters of different behaviours among the whole data space by examining the features of similarity that form each cluster. For example, in Fig. 2, the cluster on the lower right corner is characterised by the following feature states:

```
'OEE' is normal (82.5%) AND
'Mins of Preventive Maintenance' is high (58.2%) AND
'Mins of Alarms' is low (15.8%) AND 'Mins of Real Operation' is
normal (30.4%) AND 'Days from Previous Breakdown Event' is very
low (6.9%) AND 'Required Production' is low (25.3%) AND
'Actual Production' is low (30.3%)
```

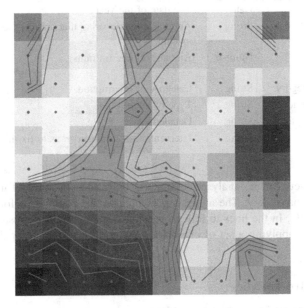

Fig. 2. The resulted U-matrix after training a SOM with OEE data

After closer observation and consulting with the manufacturer, it resulted that this cluster describes days that the factory experiences breakdown events.

In the same way, we use a SOM on the M-log dataset, this time using only 2 variables (Machine Id and Cause of Interruption). In order to examine the relationships that form between interruptions and manufacturing equipment through SOM the categorical values were transformed into binary using one hot encoder. The result is depicted in Fig. 3 and an example of the most interesting cluster is the one with the following characteristics:

```
'Machine_200',
'Machine_238',
'Machine_308',
'Machine_403',
'Cause of the Interruption:Défaut mise en position',
'Cause of the Interruption:Défaut présence pièce prise 1',
'Cause of the Interruption:Défaut présence pièce prise 2',
'Cause of the Interruption:Rivet bloqué dans revolver'
```

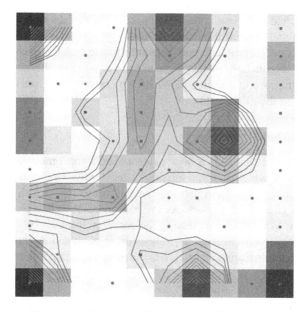

Fig. 3. The resulted U-matrix after training a SOM with M-log data

The above output tells us that the SOM algorithm detected a group of machines and causes which produce interruptions frequently occurring together. This is an interesting insight since in a complex shop floor environment with so many machines and different interruption types, is not easy for a human being to observe such patterns and correlations.

3.2 Classification Algorithms

The next step of the analysis involved the testing of the prediction power of the algorithms. The request was to predict if the factory is going to have a breakdown on the next day, given today's performance indicators. For this reason, we employed the OEE dataset, which gives us a daily overview of the production line. As a first action, we setup the dataset as a binary classification task. For this reason, we had to create labels according to whether there is a breakdown event on the next day or not, based on the "Number of breakdowns" feature input. Thus, the first class denotes a normal day without unexpected incidents, and the second class represents a day with at least one type of failure.

For the classification task we employed and tested 6 different classifiers, namely the linear Support Vector Machine (SVM), the multinomial Naïve Bayes classifier, the k-NN, Decision Trees, Random Forest, and the Multilayer Perceptron (MLP). These algorithms were selected due to their popularity and efficiency in similar predictive tasks [9, 10]. Even though different parameters were tested during the first runs, the accuracy of all classifiers did not manage to exceed the "normal day" class ratio using a k-fold cross validation evaluation. This means that the classifiers failed to capture the task at hand and find sufficient patterns within the given data space, resulting in an overfitting output that favored the major (in quantity) class. Overfitting is a common challenge in classification problems and there are a few techniques that allow an analyst to overcome it. Nevertheless, in this particular case, none of the known techniques could efficiently improve the results, so we had to come up with something different. This is described in the next section.

3.3   Improving Model Accuracy

By reviewing the data at hand, it was evident that some time-related information regarding the breakdown events was missing. This is why we introduced a metadata feature that we called "Days from previous breakdown event", which could be easily calculated by the given OEE dataset. As the experimental results prove, this feature alone gave a boost to results by increasing the accuracy from 77.7% to an impressive 95%. In fact, further feature evaluation analysis using permutation importance showed the same thing. That this feature alone carries the most important information regarding breakdowns.

Permutation importance works by randomly shuffling a single column of the dataset, leaving the target and all the other columns in place, and calculates how much the accuracy is affected by this [11]. Model accuracy is of course reduced by this method, but the aim is to see how much the loss function suffered from shuffling. This performance deterioration measures the importance of the variable that was just shuffled. In our case the results on the input features are listed in Table 3.

Table 3. Permutation importance (top-6) on input features.

Weight	Feature
0.2664 ± 0.0336	Days from Previous Breakdown Event
0.0954 ± 0.0347	Number of Breakdowns
0.0274 ± 0.0116	Mins of Real Operation
0.0129 ± 0.0103	Mins of Preventive Maintenance
0.0058 ± 0.0048	Required Production
0.0050 ± 0.0056	Total Mins of Interruptions

It is clear that the new metadata input plays the most important role in the classification outcome. The reasons why are explained in the outcome of the experimental analysis that follows.

4 Experimental Results

As already described, the experimental analysis involved 6 different classifiers, namely the linear Support Vector Machine (SVM), the multinomial Naïve Bayes classifier, k-NN, Decision Tree, Random Forest, and the Multilayer Perceptron (MLP). The input space included all features from the OEE dataset and the algorithms were evaluated using a stratified 5-fold cross validation on a shuffled dataset.

Using the newly introduced "Days from previous breakdown event" feature, the Naïve Bayes, SVM, and k-NN failed to generalise and reached a performance of 77.66%, which is precisely the rate of the first class. The MLP raised its performance slightly reaching an 80%. In contrast, the decision tree reached an accuracy of 95%, followed by random forest with 93.4%. The following table lists the results for both data scenarios examined; with and without the new metadata feature (Table 4).

Table 4. Classification results after 5-fold cross validation.

Algorithm	Accuracy (without metadata)	Accuracy (with metadata)
SVM	77.66%	77.66%
Naïve Bayes	77.66%	77.66%
k-NN (k = 6)	77.15%	77.66%
MLP	77.66%	80.20%
Decision Tree	72.58%	**95.00%**
Random Forest	70.55%	**93.40%**

It is worth mentioning that the interpretation of the decision tree outcome offers additional information in the form of rule-based knowledge, as shown below. Note that the outcome is actually a single rule of an IF-ELSE IF format:

Rule

```
    IF Days from Previous Breakdown Event > 1.5 THEN Next
day = Normal
    ELSE IF Days from Previous Breakdown Event > 0.48
THEN Next day = Breakdown
    ELSE IF Production required > 2893 THEN Next day =
Breakdown
    ELSE IF Mins of Alarms > 27.96 AND Production re-
quired < 2350 THEN Next day = Breakdown
    ELSE Next day = Normal
```

In short, the above rule claims that a day with failure is usually followed by a next day of failure, which implies either that a given malfunction may create another malfunction on the same production line or that a failure usually persists for more than 1 days. Both of these assumptions were empirically confirmed as true by the manufacturer. We should also note that, given more years of data, the predictions could be enhanced to support a greater time horizon, but still on a scale of days.

5 Conclusions and Future Work

As discussed in a very recent study [12], 97% of the manufacturing companies in Germany and Switzerland are planning to extend their activities in data analytics. Nevertheless, the manufacturing domain is still at the early stages of exploiting all available data it creates and stores, especially for predictive maintenance purposes. The analysis of real-time sensor data has been the main focus lately in the majority of the research papers, while there is a huge treasure of legacy systems data remaining untouched. Additionally, the sensor data analysis is usually applied only on a small part of a shop floor, monitoring the condition of a few machines. Legacy data on the other hand, contain information regarding the whole factory cycle and store events from all machines, even if they have sensors installed or not. And this is a gap that the UPTIME project and the proposed methodology aims to bridge, with the power of data mining technics and machine learning.

A data analytics engine is presented that allows a manufacturer to upload, examine and analyze different datasets extracted from legacy and operational systems. The datasets are required to follow a specific data model especially designed for predictive maintenance purposes. An industrial case study highlights the importance of the derived knowledge, which, in many cases, can assist and calibrate the information derived from sensorial real-time data streams. Examples of descriptive and predictive analytics are discussed, emphasizing on the experimental results on two datasets coming from a real operating factory.

One of the main practical challenges identified during this study was the fact that on an operational shop floor that already performs preventive maintenance on a fixed schedule, is very hard to obtain frequent failures or breakdowns in the data. Even more so, when a factory has newly installed equipment. Moreover, a dataset with a year's details cannot be regarded as sufficient and representative of the overall factory and machinery lifecycle and it can, therefore, reveal the potential effectiveness of the method.

The next steps of this on-going research, apart from tackling the aforementioned challenges, include the application of data analytics on a larger set of historical data from factory operations, joined by historical data generated by the installed sensors, so that the interoperability and knowledge exchange of the two data processing systems will be tested. At the same time, different factories from the manufacturing industry will be included as case studies in order for us to obtain a more generic approach that can reduce maintenance costs and improve quality, productivity and profitability for any manufacturing organisation.

Acknowledgments. This work was carried out within the UPTIME project. UPTIME project has received funding from the European Union's Horizon 2020 research and innovation programme under grant agreement No. 768634.

References

1. Choudhary, A.K., Harding, J.A., Tiwari, M.K.: Data mining in manufacturing: a review based on the kind of knowledge. J. Intell. Manuf. **20**(5), 501 (2009)
2. Harding, J.A., Shahbaz, M., Srinivas, Kusiak, A.: Data mining in manufacturing: a review. J. Manuf. Sci. Eng. Trans. ASME **128**(4), 969–976 (2006)
3. Kobbacy, K.A.H., Fawzi, B.B., Percy, D.F., Ascher, H.E.: A full history proportional hazards model for preventive maintenance scheduling. Qual. Reliab. Eng. Int. **13**(4), 187–198 (1997)
4. Lin, C.C., Tseng, H.Y.: A neural network application for reliability modelling and condition-based predictive maintenance. Int. J. Adv. Manuf. Technol. **25**(1–2), 174–179 (2005)
5. Bey-Temsamani, A., Engels, M., Motten, A., Vandenplas, S., Ompusunggu, A.P.: A practical approach to combine data mining and prognostics for improved predictive maintenance. Data Min. Case Stud. **36** (2009)
6. Wang, K.: Applying data mining to manufacturing: the nature and implications. J. Intell. Manuf. **18**(4), 487–495 (2007)
7. Kohonen, T.: Self-Organizing Maps, vol. 30. Springer, Heidelberg (2012)
8. Díaz, I., Domínguez, M., Cuadrado, A.A., Fuertes, J.J.: A new approach to exploratory analysis of system dynamics using SOM. Applications to industrial processes. Expert Syst. Appl. **34**(4), 2953–2965 (2008)
9. Romanowski, C.J., Nagi, R.: Analyzing maintenance data using data mining methods. In: Braha, D. (ed.) Data Mining for Design and Manufacturing. MACO, vol. 3, pp. 235–254. Springer, Boston (2001). https://doi.org/10.1007/978-1-4757-4911-3_10
10. Susto, G.A., Schirru, A., Pampuri, S., McLoone, S., Beghi, A.: Machine learning for predictive maintenance: a multiple classifier approach. IEEE Trans. Industr. Inf. **11**(3), 812–820 (2015)
11. Strobl, C., Boulesteix, A.L., Kneib, T., Augustin, T., Zeileis, A.: Conditional variable importance for random forests. BMC Bioinform. **9**(1), 307 (2008)
12. Groggert, S., Wenking, M., Schmitt, R.H., Friedli, T.: Status quo and future potential of manufacturing data analytics—an empirical study. In: 2017 IEEE International Conference on Industrial Engineering and Engineering Management (IEEM), pp. 779–783. IEEE (2017)

Information Extraction for Additive Manufacturing Using News Data

Neha Sehgal[1,2](✉) and Andrew Crampton[1]

[1] University of Huddersfield, Queensgate, Huddersfield, UK
[2] Valuechain, 3MBIC, Huddersfield, UK
nsehgal@valuechain.com

Abstract. Recognizing named entities like Person, Organization, Locations and Date are very useful for web mining. Named Entity Recognition (NER) is an emerging research area which aims to address problems such as Machine Translation, Question Answering Systems and Semantic Web Search. The study focuses on proposing a methodology based on the integration of an NER system and Text Analytics to provide information necessary for business in Additive Manufacturing. The study proposes a foundation of utilizing the Stanford NER system for tagging news data related to the keywords "Additive Manufacturing". The objective is to first derive the organization names from news data. This information is useful to define the digital footprints of an organization in the Additive Manufacturing sector. The existence of an organization derived using the NER approach is validated by matching their names with companies listed on the Companies House portal. The organization names will be matched using a Fuzzy-based text matching algorithm. Further information on company profile, officers and key financial data is extracted to provide information about companies interested and working within the Additive Manufacturing sector. This data gives an insight into which companies have digital footprints in the Additive Manufacturing sector within the UK.

Keywords: Named Entity Recognition · News data ·
Additive Manufacturing · Text matching · Open data

1 Introduction

Additive Manufacturing has the potential to revolutionize the global parts manufacturing and logistics landscape in the UK. It enables distributed manufacturing and the production of parts-on-demand while offering the potential to reduce cost and energy consumption; and thereby carbon footprint. This paper explores a paradigm data science approach to gather information on companies associated with Additive Manufacturing to fully exploit Additive Manufacturing growth and potential. There is no special SIC Code associated with companies

Supported by Knowledge Transfer Partnership, Innovate UK.

H. A. Proper and J. Stirna (Eds.): CAiSE 2019 Workshops, LNBIP 349, pp. 132–138, 2019.
https://doi.org/10.1007/978-3-030-20948-3_12

related to Additive Manufacturing sector, therefore it is vital to derive the list of companies, engaged with Additive Manufacturing, either digitally or registered with the UK Companies House portal. To find such companies, this paper proposes to utilize news data to find the organization being discussed in recent news articles.

In this study, the news data is collected for the keyword "Additive Manufacturing" from different open API sources. The task of extracting organizations and names of people from textual data is known as Named Entity Recognition (NER). Named entity recognition tasks generally require costly, hand-labelled training data and most existing corpora are small in size. Therefore, it is better to use the Stanford NER system to extract the names of persons and organizations listed in news articles for the keyword "Additive Manufacturing". Further, text matching is performed to match organizations derived by the NER system with companies registered at Companies House Portal.

2 Background

2.1 Named Entity Recognition

This section covers the landscape of various state-of-the-art approaches for Named Entity Recognition and Classification tasks. Historically NER systems were based on hand-made rules, but, due to the growth of big data and the popularity of machine learning in recent times, researchers have developed powerful, reliable and robust NER systems. The work related to NER has been studied extensively and considers major factors such as: Language, Textual genre and Entity type [1]. The ability to learn from previously known entity data is an essential part of any NER problem. The words, with their associated tags, compose the feature set for supervised learning.

Recent studies have utilized supervised machine learning to find insights from training data and induce rule-based systems. Major supervised learning approaches include Hidden Markov Models (HMMs), Ensemble Models, Support Vector Machines and Artificial Neural Networks. Su et al. [2] propose a Hidden Markov Model-based chunk tagger to recognize and classify names, times and numerical data. [3] employs a maximum entropy concept to use global information directly for the NER task. [4] experimented with a combination of four diverse classifiers for the NER task, including linear classifiers, maximum entropy, transformation-based learning and HMMs. [5] proposed a probabilistic approach, combined with Latent Dirichlet Allocation, to employ supervised learning using partially labeled seed entities. A study by [6] used Support Vector Machines for feature selection and for the Named Entity recognizer task.

Few researchers have employed unsupervised learning, i.e. clustering to gather named entities from clusters created based on their similarity of context [7]. Recent examples of NER applications include monitoring Twitter streams to understand user's opinions and sentiments. Li [7] presented a novel, unsupervised NER system for Twitter streams using dynamic programming followed by a random walk model. Ritter et al. [8] developed a novel T-NER system which outperformed the Stanford NER System in terms of the F1-Score by overcoming redundancy inherent in tweets using LabeledLDA.

With the rise in availability of social media data, it is difficult to analyze data, in the form of news, due to challenges including variations in spelling, linguistics, commenting, emoticons, images and the use of mixed languages. As it is difficult to annotate text data from new databases, due to time and cost constraints, it is beneficial to use the Stanford NER system (an already annotated corpus) to derive the organization being discussed and highlighted in discussions related to Additive Manufacturing. Many NER-related studies [9,10] have shown that Stanford NER generally performs better than other corpora. Therefore, this study plans to use Stanford NER for tagging and extracting organizations from corpora of news data.

3   Dataset

In order to build a picture of the Additive Manufacturing sector in the UK, data has been gathered and aggregated from multiple news API for the keywords "Additive Manufacturing". In total, 10,000 news articles are extracted which include headlines, description, paragraphs, author name and any associated tags.

The information on matched company data, after applying the NER system and text matching, has been gathered from Companies House. This information has been captured for all companies which are listed as active as of the 1st January 2019, who have a Manufacturing SIC Code. The data on company profile, officers and financial information is extracted using the Companies House API by using Python. The financial data provides details regarding the company's balance sheet, together with a few more important parameters.

Using a custom algorithm, potential company websites have been identified and scraped for: self-reported descriptions of the company; information about the sectors that the company reports they operate in; the accreditations they report that they hold; information about their capabilities; and additional links to social media accounts. This data gives an insight into which companies have digital footprints within the Additive Manufacturing sector in the UK.

3.1   Tools

Currently, there are vast amounts of tools available for data analysis and machine learning. Python has been ranked number one for the last two years on LinkedIn for being the most powerful and popular tool for data science. Python is chosen in this study as the programming language of choice due to its seemingly vast adoption in the data analysis and machine learning community.

Three major Python libraries i.e. NumPy, Panda and Scikit-learn will be used for data analysis. Panda will be used for checking the types of attributes and for relevant modifications as necessary. NumPy is useful for converting dataframes to array formats which is essential for modeling purposes. Scikit-learn is useful for clustering tasks and for splitting data into training, validation and testing groups.

4   Proposed Methodology

The news data is extracted from different news APIs. After the data has been extracted, the text data is cleaned by removing punctuation, transforming to lower case and by removing stop words. The Standford NER system is then implemented to extract names of organizations as follows:

4.1   Entity and Relation Extraction

The StanfordNER Tagger, in the NLTK library, is used for extracting the Named Entity Recognition which is a sequence of words (news data) consisting of: Name **(PERSON, ORGANIZATION and LOCATION)**; Numerical **(MONEY and PERCENTAGE)**; and Temporal **(DATE and TIME)**.

– For extracting the NER, we used the NER Model trained on an English corpus i.e., **"english.muc.7class.distsim.crf.ser"**
– For extracting the NER, we also used an NER Tagger engine i.e., **"stanford-ner.jar"** (it is also know as CRF classifier).

For applying the NER Tagger we have two techniques available:

1. Pass the refined text, obtained previously, as a parameter to the Stanford NER Tagger to get the NER tags.
2. Convert the refined text into sentences and send these as a parameter to the Stanford NER Tagger to get the NER tags.

A snapshot of the list of organizations from a news article is shown below in Fig. 1.

```
In [30]:  print(get_individuals(ne_annot_sent_7c))

          ['Deputy Group Editor', 'EOS', 'TCT Show', 'Gravity Industries', 'EOS', 'EOS', 'EOS Shared Modules', 'Evonik', 'Sieme
          ns NX', 'EOS', 'Boeing']
```

Fig. 1. Grouped NER tags on the basis of (ORGANIZATION)

The extracted names of organizations from 10,000 news articles are validated with companies registered on the Companies House Portal using a fuzzy-based text matching algorithm. The success rate for validation is 70% i.e., approx. 70% of company names extracted from online news articles had matched with Companies House data. Lastly, the data for company profiles, officers and financial information is extracted from the Companies House API. The data provides a holistic overview about UK companies working or interested in Additive Manufacturing. This data is important for start-up companies, investors and SMEs in order to understand the progress encompassing the Additive Manufacturing sector in UK.

The Companies House data on companies extracted through this methodology provides information on digital footprints and financial performance over a number of years.

5 Results

The results will be discussed in detail during the presentation. Due to data privacy, the whole analysis is not presented here in the paper. To provide an overview, a sample of 515 news articles on the topic of Additive Manufacturing are selected randomly from the corpus. The proposed methodology, based on NER, is applied to derive the list of organizations discussed in 515 news articles. There were a total of 3175 organization names extracted from 515 news articles. A sample of 750 Small and Medium Enterprises (SME) from 3175 organization names was selected for further information and data analysis. The company names are matched with a list of companies listed in the Companies House database using a fuzzy-based text matching algorithm. For this sample data, approximately 43.5% of company's names, found using the NER approach, matched with Companies House data.

The data on company profile, officers and financial (equity, assets and liabilities) are gathered from the Companies House API for 327 companies. The financial data was extracted for 192 SME companies. The remaining 135 companies are either start-up, or dormant companies or they have filed financial details in paper format; in which case their financial details are not available.

The company profile data shows that approximately 34% of additive manufacturing companies falls within the Greater Manchester Local Enterprise Partnership (LEP). The company age profile shows that 11% of additive manufacturing SMEs have recently established with an age less than 2 years. The age distribution of directors associated with additive manufacturing SME Companies shows that the majority of directors falls within the category of 45–55 years of age.

The companies are further classified based on their balance sheet banding and percentage change in shareholder funds over the last two years. The companies are categorized in four groups: Champions (Blue), Contenders (Green), Prospects (Yellow), and Strugglers (Red). The data shows that there are a high number of Prospects SME in the additive manufacturing sector. The financial matrix, as shown in Fig. 2, is helpful for investors and other key players of manufacturing sectors, looking for opportunity to expand businesses or connect with members of supply chain.

PCT_category	Equity Category				
	< 0M	[0M, 0.1M)	[0.1M, 1M)	[1M, 2M)	[2M, 5M)
>100	0	11	5	0	
[50, 100)	0	2	7	1	0
[25, 50)	0	3	20	4	0
[10, 25)	0	2	24	2	5
[2.5, 10)	0	2	21	7	6
[0, 2.5)	1	0	7	0	0
[-2.5, 0)	1	3	4	1	1
[-10,-2.5)	1	0	10	1	1
[-25, -10)	1	2	6	0	4
[-50, -25)	0	6	6	0	0
[-100, -50)	3	3	4	0	0
<-100	4	0	0	0	0

Fig. 2. Financial analysis for SME in Additive Manufacturing (Color figure online)

6   Conclusion

In the era of machine learning and big data, information extraction plays an important role for parsing and classifying billions of news articles. If the category of any company specification is not listed as one of the key SIC Codes, an alternative approach can be considered by integrating NLP and text matching algorithms. Information about organizations working or interested in the Additive Manufacturing sector can be gathered by using news articles listing the keywords "Additive Manufacturing". NER systems can help in extracting organization names from news data, which has been validated with Companies House data and thereby provides more detailed knowledge about companies by gathering information on its profile, officers and financial situation.

References

1. Nadeau, D., Sekine, S.: A survey of named entity recognition and classification. Lingvisticae Investig. **30**(1), 3–26 (2007)
2. Zhou, G.D., Su, J.: Named entity recognition using an HMM-based chunk tagger. In: Proceedings of the 40th Annual Meeting on Association for Computational Linguistics (ACL 2002), pp. 473–480. Association for Computational Linguistics, Stroudsburg (2002). https://doi.org/10.3115/1073083.1073163
3. Chieu, H.L., Ng, H.T.: Named entity recognition: a maximum entropy approach using global information. In: Proceedings of the 19th International Conference on Computational Linguistics (COLING 2002), vol. 1, pp. 1–7. Association for Computational Linguistics, Stroudsburg (2002). https://doi.org/10.3115/1072228.1072253
4. Florian, R., Ittycheriah, A., Jing, H., Zhang, T.: Named entity recognition through classifier combination. In: Proceedings of the Seventh Conference on Natural Language Learning at HLT-NAACL 2003 (CONLL 2003), vol. 4, pp. 168–171. Association for Computational Linguistics, Stroudsburg (2003). https://doi.org/10.3115/1119176.1119201
5. Guo, J., Xu, G., Cheng, X., Li, H.: Named entity recognition in query. In: Proceedings of the 32nd International ACM SIGIR Conference on Research and Development in Information Retrieval (SIGIR 2009), pp. 267–274. ACM, New York (2009). https://doi.org/10.1145/1571941.1571989
6. Isozaki, H., Kazawa, H.: Efficient support vector classifiers for named entity recognition. In: Proceedings of the 19th International Conference on Computational Linguistics (COLING 2002), vol. 1, pp. 1–7. Association for Computational Linguistics, Stroudsburg (2002). https://doi.org/10.3115/1072228.1072282
7. Li, C., et al.: TwiNER: named entity recognition in targeted Twitter stream. In: Proceedings of the 35th International ACM SIGIR Conference on Research and Development in Information Retrieval (SIGIR 2012), pp. 721–730. ACM, New York (2012). https://doi.org/10.1145/2348283.2348380
8. Ritter, A., Clark, S., Mausam, Etzioni, O.: Named entity recognition in tweets: an experimental study. In: Proceedings of the Conference on Empirical Methods in Natural Language Processing (EMNLP 2011), pp. 1524–1534. Association for Computational Linguistics, Stroudsburg (2011)

9. Kazama, J.I., Torisawa, K.: Exploiting Wikipedia as external knowledge for named entity recognition. In: Proceedings of the 2007 Joint Conference on Empirical Methods in Natural Language Processing and Computational Natural Language Learning (EMNLP-CoNLL) (2007)

10. Nothman, J., Curran, J.R., Murphy, T.: Transforming Wikipedia into named entity training data. In: Proceedings of the Australasian Language Technology Association Workshop 2008, pp. 124–132 (2008)

A Fog Computing Approach
for Predictive Maintenance

Tania Cerquitelli[1], David Bowden[2], Angelo Marguglio[3], Lucrezia Morabito[4],
Chiara Napione[4], Simone Panicucci[4], Nikolaos Nikolakis[5], Sotiris Makris[5(✉)],
Guido Coppo[6], Salvatore Andolina[6], Alberto Macii[1], Enrico Macii[7],
Niamh O'Mahony[2], Paul Becker[8], and Sven Jung[8]

[1] Department of Control and Computer Engineering,
Politecnico di Torino, Turin, Italy
{tania.cerquitelli,alberto.macii}@polito.it
[2] DELL EMC, Cork, Ireland
{david.bowden,niamh.omahony}@dell.com
[3] Engineering Ingegneria Informatica S.p.A., Palermo, Italy
angelo.marguglio@eng.it
[4] COMAU S.p.A., Turin, Italy
{lucrezia.morabito,chiara.napione,simone.panicucci}@comau.com
[5] Laboratory for Manufacturing Systems and Automation,
Department of Mechanical Engineering and Aeronautics,
University of Patras, Patras, Greece
{nikolakis,makris}@lms.mech.upatras.gr
[6] SynArea Consultants S.r.l., Turin, Italy
{guido.coppo,salvatore.andolina}@synarea.com
[7] Interuniversity Department of Regional and Urban Studies and Planning,
Politecnico di Torino, Turin, Italy
enrico.macii@polito.it
[8] Fraunhofer Gesellschaft zur Förderung der angewandten Forschung,
Aachen, Germany
{paul.becker,sven.jung}@ipt.fraunhofer.de

Abstract. Technological advances in areas such as communications, computer processing, connectivity, data management are gradually introducing the internet of things (IoT) paradigm across companies of different domain. In this context and as systems are making a shift into cyber-physical system of systems, connected devices provide massive data, that are usually streamed to a central node for further processing. In particular and related to the manufacturing domain, Data processing can provide insight in the operational condition of the organization or process monitored. However, there are near real time constraints for such insights to be generated and data-driven decision making to be enabled. In the context of internet of things for smart manufacturing and empowered by the aforementioned, this study discusses a fog computing paradigm for enabling maintenance related predictive analytic in a manufacturing environment through a two step approach: (1) Model training on the cloud, (2) Model execution on the edge. The proposed approach has been applied to a use case coming from the robotic industry.

© Springer Nature Switzerland AG 2019
H. A. Proper and J. Stirna (Eds.): CAiSE 2019 Workshops, LNBIP 349, pp. 139–147, 2019.
https://doi.org/10.1007/978-3-030-20948-3_13

Keywords: Internet of things · Predictive analytics ·
Cyber-physical system

1   Introduction

The Industrial IoT (IIoT) will massively increase the amount of data available
for analysis by organizations in a manufacturing ecosystem. In this context, data
analytics hold the promise for manufacturing companies of better understanding
their production processes and systems. In addition, predictive analytics enable
insight into machinery condition through the analysis of past data to predict
future breakdowns. This would reduce the production and/or product failure
rates, and as a result, bring down the operation costs of the manufacturer.

IoT requires an end-to-end infrastructure which is a challenge, especially for
small enterprises. Cloud solutions may provide centralized storage and higher
processing power, enabling batch processing of large amounts of data, thus suitable for the development and training of complex predictive models, such as
recurrent neural networks. On the other hand, this approach introduces latency,
depending on the network architecture and bandwidth, hence increasing the
response time of analytics-driven decision making, assuming the later is located
at an edge node in a factory. With respect to the aforementioned and towards
enabling predictive analytics at the edge, the current study discusses a two-step
approach integrating cloud and edge functionalities through a fog network where
multiple devices could be connected to the same or multiple gateways on a fog
network. First, the data aggregation and analysis is performed on a cloud node.
Then the trained models are pushed down on an edge gateway, allowing insight
generation in little time.

2   Related Work

Recent advances in ICT with the emergent rise of CPSs [10] and cloud computing [22], enable new opportunities for manufacturing enterprises [23]. Industry
4.0 has increased the significance of the maintenance process in production systems [2]. In the literature, several approaches on predictive maintenance platforms have been introduced (e.g. [12,19]), but they fail to adequately address
the fundamental tension between flexibility to host many applications, the need
of security privacy, data transmission and the user is permitted with limited
control and management. Condition-based predictive maintenance represent the
maintenance approach supported by sensor measurements [4].

An integrated predictive maintenance platform was proposed in [6], consisting
of three main pillars. A semantic framework for predictive maintenance in a
cloud environment was introduced in [17]. On a similar manner, a condition-
based maintenance policy approach was introduced in [18], that made a diagnosis
of the asset status based on wire or wireless monitored data, predicting the
assets abnormalities and executing suitable maintenance actions before serious

problems occurred. A dynamic predictive maintenance framework was presented in [21] that deals with the decision making and optimization in multicomponent systems.

Predictive analytics can be conceived as an extension of data mining technology. Enabled by historical data and high computing power they can reveal underlying information through sophisticated functions and machine learning models. The scale of such functionalities require a cloud infrastructure. However, pushing as much as possible functionality to the edge can reduce communication costs and reduce the response time for actions to be taken. Therefore new approaches are needed. Data mining [8] and management [20] techniques are one of the key enablers in the design of a condition-based maintenance capability. In general, all systems like manufacturing, automotive, oil and gas, and others dump large amounts of data periodically from different sources. Artificial intelligence involves the development of powerful reasoning algorithms and prediction techniques [16]. Advantages of cloud computing include the virtualization of the resources, parallel processing, security of the data and service integration, thus minimizing the cost and restriction for automation and maintenance infrastructure [13]. An integrated predictive maintenance platform was proposed in [5], consisting of three main pillars. The first pillar was related with data acquisition responsible for data extraction and analysis, while the second pillar was responsible for maintenance modelling knowledge modelling and representation. The final pillar has advisory capabilities on maintenance planning with emphasis given to environmental and energy performance indicators. A semantic framework for predictive maintenance in a cloud environment was introduced in [17].

In the context of smart manufacturing, fog computing can provide advanced services [14]. Fog computing [3] can be perceived as the extension of cloud computing to edge nodes of a network. Its purpose is to preserve the advantages of cloud computing, improving an integrated system's efficiency [15], security [1], sustainability [7], while reducing the amount of data transported to the cloud for processing [9]. The distributed architecture of a fog network and for computing reduces the bandwidth needed and the back-and forth communication between field devices and the cloud-based central management and orchestration node(s) [11].

3   Approach

The envisioned SERENA platform, enabling the predictive maintenance concept, will be based upon the following key technologies: (a) remote condition monitoring and control, (b) AI condition-based maintenance and planning techniques, (c) AR-based tools for remote assistance and human operator support, controlled under (d) a cloud-based platform for versatile remote diagnostics. In this paper and as part of the current platform implementation the supported functionalities that have been integrated as services include a visualization, a predictive analytics and a scheduling service. In Fig. 1 the main components of the SERENA system are presented.

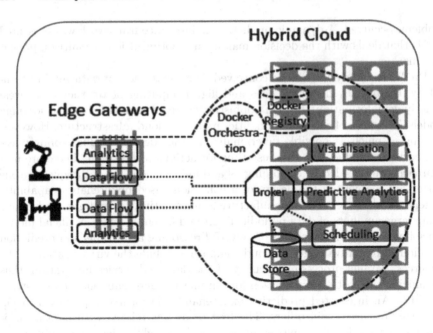

Fig. 1. SERENA system architecture.

In order to facilitate the predictive analytics deployment on a factory floor, the SERENA project proposes a distributed, lightweight and scalable architecture which through the collective use of its integrated services will provide predictive maintenance solutions to the shop floor personnel. The architecture is implemented following a micro-services architecture pattern. On top of it, docker containers are used to wrap individual services and deploy them across the network to edge gateways and through the SERENA cloud. The use of docker technologies and their distribution through the a docker orchestration manager allows software packages with its dependencies to run smoothly regardless of the underlying host. Virtual machines offer similar set of capabilities. However, while containers provide an abstraction layer at the application level, virtual machines (VM) abstract the physical hardware level, resulting in the size of containers being smaller than VMs. The adoption of same docker solutions in SERENA results in the creation of a unified architecture that can be operated and managed as a single unit. In addition, the common network interface decouples the system from its dependency on a specific technology offering technology transparency. The SERENA system and through its service oriented architecture can support its extention with additional functionalities. In this context and as at a first stage, the following functionalities were implemented and integrated to the platform.

1. Communication broker: The broker facilitates the communication between the edge gateway and the SERENA services, through multiple communication

protocols such as REST and/or MQTT. Moreover, the broker can support integration with legacy systems such as enterprise resource planning (ERP) and manufacturing execution systems (MES).

2. Edge Gateway: The gateways are collecting data from the shopfloor sensors and other systems and transfer them to the cloud through the communications broker. The gateway may also host predictive models along with additional docker containers wrapping other functionalities.

3. Orchestration and Registry: The orchestration manager or orchestrator is responsible for managing the deployment, communication and execution status of the containers. The orchestration manager deploys containers from images residing into the SERENA docker registry, ensuring availability and trustworthiness of the images.

4. Data Store: The SERENA system data required by its services are stored in this component. The Data Store is also implemented as a container. Multiple data stores can be supported by the SERENA system.

5. Predictive analytics service: This service aims to build a predictive model based on historical data through multiple machine learning techniques and apply the models in near-real time to newly arrived data streams. Through the docker containers the trained model can be pushed down at an edge "smart" gateway to support short response times of the analytics' result.

6. Visualization: A real time HTML5 Unity 3D based visualization application integrated to the SERENA system. This application is connected to the SERENA platform in order to provide real time information to the maintenance operator, as a result of the predictive analytics.

7. Scheduling: A java based scheduling service for assigning predictive maintenance activities to maintenance personnel based on a set of criteria, such as experience level, skills, availability.

The aforementioned SERENA system with its integrated functionalities has been tested in a use case coming from the robotics industry and is presented in the following section along with some first results.

4   Use Case

In order to test and validate the proposed approach, a test-bed has been built by COMAU and related to the predictive maintenance requirements of a robotic manipulator, and more specifically the incorrect belt tentioning and backlash phenomenon. This "RobotBox" consists of a motor from a COMAU medium size robot, with its associated controller. Then it is constituted by an adapter, a belt and a 5 kilos weight in place of the robot end-effector. At this point it should be mentioned that in a complete robot there are many factors affecting its physical condition, like temperature, humidity, vibrations. Hence, it is difficult to isolate single effects, especially considering that an industrial robot provides only limited monitored datasets through its controller For a COMAU robot this includes the axis position and the current required for the motor to perform the required action. With respect to the aforementioned, this initial experiment takes into account position and current of the RobotBox in order to study the belt tensioning phenomenon through the SERENA system. Raw data are transmitted in a JSON format to the edge gateway, where they are pre-processed locally to generate meaningful information named "smart" data. In this experiment, smart data include a set of 12 statistical values such as max, min, average, root mean square.

In this context, the predictive analytics service has been tailored to the belt tensionsing problem and the acquired data set. Six levels of belt tentioning have been defined by the domain expert. Then, these information along with the raw data acquired by the controller as imported to a neural network classifier to recognize the level of belt tensioning, along with an additional classifier providing qualitative status information about the backlash effect and an estimation of the remaining useful life, expressed in days.

As part of the experimental setup, presented in Fig. 2, all integrated functionalities were tested and evaluated.

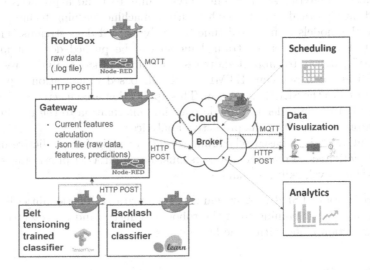

Fig. 2. SERENA system architecture

The predictive analytics model was implemented using the python tensorflow library with a training data set of 300 samples and with a hold-out validation approach. The confusion matrix of the final model is presented in Fig. 3.

The accuracy of the model was estimated at approximately 90%. Furthermore, it was noticed that the higher the environment temperature, the lower the current consumption of the motor. This can be supported by a lower friction between the components of the motor at a higher temperature.

Moreover, the analytics provide input to the visualization service that displays in real-time information about the RobotBox status as described by the input data and analytics (Fig. 4). As result the service itself provides an intuitive

		\<br\>	*Predicted*				
		0	1	2	3	4	5
	0	**1373**	0	0	0	0	0
	1	0	**2145**	0	5	0	0
Actual	2	0	0	**6673**	97	67	32
	3	0	0	36	**3718**	40	219
	4	0	0	51	230	**3302**	293
	5	0	0	0	119	30	**3530**

Fig. 3. Final predictive analytics model confusion Matrix

Fig. 4. Visualization app showing axis6 information updated in real-time.

Fig. 5. Scheduling application interface displaying measurement time series.

interface to the maintenance personnel towards enabling remote monitoring and condition evaluation of industrial equipment.

In addition, the scheduling service was tested assigning maintenance related tasks to the maintenance personnel. In the current experiment, the schedule was generated in approximately 11 ms, and included the execution of two tasks (Fig. 5).

5 Conclusions

As discussed in the paper the SERENA project proposes a lightweight fog computing architecture to enable predictive analytics and push functionalities from the cloud to the edge. Moreover, the proposed architecture has been tested with its first batch of integrated services to an industrial test-bed.

The platform itself has been designed and implemented to be scalable and support the integration of a different set of technologies. In the following period this will be tested extensive through the integration to the SERENA system of the four other industrial use cases within the project.

Finally, the analytics part is a critical aspect for enabling predictive maintenance solutions. As such, particular focus will be given on testing and improving the approaches assessed in the aforementioned testbed in the context of other demonstrators.

Acknowledgments. The research leading to these results has received funding from European Commission under the H2020-IND-CE-2016-17 program, FOF-09-2017, Grant agreement no. 767561 "SERENA" project, VerSatilE plug-and-play platform enabling REmote predictive mainteNAnce.

References

1. Alrawais, A., Alhothaily, A., Hu, C., Cheng, X.: Fog computing for the internet of things: security and privacy issues. IEEE Internet Comput. **21**(2), 34–42 (2017)
2. Alsyouf, I.: The role of maintenance in improving companies' productivity and profitability. Int. J. Prod. Econ. **105**(1), 70–78 (2007)
3. Anawar, M.R., Wang, S., Azam Zia, M., Jadoon, A.K., Akram, U., Raza, S.: Fog computing: an overview of big IoT data analytics. Wirel. Commun. Mob. Comput. **2018** (2018)
4. Colledani, M., et al.: Design and management of manufacturing systems for production quality. CIRP Ann. **63**(2), 773–796 (2014)
5. Efthymiou, K., Pagoropoulos, A., Papakostas, N., Mourtzis, D., Chryssolouris, G.: Manufacturing systems complexity review: challenges and outlook. Procedia CIRP **3**, 644–649 (2012)
6. Efthymiou, K., Papakostas, N., Mourtzis, D., Chryssolouris, G.: On a predictive maintenance platform for production systems. Procedia CIRP **3**, 221–226 (2012)
7. Fisher, O., Watson, N., Porcu, L., Bacon, D., Rigley, M., Gomes, R.L.: Cloud manufacturing as a sustainable process manufacturing route. J. Manuf. Syst. **47**, 53–68 (2018)
8. Friedman, J., Hastie, T., Tibshirani, R.: The Elements of Statistical Learning. Springer Series in Statistics, vol. 1. Springer, New York (2001). https://doi.org/10.1007/978-0-387-84858-7
9. Gupta, M.: Fog computing pushing intelligence to the edge. Int. J. Sci. Technol. Eng. **3**(8), 4246 (2017)
10. Lee, E.: The past, present and future of cyber-physical systems: a focus on models. Sensors **15**(3), 4837–4869 (2015)
11. Li, S., Maddah-Ali, M.A., Avestimehr, A.S.: Coding for distributed fog computing. IEEE Commun. Mag. **55**(4), 34–40 (2017)

12. Lindström, J., Larsson, H., Jonsson, M., Lejon, E.: Towards intelligent and sustainable production: combining and integrating online predictive maintenance and continuous quality control. Procedia CIRP **63**, 443–448 (2017)
13. Lu, C.W., Hsieh, C.M., Chang, C.H., Yang, C.T.: An improvement to data service in cloud computing with content sensitive transaction analysis and adaptation. In: 2013 IEEE 37th Annual Computer Software and Applications Conference Workshops, pp. 463–468. IEEE (2013)
14. Mahmud, R., Kotagiri, R., Buyya, R.: Fog computing: a taxonomy, survey and future directions. In: Di Martino, B., Li, K.-C., Yang, L.T., Esposito, A. (eds.) Internet of Everything. IT, pp. 103–130. Springer, Singapore (2018). https://doi. org/10.1007/978-981-10-5861-5_5
15. Mouradian, C., Naboulsi, D., Yangui, S., Glitho, R.H., Morrow, M.J., Polakos, P.A.: A comprehensive survey on fog computing: state-of-the-art and research challenges. IEEE Commun. Surv. Tutor. **20**(1), 416–464 (2018)
16. Russell, S.J., Norvig, P.: Artificial Intelligence: A Modern Approach. Pearson Education Limited, Malaysia (2016)
17. Schmidt, B., Wang, L., Galar, D.: Semantic framework for predictive maintenance in a cloud environment. Procedia CIRP **62**, 583–588 (2017)
18. Shin, J.H., Jun, H.B.: On condition based maintenance policy. J. Comput. Des. Eng. **2**(2), 119–127 (2015)
19. Spendla, L., Kebisek, M., Tanuska, P., Hrcka, L.: Concept of predictive maintenance of production systems in accordance with industry 4.0. In: 2017 IEEE 15th International Symposium on Applied Machine Intelligence and Informatics (SAMI), pp. 000405–000410. IEEE (2017)
20. Tsang, A.H., Yeung, W., Jardine, A.K., Leung, B.P.: Data management for cbm optimization. J. Qual. Maint. Eng. **12**(1), 37–51 (2006)
21. Van Horenbeek, A., Pintelon, L.: A dynamic predictive maintenance policy for complex multi-component systems. Reliab. Eng. Syst. Saf. **120**, 39–50 (2013)
22. Wang, S., Liu, Z., Sun, Q., Zou, H., Yang, F.: Towards an accurate evaluation of quality of cloud service in service-oriented cloud computing. J. Intell. Manuf. **25**(2), 283–291 (2014)
23. Zhong, R.Y., Xu, X., Klotz, E., Newman, S.T.: Intelligent manufacturing in the context of industry 4.0: a review. Engineering **3**(5), 616–630 (2017)

BIOC & FAiSE 2019

Joint Workshop on Blockchains for Inter-Organizational Collaboration and Flexible Advanced Information Systems BIOC&FAiSE 2019

Preface

In this year, the second edition of the BIOC workshop and the second edition of the FAiSE workshop are joint into one workshop.

The main goal of the BIOC workshop is to explore the means of automating inter-organizational collaborations with smart contracts and blockchain technology. The goal of this workshop is to promote, establish and speed up blockchain technology related research, and identify future research questions. Four high-quality papers have been accepted.

The paper "Blockchain Usage for Government-issued Electronic IDs: a Survey" by Michael Kuperberg, Sebastian Kemper, and Cemil Durak thoroughly analyses the state-of-the-art and opportunities of blockchain technology with respect to government-issued electronic identity documents (eIDs), including existing implementations and pilots.

The paper "Smart Contracts and Void Declarations of Intent" by Thomas Hoffmann aims at clarifying where the irreversibility of blockchain-based transactions makes no difference compared to traditional contract law solutions.

The paper "Blockchain-based Application Security Risks: A Systematic Literature Review" by Mubashar Iqbal and Raimundas Matulevičius provides an exhaustive overview of the security risks to blockchain-based applications and potential countermeasures as treated in the scientific literature.

The paper "Data Management: Relational vs. Blockchain Databases" by Phani Chitti, Jordan Murkin, and Ruzanna Chitchyan systematically compares relational databases and blockchain databases with respect to the definition and deployment of data structures, data entry and data retrieval.

The recent development in information systems, Internet of Things (IoT) technologies and the uptake of the digitalization wave in industries led to the availability of continuous flow of massive amounts of data and events. These data can be used by organizations to provide smarter and personalized services and products to people and organizations, as well as to improve the efficiency of their work and the value of their business models. The new challenges that information systems are facing in this context are related to both being able to exploit the data stemming from the IoT and the ability to react fast to the changes notified by the data and events. The main purpose of the Workshop on Flexible Advanced Information Systems (FAiSE) is to provide a forum for discussions of the synergies of the IoT, innovative technologies, and advanced information systems and thus encourage exchange between researchers and practitioners towards identifying concepts and approaches supporting the exploitation of advances in IoT towards enabling flexible information systems.

Each submission to the workshop was reviewed by four members of the program committee and two high-quality articles were selected by the PC members for publication in the workshop proceedings. One distinguishing characteristic of the workshop is its special focus on publications and presentations that report fundamental or applied research towards the reconciliation of the divide among several disparate areas in research and practice. More specifically, the accepted papers feature the following contributions.

The paper "A Generic Framework for Flexible and Data-Aware Business Process Engines" by Steven Mertens, Frederik Gailly, and Geert Poels presents a generic and high-level framework to support the execution of declarative process models with a data perspective. The framework is implemented in the DeciClareEngine-tool to demonstrate the feasibility of the proposed framework and it is applied in the context of a real-world healthcare process.

The paper "Building Information Systems by Means of Collaborative-filtering Recommendation Techniques" by Phuong T. Nguyen, Juri Di Rocco, and Davide Di Ruscio present an information system for managing and recommending books in the IoT context. The performance of their system is tested in a series of experiments.

The joint workshop took place on June 3rd, 2019 in conjunction with the 31st International Conference on Advanced Information Systems Engineering (CAiSE 2019). More information on the workshops and our joint workshop program is available at http://www.faise-workshop.com.

We would like to thank the workshop chairs of CAiSE 2019 for their support, the authors of all submitted articles for their courage to work in a new research direction and the members of the PC for the timely and valuable reviews of the submissions. We sincerely thank all Program Committee Members of the BIOC & FAiSE 2019 workshop for their time and support throughout the reviewing process.

Special thanks goes to our keynote speakers Marlon Dumas and Andreas Metzger. With his inspiring keynote "Collaborative Business Process Execution on Blockchain", Marlon shared with us his deep insights into the present and future of blockchain technology. Andreas who talked about "Data-driven AI for Self-adaptive Information Systems" gave an inspiring and insightful talk on the opportunities that Artificial Intelligence offers in building self-adaptive information systems.

April 2019

Alex Norta
Benjamin Leiding
Dirk Draheim
Dimka Karastoyanova
Luise Pufahl
Stefan Schönig

BIOC&FAiSE 2019 Organization

Organizing Committee

Alex Norta   Tallinn University of Technology, Estonia
Benjamin Leiding   University of Göttingen, Germany
Dirk Draheim   Tallinn University of Technology, Estonia
Dimka Karastoyanova   University of Groningen, The Netherlands
Luise Pufahl   HPI, University of Potsdam, Germany
Stefan Schönig   University of Bayreuth, Germany

BIOC 2019 Program Committee

Benjamin Leiding   University of Göttingen, Germany
Dirk Draheim   Tallinn University of Technology, Estonia
Alex Norta   Tallinn University of Technology, Estonia
Han van der Aa   VU University Amsterdam, The Netherlands
Mark Staples   CSIRO, Australia
Stefan Schulte   TU-Vienna, Austria
Claudio Di Ciccio   Vienna University of Economics and Business, Austria
Schahram Dustdar   TU-Vienna, Austria
Tijs Slaats   University of Copenhagen, Denmark
Xiwei Xu   UNSW Sydney, Australia
Cristina Cabanillas   Vienna University of Economics and Business, Austria
Jan Mendling   Vienna University of Economics and Business, Austria
Barbara Weber   Technical University of Denmark, Denmark
Søren Debois   IT-University of Copenhagen, Denmark
Matthias Weidlich   Humboldt-University zu Berlin, Germany
Guido Governatori   CSIRO, Australia
Mathias Weske   Hasso Plattner Institut, Germany
Manfred Reichert   University Ulm, Germany
Florian Daniel   Milano, Italy
Marcello La Rosa   University of Melbourne, Australia
Stefanie Rinderle-Ma   University of Vienna, Austria

FAiSE 2019 Program Committee

Vasilios Andrikopoulos   University of Groningen, The Netherlands
George Azzopardi   University of Groningen, The Netherlands

Hendrik Leopold	Kühne Logistics University, Germany
Francesca Zerbato	University of Verona, Italy
Maria-Eugenia Iacob	University of Twente, The Netherlands
Agnes Koschmider	Karlsruhe Institute of Technology, Germany
Patricia Lago	VU Amsterdam, The Netherlands
Andreas Metzger	PALUNO, University of Düsseldorf, Germany
Barbara Pernici	POLIMI, Italy
Pierluigi Plebani	POLIMI, Italy
Estefana Serral Asensio	Catholic University of Leuven, Belgium
Lars Ackermann	University of Bayreuth, Germany
Claudio Di Ciccio	Vienna Univ. of Economics and Business, Austria
Marco Aiello	University of Stuttgart, Germany
Michael Fellmann	University of Rostock, Germany
Nick van Beest	Data61, Australia
Artem Polyvyanyy	University of Melbourne, Australia
Fernanda Gonzalez-Lopez	Pontificia Universidad Catlica de Valparaso, Chile

Blockchain Usage for Government-Issued Electronic IDs: A Survey

Michael Kuperberg$^{(\boxtimes)}$ ⓘ, Sebastian Kemper ⓘ, and Cemil Durak ⓘ

Blockchain and Distributed Ledgers Group, DB Systel GmbH,
Frankfurt am Main, Germany
{michael.kuperberg,sebastian.kemper,cemil.durak}@deutschebahn.com

Abstract. Government IDs are traditionally plastic cards or paper-based passport booklets, sometimes with machine-readable contactless chips. Even though advanced implementations with cryptographic capabilities and online interfaces have been introduced, adoption and usage for online identification remain low. At the same time, there is a recognized need for trusted identities on the Internet, in Know-Your-Customer and Anti-Money-Laundering processes, and also in emerging blockchain-based, decentralized ecosystems. The contribution of this paper is a thorough analysis of the opportunities and state-of-the-art at the intersection of blockchain technology and government-issued electronical identity documents (eIDs), including existing implementations and pilots.

Keywords: Blockchain · eID · Government-issued electronic identities

1 Introduction

Blockchain-based applications and ecosystems require a state-of-the-art identity management. The same is true for the distributed ledger technologies (DLTs) in general, which are gaining momentum in governmental, financial and transportation areas. Most blockchain technologies have adopted the "keypair" approach to identity, where the ownership of the private key unlocks the ownership of assets and the ability to participate in the blockchain processes. Even the early, groundbreaking Bitcoin blockchain is underpinned by an advanced mechanism that relies on public-key cryptography despite being pseudonymous.

In non-permissioned blockchain implementations (such as Ethereum [12]), the keypair can be generated by anyone and joining the network is not restricted; smart contracts and the network protocols regulate the access management and the restrictions that apply to the identities (keypairs). In permissioned blockchain implementations, network participation is regulated, and keypairs are issued by authorities rather than by self-creation (cf. Certification Authorities in Hyperledger Fabric [19]). Whenever a blockchain-based application performs work that is required to be traced to a legal entity (person or legal body), the blockchain-based application must associate data (transaction in a block) with that entity. It is not imperative to maintain a blockchain keypair (identity) for

© Springer Nature Switzerland AG 2019
H. A. Proper and J. Stirna (Eds.): CAiSE 2019 Workshops, LNBIP 349, pp. 155–167, 2019.
https://doi.org/10.1007/978-3-030-20948-3_14

each legal entity: the blockchain activities can be performed by a blockchain participant that acts *on behalf of* the legal entity. However, such delegation runs counter to the original design principles of the blockchain approach, where each participant is self-sovereign in administering his/her assets, and can participate in the functioning of the network (e.g. though voting, block mining, etc.).

No matter which approach is taken, the blockchain participants in "serious" applications must be linked to verified identities. The process of establishing such as trusted identity is often compared to the Know Your Customer (KYC) process in banking, which is performed by live or online person-to-person interaction, using a physical identity document. The use of eID for KYC is very rare. Since KYC is a costly process, banks and businesses strive to reuse a verified identity across services. Identity reuse also helps to prevent stale data, but consumers are sceptical about data correlation, undesired creation of profiles, and data leaks.

Ideally, enrolling in a blockchain-based application using a trusted identity should be as easy as presenting an NFC-carrying government-issued electronic ID (eID) to a NFC-enabled smartphone. In such a case, the user would utilize multi-factor authentication (both for the phone and for the eID), and the eID would interact with the application servers. In the course of the interaction between the eID and the servers, a challenge-response pattern with cryptographic operations would be performed and a revocation list would be consulted. On successful completion, the blockchain-based application contains the association between the real-world identity and the blockchain-level keypair. In an even more advanced scenario, the eID would be used for transaction signing, and directly host the private key that is used in the scope of blockchain application.

In practice, however, such a flawless and uninterrupted workflow is hardly available, if ever. Cryptography-enabled eIDs are now widely available (cf. nPA in Germany), but the server-side integration remains challenging, and the pressure from consumers is not substantial enough. As a consequence, cryptocurrency exchanges resort to specialized service providers such as WebID [40]. In this paper, we do not consider specialized government-issued IDs which limited to narrow groups (e.g. members of parliament). Likewise, we do not consider sub-standard identification such as driver's licenses, credit cards with embossed photos, transportation smartcards or health insurance chipcards.

The contribution of this paper is to provide answers to the following question: **which eIDs, if any, are implemented using blockchain technologies or at least include blockchain-based functionality?** (such as a wallet for keypair management, participation in B2B/B2C (i.e. using smart contracts) etc.)

The remainder of this paper is structured as follows: in Sect. 2, we provide the foundations, describe state-of-the-art and set the scope for our survey. In Sect. 3, an extensive analysis of related work is provided. In Sect. 4, we define the evaluation criteria and use them to survey solutions and concepts. Section 5 summarizes the findings of our survey, concludes and provides the directions for future work.

2 Foundations

2.1 Blockchains and Distributed Ledger Technology

Blockchain is a subtype of Distributed Ledger Technology (DLT) and therefore shares similar features and characteristics with other types of DLTs. DLTs are, in general, replicated and cryptographically secured databases. In addition to the distribution of data, blockchains usually follow the *decentralization* approach: there is no single party that owns the database, and the ledger is maintained by a network of parties. Decentralized ledgers and blockchains use different fault-tolerant consensus mechanisms to ensure that a distributed network in a trustless environment can agree on a single truth about data states, transactions and a consistent state of the network, without having to rely on for central authorities or third-party intermediaries.

There are many blockchain and distributed ledger technology (DLT) products and their capabilities and maturity differ significantly. However, they all address, to differing degrees, the following key properties: tamper-proofness (immutability), programmability (through smart contracts), auditability and built-in trust.

In the context of identity management, blockchains and DLTs offer new paradigms and capabilities, such as self-sovereign identity [29], by making an identity-owning individual the final arbiter of who can access and use the personal data. By employing cryptographic algorithms and immutability, network participants can trust the records and accept them as impartial. But since identity information must be validated to be useful, a person's identity has to be verified, e.g. by having a trusted participant (or a significant number of participants) vouch for the validity of the information in a user's profile.

2.2 Identification and IDs

The terms *identity* and *ID/identifier* are used to distinguish individual entities within a group of comparable, same-typed entities. For example, a DNA can be used as an ID to distinguish two human identities. In general, the identity of a given person, organization, device etc. is the *entire* set of attribute values that enable to distinguish that entity from others in the group. An identifier is a sufficient (sub-)set of one or several attributes which forms a "primary key"; the identifier does not have to include *all* identity-forming attributes.

An identifier on its own is sufficient to denote the uniqueness of the identity in its group; it might be possible to create different identifier schemas for the same group. A global, cross-group schema for identity does not exist: each group has its own identifiers and attributes. The term *ID* is an abbreviation for "identity document"; it is often used for a physical manifestation of an identifier (e.g. a passport booklet). The term *identification* describes the process of delivering a proof, based on the given identity and using an identifier or an ID.

The identifier information can be permanently stored in a physical way as an item, which can be a passport, or a smartcard chip (i.e. computer hardware). Thus, both physical and virtual (i.e. non-material) representation of an identifier are possible. The information items that represent the identifier can be represented as digital data (such as binary encoding of a DNA) or, substantially less often, as analog data (e.g. voice recording). The term "electronic identity" is often used alongside "digital identity", since digital information is mostly processed by electronic devices such as computers. The concept of electronic and digital identities enables them for use in online services, e.g. on the Internet.

For online services, two basic types of identification are prevalent. For the first, a person *possesses* a physical item (e.g. a biometric pass, an iris scan) and *presenting* that item constitutes the identification step. For the second, a person *knows* an immaterial, non-physical secret (e.g. a password) that is *associated* with an identity; identification is performed by presenting the secret or by providing an (indirect) proof of the ownership to the secret (e.g. a digital signature computed from a secret private asymmetric key).

The difference between the two types is that the first type usually can be (temporarily) transferred as long as it maintains a physical uniqueness (unless, of course, it is too easy to duplicate or to falsify). The second type must be safeguarded because knowledge is easily replicated, while possession is not: if another person obtains the secret, he/she can impersonate as the actual identity owner. The two types are often combined into multi-factor authentication (MFA). Of course, some non-secret identification elements (such as fingerprints or dynamic 3D face models) are non-portable, or can be easily falsified (e.g. fingerprints).

In some cases, online identification is performed though third parties ("identity providers") or through secondary documents such as driving licenses, banking cards, witnesses, or bank transfers. Third parties enable identification using website technology (e.g. through OIDC, OAuth and SAML) or through B2B offerings such as PostIdent and VideoID. Identification through bank transfers can work as follows: if the bank is trusted to have performed KYC and if the account ownership is not compromised or shared, a challenge-based approach is possible: the identity requestor provides a challenge (e.g. requests a minimum-amount transfer with a case-specific purpose text) and the identity owner proves his/her identity by performing the challenge-confirming transfer.

However, the most trusted identification comes from governments, which are traditional sources of identification/lifecycle documents for humans (and animals): they issue physical identification items such as passports, ID cards, birth certificates etc. Physical passports have the disadvantage of full disclosure of information (e.g. the past entry stamps or visas are available for every inspector) and high value for thiefs, and are also easily lost or damaged. Passports are often owned by the issuing government and not by the individual person; forced confiscation of physical passports and IDs restricts not only a person's ability to travel, but also removes essential entitlements and basic citizenship capabilities - even if the citizenship itself is not removed.

Digital identification documents issued by governments are often eIDs that are either a "smart" document/chipcard with some cryptographic/electronic equipment (as in Estonia [7], Germany [13] and certain other countries), or as a centralized IT system without a physical eID (as it is the case in the

Aadhaar [1] system in India). Aadhaar employ biometric "keys" to match them to the system-stored record; a person may obtain a "printout" as a non-binding proof of identity - but the printout on its own cannot be used for identification.

Thus, the use cases of government-issued eIDs vary from country to country and serve to identify citizens in order to access services provided by the specific government. These services may include the signing documents with digital signatures, conducting payments (such as in Estonia [38]) and may even entitle the user to vote. eIDAS (electronic IDentification, Authentication and trust Services) [34] is a binding EU regulation that establish a uniform framework for cross-border uses of electronic identification.

Virtual government eIDs, also referred as "virtual residency" or "e-residency", is an approach first introduced in Estonia. Estonian e-residency includes a digital ID, but requires a personal show-up at an Estonian embassy as part of the application and payment of an administration fee. If granted, e-residency includes a PKCS11-enabled smart card with online identification, eIDAS-compliant digital signature incl. timestamping (though not a general-purpose signing certificate, and only for BDOC/DDOC container documents), electronic voting (only for full citizens) and some other services. However, it does not entitle to "normal" citizenship and does not grant conventional residency rights.

A newer aspect of eIDs is the concept of self-sovereign identities (SSI). The goal of this approach is to liberate the data from the service provider siloes and to give the end users the ultimate control over their data contents and over the sharing of their data. This "liberation" is fueled not by lawmaking or by regulation, but rather by the technical means and advances. The "Self-Sovereign Identity Working Group" is one of the interest groups driving this topic. With their project "X-Road" [20], Estonia tries to provide a system where citizens can decide which information is being shared between which institutions.

3   Related Work

In [47], Grech et al. describe how the blockchain technology can be of great use in national eID systems, especially in the context of self-sovereign identities. The authors highlight the blockchain potential for the Estonian national digital identity management system, although the focus is primarily on the uses and application of blockchain technologies in education sector. However, further eID implementations are not considered or evaluated.

In [3], Pisa et al. provide an analysis of the potential of the blockchain technologies in the framework of global economic development. Along with other topics, they also examine the blockchain technologies' suitability and role in providing and creation of secure digital ID systems by governments. While the authors describe a pilot project of a blockchain-based self-sovereign digital ID system in Canada, no other countries or solutions have been surveyed and no evaluation criteria have been defined.

[4] is an academic paper prepared for the European Union Blockchain Observatory and Forum by Third et al. It reports the use of blockchain and distributed

ledger technology for government services, with a special focus on digital identities. Among others, it introduces several use cases in national identity managements systems, specifying their maturity, the tech companies involved and so on. In [43], Lyons reports on a 2018 workshop titled "Government Services and Digital Identity". The report describes existing use cases of blockchain technologies in the public administration domain from different countries and identifies the projects of Zug residents' IDs [45] (Switzerland) as well as Estonian e-identity as priority use cases for Europe in the eID field.

In [49], Jun suggests the inevitability of replacement of bureaucracy with blockchain systems and claims the future of governments to be a blockchain government, for which he introduces four main principles. In his work, Jun lists an extensive amount of government-led blockchain projects and mentions Estonian e-identity and Zug residents' IDs. However, he does not provide detailed information on these projects, an evaluation, or any details.

4 Survey

In this section, we only consider eIDs that have a DLT-related functionality or project (there are at least 30 countries with an eID setup). eIDs have already been studied by other authors [46], and analyses of DLT/blockchains are widely available (e.g. [51]). The general topic of blockchain-supported identity management has been studied as well [50], but mostly leaves out the specifics of government-issued eIDs. In contrast to other work, our survey focuses its evaluation on the *intersection* between government-issued eIDs and blockchain/DLTs; our analysis of related work (see Sect. 3) for this intersection has shown that there is no systematic evaluation of it.

4.1 Evaluation Criteria and Scope Definition

Our contribution starts with establishing the following evaluation criteria that we apply to blockchain-empowered eID solutions:

- eID uses a DLT as storage of identity data (e.g. [encrypted] public and/or private keys, certificates, non-revokable identity attributes such as age, sex, date of birth)
- eID uses a DLT as storage of authorization data (e.g. visas, driver's licenses, data releases, attribute changes, tickets or other entitlements etc.)
- eID built-in capabilities are used for keypair generation, keypair storage, transaction signing or similar aspects of DLT cryptography
- intersection of DLT and eID, but none of the above

For each country, we indicate the technology involved (if it is known); further information is available from the cited sources. There are country-overarching initiatives (e.g. for stateless ethnic groups, such as the blockchain-based solution in [26]), we consider them in the cases where the resulting eID is nationally recognized *in lieu of* a traditional government-issued eID.

We do not consider general blockchain-backed e-government activities such as e-voting, taxing, healthcare, land administration etc. unless these activities create an eID which is usable independently. Likewise, we do not consider blockchain-based IDs which open up a "gated" ecosystem without government actors (as for example in the planned cooperation [39] of Verified.me and IBM in Canada, where a solution based on Hyperledger Fabric has been announced).

We looked at government-issued eIDs of Australia, Canada, China, Germany, Georgia, Ghana, India, Japan, Luxembourg, Netherlands, Russia, Singapore, South Korea, Sweden, Taiwan and USA, but found no relevant intersection with DLTs or Blockchains. Only the following five countries have significant projects.

4.2   Dubai, United Arab Emirates (UAE)

In October 2017, a MoU [33] was announced to develop a unified digital identity for the entire UAE within the Smart Dubai [32] initiative, based on blockchain technology. The projects aims at the integration of the UAE's SmartPass [36] verified identity service (which is also employed in airport security) with the eID-enabled Dubai ID [6] online service to form a nationwide single system, allowing users to access federal and local government services by logging in once.

The technical partner for the unified digital identity project is ObjectTech [25], a UK startup; the details of ObjectTech's technology stack have not been published yet. ObjectTech's website claims that their solution is *"fully compliant with privacy and security regulations, such as PSD2 & GDPR; it exceeds both the letter and intentions of these initiatives"* and that it is quantum resistant. The pilot program is planned to be ready by 2020 (cf. [17,30]).

UAE's federal authorities [37] issue an eID card to residents (incl. non-citizens) and also offer digital signature and identification services to companies; an SDK for developers is provided [28]. Additionally, the "UAE PASS" app [35] is provided, which turns a mobile device into a secure form of identification for UAE online services; it is not connected to the eID chipcard (unlike the Dubai ID). However, neither SmartPass nor Dubai/UAE eIDs and digital passports are *backed* by DLT technology or *integrated with* a DLT as of January 2019. In October 2018, the company behind UAE Pass has announced to follow the "strategic direction for the adoption of blockchain technologies" [2].

4.3   Estonia

Estonia has both an eID for residents/citizens [7] and a "e-residency" program [8]. The eID is issued as a PKCS11 smart "ID-Card" with the ability to sign and encrypt documents and emails, perform online login, make payments [38], use telemedicine etc. The keypair stored on the smartcard is compatible to the X.509 standard; newer cards add a contactless interface (NFC).

In addition to the "ID-Card", a separate "digi-ID" card [41] is available for those Estonian citizens who already possess a valid "ID-Card" in any case. The main differences to the "ID-Card" is that the "digi-ID" lacks any printed or embossed information, and thus can only be used in electronic environments, while the "ID-Card" also serves as a *visual* identity document.

The third eID in Estonia is the "Mobiil-ID" [42], which is small SIM-sized card for mobile phones. "Mobiil-ID" serves as a person's identification and as a digital signing solution, very similar to the two other cards. Like the previously mentioned cards it can be used to access specific e-services such as e-taxing and digitally sign documents, but with the added value of not requiring an external card reader during the process. To utilize the "Mobiil-ID", the user uses two PIN codes: the first code is needed for identification to the card and the second code is needed to unlock the signature functionality. "Smart-ID" [31] is the corresponding mobile app in order to access the "Mobiil-ID" functionalities.

According to the information on the e-Estonia project website [5], the underlying infrastructure for all these eID functionalities includes Guardtime's KSI [21] Blockchain technology for security and safety purposes. Guardtime itself states that they have succeeded in creating a "reliable service for the government that would continue to function even under cyber-attack". Even though the implementation [15] of KSI is accessible as to January 2019, it is not transparent to which specific extent the blockchain technology is used within the Estonian eID solutions described above. Guardtime has been working together with the Estonian Government on a digital signature system since 2007, and KSI is used for "independent verification of all government processes".

Beyond the above building blocks, e-Estonia also utilizes "X-Road" [20], a solution which is used to connect various public and private e-Service databases. Every data exchange over X-Road is signed, encrypted, authenticated and logged. To avoid any misunderstandings, e-Estonia officially stated that X-Road itself is not based on the blockchain-technology [44].

4.4 Finland

The Finnish eID was introduced in 1999 and was among the very first operational national eID scheme in the world; it is non-obligatory and the fees are relatively high. Currently, the Finnish eID system sees relatively low use; it does not employ or support blockchain technologies.

In 2015, independently from the general countrywide eID scheme, the Finnish Immigration Services [24] and the Helsinki-based startup company MONI [23] started a project in which the partners associate a digital identity with the prepaid MasterCard debit cards which are provided to asylum seekers and refugees who are lacking official/paper identification documents. According to [16], the debit cards are linked to corresponding unique digital identities that are created for refugees on blockchain; this turns the debit cards into a kind of government-issued eIDs. Deployed on an Ethereum blockchain platform, the solution potentially enables thousands of refugees to participate in everyday tasks [14,18,48] until they receive normal ID documents. However, the software in the trial also appears to record the financial transactions made with the card *on the blockchain*. As of January 2019, it is planned to terminate the trial until May 2019.

4.5   Luxembourg

The national eID in Luxembourg is a chipcard that also supports digital signatures, using the software provided by LuxTrust [22]. In a project called EDDITS [9], LuxTrust supports the InTech blockchain company to link Ethereum identities to conventional, CA-issued X.509 certificates - this corresponds to the third criterium in Sect. 4.1. The resulting pilot implementation can be regarded as a blockchain-supported eID on its own (even though the recognition and adoption of EDDITS are minimal); the resulting eID still fulfills the second criterium from Sect. 4.1 as authorization data is stored on a blockchain.

4.6   Switzerland

As of January 2019, the development of government-issued eID in Switzerland is still ongoing [11], but not even a pilot is available yet.

The Ethereum-based, uPort-powered resident's ID in the Swiss city of Zug has been among the pioneers of blockchain-based identity. However, as reported in [45], the validation of the app-created ID has to take place in the city office, through a human-to-human interaction; there is no national, government-issued eID to be integrated with yet. The Zug ID is only recognized in the city itself.

Another project is the "Schaffhauser eID+" blockchain-secured [27] electronic identity solution. The system, which has been implemented jointly by Swiss e-government specialist Procivis [10] and the IT services of the canton and town of Schaffhausen (KSD), is in production use. In fact, we consider it to be an interesting case of an intersection between a government-issued eID and the DLT technology, even though it does not use a "traditional" card-shaped eID. As for the classification in Sect. 4.1, the second scenario (DLT stores authorization data) is explicitly supported; support of the other two scenarios (DLT stores identity data; eID capabilities are used for DLT cryptography) is not declared.

5   Conclusions

Table 1 summarizes our findings. The most developed use case of government-issued eIDs and blockchain technology can be found in Estonia (EE), with the e-Identity ID card which is deployed on the KSI Blockchain, and trials/pilots are ongoing or in development in Switzerland (CH), Luxembourg (LU), Finland (FI) and United Arab Emirates (UAE). For the Estonian eID, the details of what data exactly is stored on the blockchain (and how) have not been published yet.

The EDDITS project (Luxembourg) [9] is a pilot that utilizes the eID functionality to create trusted on-blockchain identities. For the Ethereum-based Zug ID pilot, an electronic identity is created on-chain, but it does not interact with a government-issued eID document/certificate. Transaction signing, or even key storage on the eID cards, remain a vision for the future. None of the studied government-issued eID solutions declares that it stores primary identity data (such as keys, certificates or attributes) on a DLT or blockchain, even in encrypted form.

Table 1. Comparison table of eID-using blockchain solutions (see Sect. 4.1 for a definition of "identity data" and "authorization data")

Authority that issues eID	United Arab Emirates Governm.	Estonian Governm.	Finnish Immigration Services	Governm. of Luxembourg via LuxTrust	Switzerland City of Zug	Switzerland Canton of Schaffhausen
Rollout status	Pilot starting 2020	In use	In use till 30.04.2019	Pilot phase	Pilot phase	In use
Level	National	National	National	National	Municipal	Canton
Solution used for	Digital passport; "ID locker"	Data integrity, timestamp	Unique Digital Identities	Trusted blockchain identities	Self-sovereign identities	Self-sovereign identities
DLT stores identity data	No	No	No	No	No	No
DLT stores authorizations for eID	Planned	No (but the DLT acts as an access log)	No (but the DLT stores payment transaction history)	No	No	Yes
eID capabilities for DLT cryptogr.	No	No	No	Yes	Yes	Unspecified
GDPR	Compliant	Compliant	Unspecified	Unspecified	Compliant	Unspecified
eID Type	Mobile app	Multiple	Multiple	X.509 cert.	Mobile app	Mobile app
Implem. Partner	ObjectTech	Guardtime	MONI	Intech	uPort and ti&m	Procivis
Blockch. Type	Unspecified (Q1/19)	Private	Unspecified	Public testnet: Kovan	Public	Unspecified
Blockch. Technol.	Unspecified	KSI Blockchain	Ethereum Blockchain	Ethereum; ERC-725 ERC-735	Ethereum + uPort	Unspecified

For our future work, we plan to address the following question: which eIDs are *suitable* for use in blockchain-/DLT-based applications? Additionally, we plan to study how blockchain transactions can be (co-)signed by eIDs.

Acknowledgements. Moritz Stumpf provided additional insights to the Estonian eID landscape.

References

1. Aadhaar Online Services. https://uidai.gov.in
2. ADSSSA showcases blockchain implementation in bid to accelerate 'One Government' services model. https://www.darkmatter.ae/press-release/adsssa-showcases-blockchain-implementation-in-bid-to-accelerate-one-government-services-model/
3. Blockchain and economic development: hype vs. reality. https://www.cgdev.org/sites/default/files/blockchain-and-economic-development-hype-vs-reality_0.pdf
4. Blockchain for government and public services. https://www.eublockchainforum.eu/sites/default/files/reports/eu_observatory-_blockchain_in_government_services_v1_2018-12-07.pdf
5. Blockchain for Smart-ID. https://e-estonia.com/egoverment-blockchain-guardtime/
6. Dubai ID. https://www.dm.gov.ae/en/Pages/Login.aspx
7. e-Identity of Estonia. https://e-estonia.com/solutions/e-identity/id-card/
8. E-residency 2.0 White Paper. https://s3.eu-central-1.amazonaws.com/ereswhitepaper/e-Residency+2.0+white+paper+English.pdf
9. EDDITS. https://eddits.io/
10. eID+. https://procivis.ch/eid
11. Etablierung einer national und international gültigen elektronischen Identität (E-ID). https://www.egovernment.ch/de/umsetzung/schwerpunktplan/elektronische-identitat/
12. Ethereum. https://www.ethereum.org
13. The German National Identity Card (nPA). https://www.personalausweisportal.de/EN/Home/
14. Government services and digital identity. https://www.eublockchainforum.eu/sites/-default/-files/research-paper/20180801_government_services_and_digital_identity.pdf
15. Guardtime KSI on Github. https://github.com/guardtime/ksi-tool#start-of-content
16. How Blockchain is Kickstarting the Financial Lives of Refugees. https://www.technologyreview.com/s/608764/how-blockchain-is-kickstarting-the-financial-lives-of-refugees/
17. How blockchain is used by governments as a form of national identity. https://medium.com/@bryzek/how-blockchain-is-used-by-governments-as-a-form-of-national-identity-e24a4eefb7d8
18. How Finland is Using the Blockchain to Revolutionise Financial Services for Refugees. https://reliefweb.int/report/finland/how-finland-using-blockchain-revolutionise-financial-services-refugees
19. Hyperledger Fabric. https://www.hyperledger.org/projects/fabric
20. Interoperability Services. https://e-estonia.com/solutions/interoperability-services/x-road/
21. KSI Technology Stack. https://guardtime.com/technology
22. Luxembourg based company InTech launches innovative blockchain-based on-line service. https://www.luxtrust.com/luxembourg-based-company-intech-launches-innovative-blockchain-based-on-line-service-eddits-for-associating-strong-digital-identities-with-ethereum-addresses-in-partnership-with-lux/
23. Moni. https://www.moni.fi

24. Moni-based Reception allowance for Refugees. https://migri.fi/en/reception-allowance
25. ObjectTech. https://www.objecttechgroup.com/
26. Procivis and the Rohingya Project partner to provide electronic identity to the Rohingya diaspora. https://procivis.ch/2018/04/04/procivis-and-the-rohingya-project-partner-to-provide-electronic-identity-to-people-without-legal-documentation/
27. Procivis eID+. https://www.cnlab.ch/fileadmin/documents/Publikationen/2018/Procivis_eID__Herbsttagung_2018-09.pdf
28. SDK for UAE eID. http://sdk.emiratesid.ae
29. Self-Sovereign Identity Working Group. https://blockchainhub.net/self-sovereign-identity/
30. Smart Dubai to launch a unified digital identity card. https://embeddedsecurity-news.com/2017/10/uae-tra-smart-dubai-to-launch-a-unified-digital-identity-card/
31. Smart-ID App. https://e-estonia.com/solutions/e-identity/smart-id/
32. SmartDubai. https://smartdubai.ae
33. Telecommunications Regulatory Authority and Dubai Smart Government Sign MoU to launch unified digital identity. https://www.ica.gov.ae/en/media-centre/news-and-reports/news.aspx
34. Trust Services And Electronic Identification (eID). https://ec.europa.eu/digital-single-market/en/trust-services-and-eid
35. UAE PASS Mobile App. https://smartdubai.ae/apps-services/details/uae-pass
36. UAE SmartPass. https://smartpass.government.ae/
37. United Arab Emirates eID. https://www.ica.gov.ae/en/home.aspx
38. Using ID-cards for Payments. https://eid.eesti.ee/index.php/Using_ID-card_for_payments
39. Verified.me. https://verified.me/
40. WebID Identity Company. https://www.webid-solutions.de/en/
41. What is Digi-ID. https://www.id.ee/index.php?id=34410
42. What is Mobiil-ID. https://www.id.ee/index.php?id=36892
43. Workshop report government services and digital identity. https://www.eublockchainforum.eu/sites/default/files/reports/workshop_3_report_--_government_services2fdigital_id.pdf
44. X-Road not to be confused with blockchain. https://e-estonia.com/why-x-road-is-not-blockchain/
45. Zug ID: Exploring the First Publicly Verified Blockchain Identity. https://medium.com/uport/zug-id-exploring-the-first-publicly-verified-blockchain-identity-38bd0ee3702
46. Carretero, J., Izquierdo-Moreno, G., Vasile-Cabezas, M., Garcia-Blas, J.: Federated identity architecture of the European eID system. IEEE Access **6**, 75302–75326 (2018). https://doi.org/10.1109/ACCESS.2018.2882870
47. Grech, A., Camilleri, A.F.: Blockchain in education, vol. 33, p. 132. Publications Office of the European Union, Luxembourg, January 2017. https://doi.org/10.2760/60649
48. Guggenmos, F., Lockl, J., Rieger, A., Fridgen, G.: Challenges and Opportunities of Blockchain-Based Platformization of Digital Identities in the Public Sector (Research in Progress), June 2018
49. Jun, M.: Blockchain government - a next form of infrastructure for the twenty-first century. J. Open Innov.: Technol. Market Complex. **4**, 7 (2018). https://doi.org/10.1186/s40852-018-0086-3

50. Lim, S.Y., et al.: Blockchain technology the identity management and authentication service disruptor: a survey. Int. J. Adv. Sci. Eng. Inf. Technol. **8**, 1735 (2018). https://doi.org/10.18517/ijaseit.8.4-2.6838
51. Zheng, Z., Xie, S., Dai, H.N., Chen, X., Wang, H.: Blockchain challenges and opportunities: a survey. Int. J. Web Grid Serv. **14**(4), 352–375 (2018)

Smart Contracts and Void Declarations of Intent

Thomas Hoffmann[(✉)]

Tallinn Law School, Tallinn University of Technology,
Ehitajate tee 5, 19086 Tallinn, Estonia
thomas.hoffmann@ttu.ee

Abstract. Among the characteristics of blockchain-based Smart Contracts, the aspect of irreversibility of blockchain transactions is one of the most controversially commented features from a legal perspective – taking into account that "traditional" contracts can be void or voidable for various reasons. But while there are indeed cases where existing private law concepts struggle to provide sound and predictable solutions to Smart Contract-induced problems, many of these controversies derive either from the use of disambiguous terminology in interdisciplinary communication, the diversity of the instrument of voidness and avoidance from a comparative perspective (and thus not the Smart Contract as such) or a general "misconception" of the irreversability of traditional forms of performance. This contribution intends to clarify where the irreversability of blockchain-based transactions does – against all odds – not make a difference compared to traditional contract law solutions, but also determines where legal conflicts indeed may arise from Smart Contracts and mistake.

Keywords: Smart contracts · Blockchain · Declarations of intent · Avoidance

1 Apparent Legal Challenges to Smart Contracts

From a legal perspective, a "Smart Contract" – as defined by Szabo as "a set of promises, specified in digital form, including protocols within which the parties perform on these promises" [13] – is not necessarily a contract. In law, in most legal systems a contract consists of two (usually formless) corresponding declarations of intend – offer and acceptance – which provide sufficient information on the *essentialia negotii*, i.e. parties to the contract, object of the agreement, modes of performance etc. The Smart Contract, on the other hand, is simply a software-based log of actions which may have legal significance (in that case, it protocols a declaration of intent) and which – if respectively programed – effectuates an additional transaction.

The term Smart Contract has gone somewhat rogue, as even oracles are labelled Smart Contracts, although their purpose is restriced to collecting and distributing publically accessible digital data and does not include/refer to any declaration of intent (and not even another party). But also beyond these obvious cases, the typical feature of a Smart Contract – its self-execution – does not constitute a contract itself, but rather the performance of an (eventually previously concluded, otherwise incorrectly alleged) contract. Legally, Smart Contracts do in that respect not differ from mechanical

© Springer Nature Switzerland AG 2019
H. A. Proper and J. Stirna (Eds.): CAiSE 2019 Workshops, LNBIP 349, pp. 168–175, 2019.
https://doi.org/10.1007/978-3-030-20948-3_15

vending machines, where an inserted coin triggers the ejection of e.g. a bubble gum – or of sacred water, as in the case of the first document mechanical vending machine developed by Hero of Alexandria and documented in the journal "Pneumatika" in 62 AD [9].

1.1 Declarations of Intent Reflected in Smart Contracts

Whether a Smart Contracts contains a log of an existing contract depends thus of the question whether an offer and a respective acceptance have been issued and received by the parties. This question can be controversial if the Smart Contract has been set up on a blockchain consensus architecture, as it is today usually the case.

In the blockchain, the issuance of such declarations of intent take place by expressing the intent via completing the respective actions on the interface; while the private key enables the party to access the system, the public key serves to determine the declarant party form the receiver's perspective. Legally binding this declaration will, however, only be from that point of time when the action has been "enchained" by the hash of a subsequent block, as eventual forks arising during calculation of the hash on separate servers until that point of time prevent a clear determination of the declaration. In other words, "enchaining" the transaction into the blockchain makes it also legally irrevocable and thus binding [2].

The Common law postal rule, however, may face a certain revival after its significance had steadily deceased in digitally assisted transactions so far. The postal rule – which traditionally regarded the acceptance as binding already when posted by the party (instead of when received by the offeror) – did so far not apply on declarations where submission and receipt match chronologically, as among persons present or on the phone – or declarations send via e-mail or telex. Declarations entering the blockchain via PKI would generally be seen as comparable to e-mails, but as receipt of the declaration could be interpreted either as effectuated once it has been "received and authenticated through consensus of network users, or once it is coded and added to the blockchain" [1], the previous congruence of submission and receipt is split up by the nature of the blockchain mechanism, and the mailbox rule could be seen as a criteria providing far more legal certainty, as the determination of the point of time of submission of the declaration would be far less controversial.

1.2 Performance of Non-existing Contracts

The content of contracts is determined by the interpretation of the respective actions taken by the parties, taking the perspective of an objective oberserver. If these actions qualify to be interpreted as declarations of intent to mutually enter into a binding contract, a contract exists; if any of the criteria presented above are lacking, there legally is no contract, and the protocol does not represent the correct legal status between the parties. If – based on that protocol – the alleged contract has nevertheless been performed (another transaction has been triggered, e.g. money has been transferred, a door lock been opened etc.), this transaction is at least in those legal system which are governed by the abstraction principle [3] (e.g. Germany or Estonia) legally effective in spite of the lack of an underlying contractual obligation, and the party to whose benefit the transaction has taken place is unjustly enriched and has to return all which has been received – but this has been so since Roman times already. This return is legal not an "annihilation" of the performance, but a new performance which restitutes to previous status. Returning to the bubble gum example, the dispenser is also in this respect similar to the blockchain, as the mechanism technically prevents re-inserting the gum, even if it has been triggered by unlawful means as e.g. punching the machine. The party claiming return of all undue enrichment – here the owner of the dispensing machine and previous owner of the dispensed bubble gum– would be entitled to retransfer of the property in the bubble gum instead of simply restituting possession in it.

1.3   The Impact of Void Declarations of Intent

In Smart Contracts in its legal sense – i.e. in those Smart Contracts designed for fhe purpose of protocollingand executing synallagmatic contracts – this risk of a lack of the essentialia negotii is technically generally prevented, i.e. the transaction is only exe-cuted if it can be assumed that legally a contract to be performed has been concluded (e.g. parties have been identified by providing their personal keys etc.). Practically more important are those cases where formally complete and effective declarations of intent have been issued by the parties, but these are either initially void by law or by declaration by a party (avoidance).

Initially Void Declarations. It has been often argued [10] that there is a tension between today's private law concepts and the blockchain-generated Smart Contracts, as law provides for various situations where a transaction – or an individual declaration of intent – is void ex tunc, i.e. from the beginning. In German law, for instance, legal transactions which "violate a statutory prohibition" (sec. 134 BGB, BGB being the German Civil Code) or which "is contrary to public policy" (sec. 138 BGB) are initially void. While certain statutory prohibitions could theoretically be implemented as algorithms into the blockchain environment (or at least in form of standard business terms imposed on all users of an individual blockchain facility, e.g. that the birth date guaranteeing age of consent have to be disclosed in order to receive a private key initially), many other legal restrictions and certainly all cases of sec. 138 BGB require a full-scale legal evaluation, and the voidness of violating transactions will become apparent only when the transactions have been confirmed in the blockchain.

The blockchain in this situation does not reflect the correct legal status of the transaction any more. This has been, however, always be standard situation with other documents designed to provide evidence (and not constituting it, as land registers for instance) for the distribution of rights. A vehicle title document, for instance, which has been issued upon application to a car thief (who pretended to be the real owner at the authorities) will continue to show him as car owner to anybody to whom he presents this document as long as nobody takes action. The real owner may (and will), of course, let the thief's document be declared void – but the paper will still be physically there.

The blockchain is not different to that. A void transaction may still be in the blockchain record, but the only legal information that the chain contains is that at a certain point of time a person equipped with a private key has taken actions which are mirrored in form of a respective blog of these actions in the blockchain. This blog may represent a strong assumption that the underlying transaction complies with the law and is thus effective (just as the car title document), but nothing else.

In this respect, the conflict between traditional law and blockchain smart-contracts does in terms of void transactions/declarations of indeed not impose major challenges.

Avoidance. Transactions may not only be void by law, but also upon the explicit declaration of a party to the transaction. As consent of both parties is the constitutive element of an agreement, a party who realizes that it actually did not agree on the essence of the contract for reasons as e.g. mistake or deceit/duress by the other party, may declare this defect of its declaration in form of avoidance, making the party's declaration initially void and thus collaps the entire transaction basing in the alleged declaration. The avoidance does thus not address the transaction itself, but targets only the proper declaration of intent.

In contrast to the rather uniform rules on formation of contracts, the national law's conditions imposed on avoidance differ considerably worldwide. In common law, for instance, "mistakes were, in principle, considered relevant only when they were attributable to the other party (misrepresentation, undue influence). Apart from that, appropriate solutions could in most cases be found by means of interpretation (implied terms)" [4]. Zimmermann concludes that "the will-theoretical model of most continental European countries, according to which a contract should be based upon the real intentions of the contracting parties, stands in contrast to the significantly more contract-friendly conceptions of the common law, Austrian law and the Scandinavian legal systems" [4].

While the ways to archive an avoidance may considerably differ, the impact – the transaction being void ab initio – is a common consequence internationally which legally does not lead to different results than in the case of initially void contracts. For publicity reasons it would be advisable that the declaration of avoidance would be disclosed in the same way as the avoided declaration had been submitted, i.e. via the blockchain within a separate block [2]. This will obviously not make the previous declaration void, but that way the legal status of the parties would then again be correctly reflected in the blockchain – just as (taking up the traditional-law example presented above) the re-issuance of a correct car title document to the real owner by the respective authorities does not make the incorrect thief's document decompose automatically into ashes, but simply "updates" (here in form of correction) the documentation on a certain legal status.

In that respect, there is from a legal perspective also no need for reverse transactions or other measures contradicting the nature and advantages of the blockchain.

2   Existing Legal Challenges for Smart Contracts

While a simple Smart Contract is thus legally about as complex as a bubble gum dispenser, there are indeed also aspects where our existing legal concepts reach short when it comes to providing tools and regulations for smart-contract driven transactions which go beyond contractual performance.

Taking into account the range of transactions Smart Contracts are able to undertake – see e.g. Ethereum –, the combination of Smart Contracts with software agents would fully uncover the potential of Smart Contracts. Technically, a Smart Contract is not restricted to transactions performing contractual duties, but the triggered action can also consist of the composition and submission of a message which an objective observer would interpret as a declaration of intent – a declaration which itself can be embedded into a Smart Contract, if programed respectively ("follow-on" contracts).

Just as with Smart Contracts, there is much controversy caused by not sufficiently specified (or inappropriately applied) terminology when it comes to declarations of intend which have been generated (and not only documented) by software.

From a contract law perspective, the essential question is to which degree both the *essentialia negotii* of the contract as well as the individual other contract partner are determined by the software rather than by the human individual making use of the software. The scope reaches from simple calculations on base of human-set parameters over software agents to fully software-generated autonomous declarations [14] of intent based on weak and – in a future not too distant – strong Artificial Intelligence.

2.1   Interpreting Computer Declarations

The legally most challenging aspect of software agents and AI-generated declarations is the question of attribution of these declarations of intent to the respective human behind the system. But already on the simplest level – where the attribution is still obvious – the mere perspective of interpretation of such a declaration of intent causes considerable problems, as following recent case decided by the German Federal Court of Justice (BGH, Bundesgerichtshof) illustrates:

In its case BGHZ 195, 126 (Judgement of 16 October 2012, X ZR 37/12), which dealt with an online purchase of flight tickets, the buyer typed – after having bought his proper ticket the regular way - "to be determined" in the name field of an airline company's flight booking page, assuming that he could supplement a name of his companion later, and confirmed his intend to buy this additional flight by clicking on the respective button. The system accepted this offer automatically, although the airline company had declared in its standard business terms available on the same site that it would agree only to sell tickets exclusively upon final specification of the name of the individual passenger (as it is standard airline practice). The buyer was hindered by the airline company to supplement the name later and had therefore to waive the second flight altogether and claimed return of the price for the second ticket.

The Federal Court decided that no contract had been concluded between the parties, arguing that even though the human individual on the buyer's side knows that a computer program will interpret the declaration of intent, the declaration would have to be interpreted as if the "represented" airline company board of directors itself would have read this declaration, and they obviously would not have accepted this offer. According to Sutschet, the BGH's approach is not convincing, as it deliberately follows two different interpretation perspectives for computer-processed declaration of intent: If the computer *receives* a declaration (here the offer), the human recipient's perspective shall be deemed decisive (here the airline); if on the other hand the computer *submits* a declaration (here the acceptance), it shall be again recipient (again the airline) whose human perspective is deemed relevant [14]. Both interpretations do besides explicitly contradict the literal meaning of the declarations in question, which are "to be determined" as passenger name and "offer accepted" respectively. Sutschet proposes to solve the problem by avoidance, as the airline company was not aware about the objective content of the declaration issued on its behalf, which seems plausible.

If the airline had used Smart Contracts for their sales mechanism – which would be a reasonable and efficient approach –, this interpretation dilemma remains.

2.2 Attributing Autonomous Software Declarations

While simple Smart Contracts are automated systems, follow-on contracts would be seen as autonomous systems; the computer starts acting itself in form of a so-called "software agent". In general, a software agent is an IT-based mechanism (computer program) which generate autonomous – i.e. non-determined – declarations of intent on behalf of its user on base of algorithms or other data input. In contrast to computer declarations, the essentialia negotii/the individual contract partner are exclusively determined by the software. Legal challenges arise here first of all in the question in how far agency instruments should be applied by analogy on these declarations, which in ths case also in a broad interpretation can not be considered any more as a declaration composed by the human making use of the algorithm. While the consequence – considering the software as the author of the declaration of intent, comparable to a representative – has long time not found much support [2], there is a trend of making use of the indeed technically very suitable mechanisms of agency by focussing on a distribution of legal capacity by the society onto a legal entity [11] rather than deriving this legal capacity from a legal subject.

The aspect of attribution, however, does play less of a role when it comes to void declarations of intent as covered by this paper.

3   Conclusion

Legal implications arising from Smart Contracts and void declarations of intent are not caused by the use of blockchain-based Smart Contracts as such. Smart Contracts do only reflect contractual relations which exist beyond them, and their legal shortcomings are reflected with them. For practice, this means that the branch of "Rechtsgeschäftslehre" (formation of contracts) does not have a diferent impact on Smart Contracts than it has on traditional contracts.

But Smart Contracts could provide an opportunity to reduce existing wekanesses in present legal practice, as questions of party verification, complying with legal restrictions etc. – either by implementing possibilities for "public or governmental entities to take responsibility for clarifying the legal status of Smart Contracts" or obliging "industries (…) to take preemptive measures and create model contract terms that support the exploitation of Smart Contracts", as recently proposed by Lauslahti et al. [7].

Anyhow, the overall potential of Smart Contracts for contract law should also not overestimated. Firstly, contracts do have in society by far more functions than creating enforceable obligations, as addressed in detail by Levy, who points out that people use contracts also as indirect, but very efficient means of regulating their legal relations by e.g. including facially unenforceable terms or purposefully underspecified terms into contracts or willfully not enforcing enforceable terms [8]. Also the call for Smart Contracts to be used for public registries – as e.g. land registries – reduces their function to mere records, neglecting the essential significance of the historical genesis of a property right e.g. in cases of acquisition of property in good faith [15]. The societal advantages incurred by Smart Contracts in terms of efficiency, legal certainty and practicability have, finally, to be juxtaposed to the considerable potential of Smart Contracts for criminal schemes [5].

Either way, the digitalisation of legal professions [6] will inevitably and increasingly force lawyers and other legal practitioners to get acquainted with Smart Contracts and the blockchain architecture. But a sober analysis of the elementary contract tools in this environment – as intended to be provided by this contribution – reveals that in terms of void declarations of intent the existing legal tools and mechanisms are apt to fully cover Smart Contract solutions.

References

1. Giancaspro, M.: Is a 'smart contract' really a smart idea? Insights from a legal perspective. Comput. Law Secur. Rev. **33**, 825–835 (2018)
2. Heckelmann, M.: Zulässigkeit und Handhabung von Smart Contracts. Neue Juristische Wochenschrift **71**, 505–510 (2018)
3. Hoffmann, T., Kelli, A., Värv, A.: The abstraction principle: a pillar of the future Estonian intellectual property law? Eur. Rev. Priv. Law **21**(3), 823–842 (2013)
4. Jansen, N., Zimmermann, R.: Contract formation and mistake in European contract law. Oxf. J. Leg. Stud. **31**(4), 625–662 (2011)
5. Juels, A., Kosba, A.E., Shi, E.: The Ring of Gyges: Using Smart Contracts for Crime. http://www.arijuels.com/wp-content/uploads/2013/09/Gyges.pdf. Accessed 27 Mar 2017
6. Kerikmäe, T., Hoffmann, T., Chochia, A.: Legal technology for law firms: determining roadmaps for innovation. Croat. Int. Relat. Rev. **24**(81), 91–112 (2018)
7. Lauslahti, K., Mattila, J., Seppälä, T.: Smart Contracts – How will Blockchain Technology Affect Contractual Practices? ETLA (Research Centre of the Finnish Economy) reports, p. 68 (2017)
8. Levy, K.: Book-smart, not street-smart: blockchain-based smart contracts and the social workings of law. Engag. Sci. Technol. Soc. **3**, 1–15 (2017)

9. Savelyev, A.: Contract law 2.0: 'Smart' contracts as the beginning of the end of classic contract law. Inf. Commun. Technol. Law **26**(2), 116–134 (2017)

10. Schrey, J., Thalhofer, T.: Rechtliche Aspekte der Blockchain. Neue Juristische Wochenschrift, 1431–1436 (2017)

11. Specht, L., Herold, S.: Roboter als Vertragspartner? Gedanken zu Vertragsabschlüssen unter Einbeziehung automatisiert und autonom agierender Systeme. Multimedia und Recht, 40–44 (2018)

12. Sutschet, H.: Anforderungen an die Rechtsgeschäftslehre im Internet. Neue Juristische Wochenschrift **67**, 1041–1047 (2014)

13. Szabo, N.: Formalizing and securing relationships on public networks. First Monday **2**(9) (1997). http://ojphi.org/ojs/index.php/fm/article/view/548/469. Accessed 27 Mar 2017

14. Taeger, J.: Die Entwicklung des IT-Rechts im Jahr 2016. Neue Juristische Wochenschrift, 3764

15. Wilsch, H.: Die Blockchain-Technologie aus Sicht des deutschen Grundbuchrechts. Deutsche Notar-Zeitschrift, 761–787 (2017)

Blockchain-Based Application Security Risks: A Systematic Literature Review

Mubashar Iqbal[✉] and Raimundas Matulevičius

Institute of Computer Science, University of Tartu, Tartu, Estonia
{mubashar.iqbal,raimundas.matulevicius}@ut.ee

Abstract. Although the blockchain-based applications are considered to be less vulnerable due to the nature of the distributed ledger, they did not become the *silver bullet* with respect to securing the information against different security risks. In this paper, we present a literature review on the security risks that can be mitigated by introducing the blockchain technology, and on the security risks that are identified in the blockchain-based applications. In addition, we highlight the application and technology domains where these security risks are observed. The results of this study could be seen as a preliminary checklist of security risks when implementing blockchain-based applications.

Keywords: Blockchain · Blockchain-based applications · Decentralized applications · Security risks

1 Introduction

Blockchain is a distributed immutable ledger technology [34]. It gives participants an ability to share a ledger by peer-to-peer replication and updates every time when a transaction occurs. A ledger contains a certain and verifiable record of every single transaction ever made [22]. Security engineering is concerned with lowering the risk of intentional unauthorized harm to valuable assets to that level which is acceptable to the system's stakeholders by preventing and reacting to malicious harm, misuse, threats, and security risks [14]. Security plays an important role in the blockchain-based applications. Those applications are acknowledged to be less vulnerable because the use of a decentralized consensus paradigm to validate the transactional information. They also backed by cryptography technology. However, the blockchain technology is continuously penetrating various fields and the involvement of the monetary assets raised the security concerns, mainly when the attackers stole the monetary assets or damage the system. For example, the reentrancy attack on the Ethereum based decentralized autonomous organization (DAO) smart contracts when an adversary gained control on $60 million Ethers [4,26].

Blockchain technology promises to overcome the security challenges, enhance the data integrity and to transform the transacting process into a decentralized,

© Springer Nature Switzerland AG 2019
H. A. Proper and J. Stirna (Eds.): CAiSE 2019 Workshops, LNBIP 349, pp. 176–188, 2019.
https://doi.org/10.1007/978-3-030-20948-3_16

transparent and immutable manner. The recent progression of blockchain technology captured the interest of various sectors to transform their business processes by using blockchain-based applications. Hence, the security challenges are debatable and there is no comprehensive (or standardized) overview of security risks which can potentially damage the blockchain-based applications. There exist few studies reporting on security challenges in the blockchain platforms [4,24], but there is still a lack of focus on the blockchain-based applications security.

In this paper, we present a systematic literature review (SLR) following the guidelines of [20]. Our research objectives are twofold. Firstly, we explain what security risks of the centralized applications are mitigated by introducing the blockchain-based applications. Secondly, we report the security risks of the blockchain-based applications which appear after introducing the blockchain technology. The main contributions of our study are: (1) a list of security risks in the blockchain-based applications which are mitigate or inherit by incorporating the blockchain technology/platform, (2) aggregate a list of possible countermeasures and (3) an overview of the prominent research domains which are nourishing by the blockchain. The results of this study could be seen as a preliminary checklist of security risks when implementing the blockchain-based applications.

The rest of the paper is structured as follows: Sect. 2 provides the overview of the blockchain and related work. Section 3 presents the contributions which explains the SLR process and Sect. 4 discuss its results. In Sect. 5, conclusion and future research directions are conferred.

2   Background

In this section, first, we introduce the blockchain technology. Second, we present an overview of related work.

2.1   Overview of Blockchain Technology

Blockchain forms a chain by a sequence of blocks that replicates over a peer-to-peer (P2P) network. In blockchain, each block is attached to the previous block by a cryptographic hash, a block contains block header and a list of transactions as a Merkle tree. Blockchain is classified as a permissionless or permissioned [31]. In permissionless blockchain anyone can join or leave the network and transactions are publicly available. In permissioned blockchain only predefined verified nodes can join the network and transactions visibility is restricted [2,31].

In blockchain a smart contract (SC) is a computer program [4,7] which constitutes a digital contract to store data and to execute functions [28] when certain conditions are met. In ethereum platform, developers use *Solidity* programming language to write smart contract and to build decentralized applications [7]. In Hyperledger fabric, smart contract is called chaincode. Similarly other blockchain platforms introduces the smart contracts to perform contractual agreements in a digital realm. The smart contracts are the high-level programming language-based programs and those can be error-prone where security flaws could be introduced (e.g. the reentrancy bug [26]).

Blockchain eliminates the trusted intermediary and follows the decentralized consensus mechanism to validate the transactional information. Different blockchains use various consensus mechanism. Proof of Work (PoW) is a widely use computational rich energy-waste consensus strategy where special nodes called miners validate transactions by solving the crypto puzzle. Proof of Stake (PoS) is an energy-efficient consensus strategy [42] where miners become validators [12] and lock a certain amount of cryptocurrency to show an ownership to participate in the consensus process. There are other consensus mechanisms, for example, Delegated Proof of Stake (DPoS), Proof of Authority (PoA), Proof of Reputation (PoR) and Proof of Spacetime (PoSt).

The number of blockchain platforms is rapidly growing and thus, the security becomes an important factor of the successful blockchain-based applications. In this paper, we focus on three frequently used blockchain platforms (Bitcoin, Ethereum, Hyperledger fabric). In addition, we also look at customised permissioned & permissionless platforms (see Table 3). Our goal is to learn which security risks and threats are considered in the applications of these platforms.

2.2 Related Work

There exists a few surveys, which consider blockchain platforms security risks. For instance, Li et al. [24] overview the security attacks on the blockchain platforms & summarise the security enhancements. In our work, we consider the security risks on the *blockchain-based applications* and their countermeasures.

Another related study [4] is conducted on Ethereum *smart contracts* security. It reports on the major security attacks, and presents a taxonomy of common programming pitfalls, which could result in different vulnerabilities. This study focuses on the security risks in the Ethereum smart contracts, further investigation is required to explore possible security risks in *smart contracts based decentralized applications* and their viable countermeasures.

The main attributes of blockchain are integrity, reliability and security [21] which are also important in the IoT systems. The conventional approaches and reference frameworks of IoT network implementation are still unable to fulfill the requirements of security [19]. Khan et al. [19] survey major security issues of IoT and discuss different countermeasures along with the blockchain solution. This study however does not detail security challenges in the *blockchain-based IoT applications*. Our study reviews the different blockchain-based IoT applications, discusses their security risks and potential countermeasures.

3   Survey Settings

In [20], a comprehensive approach is presented to perform a SLR. In this section, we apply it to conduct a SLR on the security risks in the blockchain-based applications.

3.1   Review Method

In order to achieve the objectives of this study, we consider four research questions: (i) What are the domains where blockchain solutions are applied? (ii) What security risks are mitigated by the blockchain solutions? (iii) What do security risks appear within the blockchain-based applications? (iv) What are the countermeasures to mitigate security risks in the blockchain-based applications?

Selection of Databases. The selection of electronic databases and literature search is carried out by consulting with the experts of software security. Literature studies are collected from: ACM digital library, IEEE digital library, ScienceDirect, SpringerLink and Scopus. The **search queries** (including some alternative terms and synonyms) are formulated as follows:

> *Blockchain applications security (risks, threats, gaps, issues, challenges), permissioned blockchain applications security, permissionless blockchain applications security, public blockchain applications security.*

Relevance and Quality Assessment. The inclusion and exclusion criteria listed in Table 1. In this study, we only include the peer-reviewed literature because most of the grey literature is based on assumptions, abstract concepts and prejudices towards their applications security. Based on these shreds of evidence the grey literature could lead to the publication bias and erroneous results, so in order to eliminate these concerns only peer-reviewed literature is considered.

Table 1. Inclusion and exclusion criteria.

Inclusion Criteria	Exclusion Criteria
Only the peer-reviewed literature	Literature that does not subject to peer review
Literature studies that discuss security risks in the blockchain-based applications	Grey literature or informal studies with no concrete evidence

The selection of the studies was made after reading the paper *title, abstract, introduction and conclusion* sections. Finally, following the quality guidelines of [20] and research scope of our study we have assessed the quality of studies using following questions:

- Are the goals and purpose of a study is clearly stated?
- Is the study describes security risks on the blockchain-based applications?
- Is the study provide the countermeasures to mitigate security risks?
- Is the study answered the defined research questions?
- How well the research results are presented?

The answers to above questions are scored as follows: $1 =$ Fully satisfy, $0.5 =$ Partially satisfy, $0 =$ Not satisfy. The studies with 2.5 or more points are included.

3.2   Screening Results

Table 2 presents the screening results. Initially, total 141 studies were collected. Later 73 studies were excluded by applying inclusion/exclusion and quality assessment criteria. Finally, 68 studies remained[1]. The extracted information outlines the study identification, research problem, security risks and countermeasures.

Table 2. Literature studies.

Database	Total	Excl.	Incl.
ACM	21	11	10
IEEE	31	9	22
ScienceDirect	22	15	7
SpringerLink	23	12	11
Scopus	44	26	18
Total	141	73	68

4   Results and Discussion

In this section, we present the SLR results. Table 3 shows how the field of blockchain-based applications is emerging every year. We observe that *Ethereum-based* applications are gaining popular-

Table 3. Statistics of literature studies as per year.

	Permissionless			Permissioned			
	Bitcoin	Ethereum	CPL	HLF	CP	Generic	Total
2016	2	0	0	0	0	0	2
2017	7	3	8	1	2	1	22
2018	9	15	3	8	8	1	44
Total	18	18	11	9	10	2	68

ity among the others. Also, permissioned blockchain platforms (*Hyperledger Fabric (HLF) & Customised Permissioned (CP)*) are arising because those support various industry-based use cases beyond cryptocurrencies. Practitioners also presented various *Customised Permissionless (CPL)* platforms to achieve customised tasks and to overcome the limitations of other platforms. The term *Generic* refers to studies where the blockchain type and platform is not mentioned.

4.1   Applications Domains

Table 4 presents the quantity of *applications domains & technology solutions* based on the different blockchain platforms. It shows *Healthcare* is mostly studied application domain and *security layer* as a technology solution. Also, it indicates that Ethereum is widely used blockchain platform for building the decentralized applications.

4.2   Security Risks

Security risks result in a harm to the system and its components [18]. In our study, the identified security risks are classified into two categories. (i) Security risks which are mitigated by introducing the blockchain-based applications (see Table 5), and (ii) Security risks which are appear within the blockchain-based applications (see Table 6). Table 5 presents the most common security risks which

---

[1] Here is a list of this SLR studies: http://datadoi.ut.ee/handle/33/89.

Table 4. Research areas based on different blockchain platforms.

| | Permissionless | | | Permissioned | | | |
	Bitcoin	Ethereum	CPL	HLF	CP	Generic	Total
Applications domains where blockchain is used							
Healthcare	0	3	1	2	4	1	11
Resource monitoring & Digital rights management	1	3	2	0	2	1	9
Financial	2	1	1	1	0	0	5
Smart vehicles	1	0	1	1	2	0	5
Voting	1	1	0	2	0	0	4
Technology solutions where blockchain is used							
Security layer	6	7	1	0	1	0	15
IoT	2	2	1	2	2	0	9
Total	13	17	7	8	11	2	58

Table 5. Security risks which are mitigated by introducing blockchain applications.

| | Permissionless | | | Permissioned | | | |
	Bitcoin	Ethereum	CPL	HFL	CP	Generic	Total
Data tampering attack	7	8	4	7	5	1	32
DoS/DDoS attack	7	7	5	3	2	1	25
MitM attack	3	6	2	2	0	1	14
Identity theft/Hijacking	1	0	3	0	0	1	5
Spoofing attack	2	0	1	0	1	0	4
Other risks/threats	6	4	2	1	2	2	17
Total	26	25	17	13	10	6	97

show that the researchers are utilizing the blockchain-based applications to overcome the limitations of centralized applications. For example, *data tampering attack* is mitigated in *Healthcare* applications and DDoS attack/Single point failure is resisted by decentralized distributed property of blockchain.

In addition to risks in Table 5, other risks (found once or twice in the studies) are: Side-channel attack, Impersonation attack, Phishing attack, Password attack, Cache poisoning, Arbitrary attack, Dropping attack, Appending attack, Authentication attack, Signature forgery attack, Keyword guess attack, Chosen message attack, Audit server attack, Inference attack, Binding attack and Bleichenbach-style attack.

Table 6 represents the most common security risks which appear within the blockchain-based applications after introducing the blockchain technology. The table indicates the security risks, which have a high probability to make the blockchain-based applications vulnerable to attack.

Table 6. Security risks which appear within the blockchain applications.

| | Permissionless | | | Permissioned | | | |
	Bitcoin	Ethereum	CPL	HLF	CP	Generic	Total
Sybil attack	5	1	1	4	1	1	13
Double spending attack	4	1	2	2	0	1	10
51% attack	3	3	1	0	0	1	8
Deanonymization attack	2	1	3	0	0	1	7
Replay attack	2	4	1	0	0	0	7
Quantum computing threat	0	1	1	2	0	1	5
Selfish mining attack	1	0	2	1	0	0	4
SC reentrancy attack	0	2	0	0	0	1	3
Other risks/threats	6	1	6	3	1	3	20
Total	23	14	17	12	2	9	77

Hence the *Sybil attack*, *Double spending attack* and *51% attack* are the most appeared security risks after incorporating the blockchain technology. Other security risks which are appeared once or twice in the studies are: Eclipse attack, BWH attack, 25% attack, Stake grinding attack, Block Discarding attack, Difficulty Raising attack, Pool-hopping attack, Node masquerading attack, Timestamp attack, Balance attack, Signature forgery attack, Confidentiality attack, Private keys compromise, Overspending attack, Collusion attack and Illegal activities.

In Table 7 we encompass the security risks along with the blockchain-based applications research areas to show which security risks are more frequently occurring on different blockchain-based applications. Most frequently the security risks expose in *Resource monitoring and digital rights management* applications, followed by the *Financial, Healthcare, Smart vehicles* and *Voting* applications. Also, blockchain is presented as a technology solution where researchers incorporated the blockchain as a security layer to protect against the listed security risks. However, Table 7 shows 34 different security risks *(combining both security risks which are mitigated and appear by introducing the blockchain solution)*. Furthermore, blockchain technology solution for IoT based applications is rapidly increasing because it provides integrity, reliability and security [19] and these are important for IoT based solutions to reach high requirements of security. By the results, the most common security risks in IoT based applications are mitigated by implementing the blockchain-based solution and only 3 different security risks are inherited after introducing the blockchain solution. The *other* column represents the generic blockchain-based applications and blockchain technology solutions where no specific domain is studied.

Table 7. Security risks based on the research areas.

	Applications					Technology			
	Healthcare	Resource monit.	Financial	Smart vehicles	Voting	Security layer	IoT	Other	Total
Security risks which are mitigated by introducing blockchain applications									
Data tampering attack	6	5	1	4	3	2	5	6	32
DoS/DDoS attack	0	5	1	3	1	7	3	5	25
MitM attack	1	4	1	1	1	2	2	2	14
Identity theft/Hijacking	1	2	0	0	0	0	1	1	5
Spoofing attack	0	0	0	0	1	0	1	2	4
Other risks/threats	2	0	1	0	1	5	5	3	17
Security risks which appear within the blockchain applications									
Sybil attack	1	1	1	1	2	1	1	5	13
Double spending attack	0	4	2	0	0	2	0	2	10
51% attack	0	4	0	0	1	1	0	2	8
Deanonymization attack	0	2	1	1	1	1	1	0	7
Replay attack	0	2	1	0	0	4	0	0	7
Quantum comp. threat	1	0	0	0	0	2	0	2	5
Selfish mining attack	0	1	1	0	0	2	0	0	4
SC reentrancy attack	0	0	0	0	0	3	0	0	3
Other risks/threats	0	11	5	0	0	2	1	1	20
Total	12	41	15	10	11	34	20	31	174

4.3   Countermeasures

In this section, we overview countermeasures to mitigate the security risks listed in Table 5 and 6.

Countermeasures Introduced with Blockchain Solution. The security risks presented in Table 5 are mitigated by implementing the blockchain-based applications together with the techniques to mitigate these risks. For instance, *Data tampering attack* poses threat to the data sensitive applications. In [40,41] authors implement the smart contract to mitigate votes tampering. In [35,40] authors encrypt information and associate a unique hash. Chen et al. [9] propose a random oracle model with strong RSA. And Li et al. [23] introduce a elliptic curve digital signature algorithm (ECDSA) based signature scheme for anonymous data transmission along Merkle hash tree based selective disclosure mechanism. Han et al. [16] propose to use permissioned blockchain where only the authorized nodes are able to access the data as well as generate a cipher-text by using digital signatures.

DoS/DDoS attack is another exploitable cyber-attack, it is resisted by distribution of service on different nodes [40]. The [11,25] authors implement an access control scheme to prevent an unauthorized requests. Androulaki et al. [3] propose a block-list to track suspicious requesting nodes and the authors of [3,32] incorporate the transaction fee to resist it. In order to resist the *MitM attack*, authors suggest to encrypt an information [10,40] and publish on the blockchain [40]. In [25,38] research studies, an authentication scheme is introduce to verify each communication node. *Identity theft/Hijacking* based risks are mitigated by information authentication and message generation time-stamping [13]. Mylrea et al. [30] suggest a permission based solutions (e.g. KSI). *Spoofing attack* is mitigated by introducing an anonymous communication among nodes [8] and Keyless Signature Infrastructure (KSI) based distributed & witnesses trust anchor [30].

Countermeasures to Mitigate Security Risks of Blockchain Solutions. The blockchain solution comes with a few trade-offs and inherit several security risks (see Table 6) of blockchain technology which are mitigated by implementing the various techniques, those techniques are listed below as countermeasures. In order to mitigate the *Sybil attack*, in [15,41] authors suggest the permissioned blockchain-based application. Bartolucci et al. [5] incorporate the transaction fee & identification system to allow only an authorized users to perform different operations. In [32], authors use the PoR scheme and Liu et al. [27] implement the customised blockchain to control the computing power. *Double spending attack* is mitigated by the transaction verification based on unspent transaction state [3]. In [1] authors resisted this attack by PoA scheme and in [6] by PoW complexity. Also, the Muzammal et al. [29] append the nonce with each transaction. Another frequent security risk on the blockchain-based applications is *51% attack* which is resisted by implementing trusted authorities control [43] and Hjalmarsson et al. [17] customised the Ethereum blockchain to permissioned blockchain.

In order to mitigate *Deanonymization attack*, in [25] authors propose a solution to obtain identity information only after an authorization. Bartolucci et al. [5] propose the mixer for mixing the position of output addresses. In [33,37] authors propose another solution to mitigate this attack by using the fresh key for each transaction. *Selfish mining attack* is mitigated by PoR scheme [32] and by raising the threshold [37]. No countermeasure is found for *Replay attack*. In order to overcome the *Quantum computing threats*, Yin et al. [39] implement the lattice cryptography and in [6] authors suggest an additional digital signatures or a hard fork in the post-quantum era. Decusatis et al. [11] propose a need of quantum blockchain. To eliminate the chances of *Smart contract reentrancy attack*, authors of [26] present the automation tool to detect smart contract bugs via run-time trace analysis and in [36] authors built a static analysis tool that detects reentrancy bugs in smart contract and translates solidity source code into an XML-based intermediate representation and checks it against XPath patterns.

5   Conclusion and Future Work

In this paper, we present a systematic literature review on the blockchain-based applications security risks to explain what security risks are mitigated by introducing the blockchain-based applications, and what security risks are reported in the blockchain-based applications. Our result is a preliminary checklist to support developers' decisions while developing the blockchain-based applications.

Our current study has a few limitations: (i) Applications which are built on the blockchain platforms are mostly in the prototype phase. Thus the research studies present only the conceptual illustrations of different security risks and their countermeasures but not the real life applications. (ii) The field of decentralized applications is relatively new but continuously evolving. Not all the possible security risks are researched in the blockchain-based applications which show the possibility that a wide range of security risks will emerge in upcoming years. (iii) This study found that a lot of security risks and their countermeasures are either obscure or the practical implementation is still not available. Overcoming these limitations could possibly result in the interesting insights and contribute to the explaining the blockchain-based application security risks, their vulnerabilities and the countermeasures for more in-depth.

As a part of the future work, our aim is to build a comprehensive reference model for security risk management to systematically evaluate the security needs. This model would explain the protected assets of the blockchain-based applications, and countermeasures to mitigate their risks.

Acknowledgement. This research has been supported by the Estonian Research Council (grant IUT20-55).

References

1. Alcarria, R., Bordel, B., Robles, T., Martín, D., Manso-Callejo, M.Á.: A blockchain-based authorization system for trustworthy resource monitoring and trading in smart communities. J. Sens. (Switzerland) **18**(10), 3561 (2018)
2. Ali, S., Wang, G., White, B., Cottrell, R.L.: A blockchain-based decentralized data storage and access framework for PingER. In: Proceedings of 17th IEEE International Conference on Trust, Security and Privacy in Computing and Communications and 12th IEEE International Conference on Big Data Science and Engineering, Trustcom/BigDataSE, pp. 1303–1308 (2018)
3. Androulaki, E., et al.: Hyperledger fabric: a distributed operating system for permissioned blockchains. In: Proceedings of EuroSys 2018 Thirteenth EuroSys Conference, Article No. 30 (2018)
4. Atzei, N., Bartoletti, M., Cimoli, T.: A survey of attacks on ethereum smart contracts (SoK). In: Maffei, M., Ryan, M. (eds.) POST 2017. LNCS, vol. 10204, pp. 164–186. Springer, Heidelberg (2017). https://doi.org/10.1007/978-3-662-54455-6_8
5. Bartolucci, S., Bernat, P., Joseph, D.: SHARVOT: secret SHARe-based VOTing on the blockchain. In: Proceedings of ACM/IEEE 1st International Workshop on Emerging Trends in Software Engineering for Blockchain, pp. 30–34 (2018)
6. Buchmann, N., Rathgeb, C., Baier, H., Busch, C., Margraf, M.: Enhancing breeder document long-term security using blockchain technology. In: Proceedings of International Computer Software and Applications Conference, vol. 2, pp. 744–748 (2017)
7. Buterin, V.: A next-generation smart contract and decentralized application platform (2014). https://github.com/ethereum/wiki/wiki/White-Paper
8. Cebe, M., Erdin, E., Akkaya, K., Aksu, H., Uluagac, S.: Block4Forensic: an integrated lightweight blockchain framework for forensics applications of connected vehicles. J. IEEE Commun. Mag. **56**(10), 50–57 (2018)

9. Chen, L.: EPBC: efficient public blockchain client for lightweight users. In: Proceedings of SERIAL 2017 1st Workshop on Scalable and Resilient Infrastructures for Distributed Ledgers, Article No. 1 (2017)

10. Dagher, G.G., Mohler, J., Milojkovic, M., Marella, P.B.: Ancile: privacy-preserving framework for access control and interoperability of electronic health records using blockchain technology. J. Sustain. Cities Soc. **39**(December 2017), 283–297 (2018)

11. Decusatis, C., Lotay, K.: Secure, decentralized energy resource management using the ethereum blockchain. In: Proceedings of 17th IEEE International Conference on Trust, Security and Privacy in Computing and Communications and 12th IEEE International Conference on Big Data Science and Engineering, Trustcom/BigDataSE, pp. 1907–1913 (2018)

12. Fabian Vogelsteller, V.B.: Proof of Stake FAQs (2018). https://github.com/ethereum/wiki/wiki/Proof-of-Stake-FAQs

13. Fan, K., et al.: Blockchain-based secure time protection scheme in IoT. J. IEEE Internet Things **PP**(c), 1 (2018)

14. Firesmith, D.G.: Engineering Security Requirements. Journal of Object Technology **2**(1), 53–68 (2003). Published by ETH Zurich, Chair of Software Engineering ©JOT, 2003

15. Gallo, P., Quoc Nguyen, U.: BlockSee: blockchain for IoT video surveillance in smart cities Suporn Pongnumkul NECTEC Thailand. In: Proceedings of IEEE International Conference on Environment and Electrical Engineering and 2018 IEEE Industrial and Commercial Power Systems Europe (EEEIC/I&CPS Europe), pp. 1–6 (2018)

16. Han, H., Huang, M., Zhang, Y., Bhatti, U.A.: An architecture of secure health information storage system based on blockchain technology. In: Sun, X., Pan, Z., Bertino, E. (eds.) ICCCS 2018. LNCS, vol. 11064, pp. 578–588. Springer, Cham (2018). https://doi.org/10.1007/978-3-030-00009-7_52

17. Hjalmarsson, F.P., Hreioarsson, G.K., Hamdaqa, M., Hjalmtysson, G.: Blockchain-based e-voting system. In: Proceedings of IEEE 11th International Conference on Cloud Computing (CLOUD), pp. 983–986 (2018). https://ieeexplore.ieee.org/document/8457919/

18. Jouini, M., Rabai, L.B.A., Aissa, A.B.: Classification of security threats in information systems. Procedia Comput. Sci. **32**, 489–496 (2014)

19. Khan, M.A., Salah, K.: IoT security: review, blockchain solutions, and open challenges. J. Futur. Gener. Comput. Syst. **82**, 395–411 (2018)

20. Kitchenham, B., Charters, S.: Guidelines for performing systematic literature reviews in software engineering version 2.3. Engineering **45**(4ve), 1051 (2007)

21. Koteska, B., Mishev, A.: Blockchain implementation quality challenges: a literature review. In: Proceedings of the SQAMIA 2017: 6th Workshop of Software Quality, Analysis, Monitoring, Improvement, and Applications, pp. 11–13, September 2017

22. Lewis, A.: Blockchain technology explained (2015). http://www.blockchaintechnologies.com/blockchain-definition

23. Li, H., Lu, R., Misic, J., Mahmoud, M.: Security and privacy of connected vehicular cloud computing. J. IEEE Netw. **32**(3), 4–6 (2018)

24. Li, X., Jiang, P., Chen, T., Luo, X., Wen, Q.: A survey on the security of blockchain systems. J. Futur. Gener. Comput. Syst. (2017)

25. Lin, C., He, D., Huang, X., Choo, K.K.R., Vasilakos, A.V.: BSeIn: a blockchain-based secure mutual authentication with fine-grained access control system for industry 40. J. Netw. Comput. Appl. **116**(February), 42–52 (2018)

26. Liu, C., Liu, H., Cao, Z., Chen, Z., Chen, B., Roscoe, B.: ReGuard: finding reentrancy bugs in smart contracts. In: Proceedings of International Conference on Software Engineering, pp. 65–68 (2018)
27. Liu, M., Shang, J., Liu, P., Shi, Y., Wang, M.: VideoChain: trusted video surveillance based on blockchain for campus. In: Sun, X., Pan, Z., Bertino, E. (eds.) ICCCS 2018. LNCS, vol. 11066, pp. 48–58. Springer, Cham (2018). https://doi.org/10.1007/978-3-030-00015-8_5
28. Macrinici, D., Cartofeanu, C., Gao, S.: Smart contract applications within blockchain technology: a systematic mapping study. J. Telemat. Inform. (October), 0–1 (2018). https://linkinghub.elsevier.com/retrieve/pii/S0736585318308013
29. Muzammal, M., Qu, Q., Nasrulin, B.: Renovating blockchain with distributed databases: an open source system. J. Futur. Gener. Comput. Syst. **90**, 105–117 (2018)
30. Mylrea, M., Gourisetti, S.N.G.: Blockchain for smart grid resilience: exchanging distributed energy at speed, scale and security. In: Proceedings of 2017 Resilience Week, RWS 2017, pp. 18–23 (2017)
31. Pradeepkumar, D.S., Singi, K., Kaulgud, V., Podder, S.: Evaluating complexity and digitizability of regulations and contracts for a blockchain application design. In: Proceedings of 2018 ACM/IEEE 1st International Workshop on Emerging Trends in Software Engineering for Blockchain, no. 1, pp. 25–29 (2018)
32. Qin, D., Wang, C., Jiang, Y.: RPchain: a blockchain-based academic social networking service for credible reputation building. In: Chen, S., Wang, H., Zhang, L.-J. (eds.) ICBC 2018. LNCS, vol. 10974, pp. 183–198. Springer, Cham (2018). https://doi.org/10.1007/978-3-319-94478-4_13
33. Saritekin, R.A., Karabacak, E., Durğay, Z., Karaarslan, E.: Blockchain based secure communication application proposal: Cryptouch. In: Proceedings of 6th International Symposium on Digital Forensic and Security, ISDFS 2018, vol. 2018-Janua, pp. 1–4 (2018)
34. Sato, T., Himura, Y.: Smart-contract based system operations for permissioned blockchain. In: Proceedings of 2018 9th IFIP International Conference on New Technologies, Mobility and Security, NTMS 2018, vol. 2018-Janua, pp. 1–6 (2018)
35. Sylim, P., Liu, F., Marcelo, A., Fontelo, P.: Blockchain technology for detecting falsified and substandard drugs in distribution: pharmaceutical supply chain intervention. J. Med. Internet Res. **20**(9), e10163 (2018)
36. Tikhomirov, S., Voskresenskaya, E., Ivanitskiy, I., Takhaviev, R., Marchenko, E., Alexandrov, Y.: SmartCheck: static analysis of ethereum smart contracts. In: Proceedings of the 1st International Workshop on Emerging Trends in Software Engineering for Blockchain - WETSEB 2018, pp. 9–16 (2018)
37. Tosh, D.K., Shetty, S., Liang, X., Kamhoua, C.A., Kwiat, K.A., Njilla, L.: Security implications of blockchain cloud with analysis of block withholding attack. In: Proceedings of 17th IEEE/ACM International Symposium on Cluster, Cloud and Grid Computing, CCGRID 2017, pp. 458–467 (2017)
38. Yao, H., Wang, C.: A novel blockchain-based authenticated key exchange protocol and its applications. In: Proceedings of IEEE 3rd International Conference on Data Science in Cyberspace, DSC 2018, pp. 609–614 (2018)
39. Yin, W.E.I., Wen, Q., Li, W., Zhang, H.U.A., Jin, Z.: An anti-quantum transaction authentication approach in blockchain. J. IEEE Access **6**, 5393–5401 (2018)
40. Yu, B., et al.: Platform-independent secure blockchain-based voting system. In: Chen, L., Manulis, M., Schneider, S. (eds.) ISC 2018. LNCS, vol. 11060, pp. 369–386. Springer, Cham (2018). https://doi.org/10.1007/978-3-319-99136-8_20

41. Zhang, W.: A privacy-preserving voting protocol on blockchain. In: Proceedings of IEEE 11th International Conference on Cloud Computing, pp. 401–408 (2018)
42. Zheng, Z., Xie, S., Dai, H.N., Chen, X., Wang, H.: Blockchain challenges and opportunities : a survey. Int. J. Web Grid Serv. **14**(4), 1–24 (2016). http://inpluslab.sysu.edu.cn/files/blockchain/blockchain.pdf
43. Zhu, L., Wu, Y., Gai, K., Choo, K.K.R.: Controllable and trustworthy blockchain-based cloud data management. J. Futur. Gener. Comput. Syst. **91**, 527–535 (2018). https://linkinghub.elsevier.com/retrieve/pii/S0167739X18311993

Data Management: Relational vs Blockchain Databases

Phani Chitti, Jordan Murkin, and Ruzanna Chitchyan[✉]

Department of Computer Science, University of Bristol,
MVB Building, Woodland Road, Bristol BS8 1UB, UK
{sc18092,jordan.murkin,r.chitchyan}@bristol.ac.uk

Abstract. This paper presents an initial exploitative study of how the relational and blockchain databases compare in defining and deploying data structures, populating these with new entries, and retrieving the relevant data for further use. The aim of this study is to better inform the software developers in general and the distributed application developers in particular.

Keywords: Data management · Blockchain · RDBMS ·
Smart contract · Distributed ledger

1 Introduction

Traditionally software systems store data in relational database management systems (RDBMS), occasionally using other means of storing data like File systems (for storing documents). Off late No-SQL databases for storing discrete data like documents, search results etc. have gained popularity. Yet, the RDBMSs continue to be preferred for storing data generated out of enterprise systems. Under these solutions the responsibility for maintaining the database, ensuring data integrity and providing secured access to different users based on their roles, lies with a select set of people - called administrators - who are employed by the database owners. This centralized authority which maintains the database also ensures the administrative activities, like regular backups etc.

On the other hand, (public) distributed ledger technologies (a.k.a. blockchains) are gaining more recognition as decentralized data stores and as an alternative to the traditional data storage systems. Initially these technologies arose to support cryptocurrencies [14]. However, their distinguishing features - distributed consensus, non-dependency on a centralized authority, built-in trust, low entry barriers for joining the network - are attracting many diverse domains to adapt this technology. Yet, in order to confidently develop an enterprise application that would rely on a distributed ledger solution as it's main database, we must have confidence that all the necessary services supported by

This research is funded by the UK EPSRC Refactoring Energy Systems fellowship (EP/R007373/1).

H. A. Proper and J. Stirna (Eds.): CAiSE 2019 Workshops, LNBIP 349, pp. 189–200, 2019.
https://doi.org/10.1007/978-3-030-20948-3_17

the current solutions (primarily RDMSs) can be adequately delivered through the distributed ledger solutions.

To this end we present an initial exploitative study of how the relational and blockchain databases compare in defining and deploying data structures, populating these with new entries, and retrieving the relevant data for further use.

One of the most popular distributed ledger environments today is the blockchain-based Ethereum platform which supports building decentralized applications [1], and provides the flexibility of writing arbitrary state transition functions via scripts. The scripts are executed by the Ethereum Virtual Machine (EVM). In Ethereum the state is made of two types of accounts: External (private key) accounts, and Contract (contract code) accounts [2]. External accounts can send messages, by creating transactions, to Contract accounts. Contract accounts, upon receipt of the transaction request messages, execute their contract code with the given transaction parameters. Contract accounts also can send messages to other contracts. The contract accounts contain their contract code and store the values of persistent variables. Each action undertaken by a contract account when executing code, storing a data value, or calling another contract account, should be paid for by the initiator of the contract's transaction.

As Ethereum is the most used blockchian development platform today, we too use it for our exploitative study. As a relational database counterpart to Ethereum we use the MySQL RDBMS. MySQL provides a comprehensive set of advanced RDBMSs features, and, in its own right, is also one of the most well used RDBMSs.

This paper discusses an experiment where we set out to create a set o data structures for an application using both RDBMS and a blockchain-based solution. We aim to identify the correspondent activities needed to carry out a given task with these two alliterative technologies (as discussed in Sect. 2). We then draw out the challenges and opportunities identified through this exploitative comparison (see Sect. 3) and discuss these. The aim of this study is to better inform the software developers in general and the distributed application developers in particular on the issues that one has to address when using either of these technologies as a main database.

2   Experiment

This section describes the experiment that is conducted to evaluate each of above discussed database solution alternatives. The experiment is carried out using the context of a peer-to-peer energy trading scenario [13].

Energy Trading Scenario: A number of households (or farms, and other non-energy small businesses) generate renewable energy (e.g., via solar PV panels, wind turbines, etc.) for own use, and wish to sell the excess generation to other households. For this the excess generation is advertised through "sell requests" over a trading platform. Similarly, those wishing to purchase a certain amount of energy advertise their "buy requests". A peer-to-peer energy trading algorithm (ETA) [13] that runs on the trading platform, works to match the sell and buy requests declared by the market participants for a given time period. The sell and buy requests are matched on the basis of scores calculated by the ETA for all trade participants. The scores are based on participants' preferences, which are provided by the participants when they join the trading platform (e.g., sell cheaper if buyer is local, e.g., within 2 miles, buy solar if possible, etc.).

The experiment consists of:

- Defining data structures to represent sellers and buyers: Each participant will have name, address, physical location details like longitude and latitude, contact details, as well as preferences on how (s)he wants to trade.
- Deploying the data structures: enabling their use either through a relational database or a blockchain;
- Storing the data generated per data structure: to replicate participation of a large number of users (here we use the Random() function to randomly generate values for user data).
- Retrieving the stored data to carry out transactions: data will be retrieved in order to form transactions between sellers and buyers. The transactions will be formed via the a Peer-To-Peer (P2P) energy trading algorithm (ETA).
- Storing trade transactions back into the databases.

Figures 1 and 3 depict the process of experiment realisation using a traditional relational database (MySQL RDBMS) and a blockchain-based solution (Ethereum). Both of these solutions are chosen due to their widespread popularity and availability of free access.

2.1   Implementing with MySQL RDBMS

As in any relational database, the data structures in MySQL are to be represented via relations (i.e., tables in a database). As shown in Fig. 1, the process starts with:

Fig. 1. Data storage and retrieval with MySQL

Defining tables and relationship among them. This requires that the data must be normalised and related, where:

- Normalization is the removal of the redundancy in data, leading to assured cohesion among entities and increased consistency.
- After normalization the data is arranged into a set of related entities (also called relations, tables). The relations for this study are depicted in Fig. 2. Unique identifiers (called keys) are defined for each record entry; these keys are referred in other records when a link is to be established between two pieces of data. Use of such keys ensures referential integrity between entities (i.e., making sure that the data integrity is preserved when two or more pieces of data need to refer to each other).

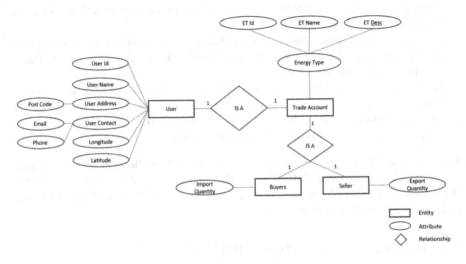

Fig. 2. Entities and relationships identified after normalization

With MySQL all the steps of our experiment (i.e., relation definition, deployment, data storage, and retrieval) are fully supported by the database management system itself, where a command line and/or a web interface tool/site can be used to carry out all the required actions. Thus:

- *Deployment* of the relations is reduced to CREATE TABLE command within the RDBMS (e.g., for a user table: CREATE TABLE IF NOT EXISTS User (UserId varchar(255) NOT NULL, UserName varchar(255) NOT NULL, UserAddress varchar(255) NOT NULL, Postcode varchar(255) NOT NULL, UserEmail varchar(255) NOT NULL, UserPhone varchar(255) NOT NULL, Longitude FLOAT NOT NULL, Latitude FLOAT NOT NULL, PRIMARY KEY (UserID));

- *Data storage* is reduced to INSERT command with reference to the specific table name, and a new record line is inserted and stored in the referenced table (e.g., INSERT INTO EnergyType VALUES (1, 'PV', 'Solar Energy')).
- *Retrieval of particular records* is carried out through the SELECT command by referencing the unique keys within each data record, whereby the related data is identified by repeated use of this same key in other tables.

2.2 Blockchain Based Approach

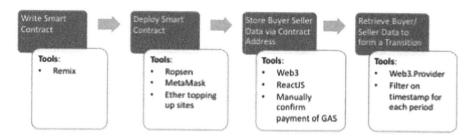

Fig. 3. Data storage and retrieval with Blockchain. Note: Tools listed here were used in this experiment, other tools could be chosen instead.

With the Ethereum alternative:

Defining the data structures is carried out through the creation of smart contracts (as shown in Listing 1.1) which will also contain the data to be stored in the blockchain. Hence, for this purpose, smart contracts are equivalent to tables in RDBMS.

Ethereum allows for the removal of duplication (akin to data normalisation in RDBMS) to be carried out by breaking data structures into multiple contracts then each refer to the other. As contracts may include references to other contracts via their contract addresses, this parallels to a kind of foreign key referencing. However, these references point to the whole of the contract (and its' entire data)and not to individual records; this is a contrast to the per individual record referencing of the RDBMSs.

Contracts may also emit events. An event affiliated to a contract, defines an indexing for quick filtering of the contract's data for outside of the blockchain access.

```
contract ETPAccount {
  bytes18 public postcode;
  bytes32 public latitude;
  bytes32 public longitude;
  uint16 public pricePreference;
  uint16 public distancePreference;

  event ElectricityExported(uint period, uint exports);
  event ElectricityImported(uint period, uint imports);

  constructor(bytes18 _postcode, bytes32 _lat,bytes32 _lng,
              uint16 _ppref, uint16 _dpref) public {
    postcode = _postcode;
    latitude = _lat;
    longitude = _lng;
    pricePreference = _ppref;
    distancePreference = _dpref;
  }

  function setPricePreference(uint16 _ppref) external {
    pricePreference = _ppref;
  }

  function setDistancePreference(uint16 _dpref) external {
    distancePreference = _dpref;
  }

  function storeExports(uint _period, uint _exports) external {
    emit ElectricityExported(_period, _exports);
  }

  function storeImports(uint _period, uint _imports) external {
    emit ElectricityExported(_period, _imports);
  }
}
```

Listing 1.1. Listing of smart contract for seller's data.

Deployment

Interaction with a blockchain is divided into two categories, *calls* - read-only interactions - and *transactions* - potentially state changing interactions. The reason for this distinction is the way each is processed. A call reads directly from a blockchain node and therefore does not require the involvement of the other parties in the network. Instead, a transaction must be broadcast, processed and included inside the distributed ledger. To account for this processing and storage requirement of other nodes in the network, transactions must be signed by an external account. This external account must have sufficient funds to pay for the costs incurred by the network.

Deployment of a smart contract therefore must take place via a transaction to a blockchain network which will record it into a permanent register (the chain) and validate that it concurs with the expected formats and rules (e.g., set by the consensus protocol). As noted before, our experiment was carried out on the Ethereum platform. Our contracts were deployed on the Ropsten test network [4] - an Ethereum test network that replicates the main network but provides free funds to accounts.

MetaMask – a Chrome browser extension – was used to create the external account in this experiment. The new account always contains zero funds balance. However, as noted before, use of the Ropsten network is free, so it provides test websites (https://faucet.metamask.io/ and https://faucet.ropsten.be/) to top up the testing pseudo-funds in the newly created external accounts.

Once the contract is deployed to the network, a contract address (e.g., "0xb0665117611910d3623358148dc6585f90ed7c3c5") will be provided that identifies it on the network.

Data Storage: Using the contract address, we can then interact with the public methods of the deployed smart contract. For example, in the smart contract (Listing 1.1) we could create transactions to supply data to our 'storeExports()'function which would permanently store the data in an accessible manner on the blockchain (in terms of an RDBMS, this corresponds to inserting rows of data into the newly created data structure).

In this experiment, to insert Buyer/Seller Data into the blockchain, we developed a single-page application (SPA, using HTML and JavaScript via React JS and Web3 tools). While inserting seller details (e.g.: "BS81UB", "−2.345672", "50.234098", "10", "12.31", "v10", "1"), a new transaction would be created by the blockchain network. This transaction would be placed into a block, along with many other transactions so as the pre-defined size of the block is achieved. The block is then validated (or, in other words, *mined*) by the miners of the network. The validated block will then be inserted into the Blockchain under the contract's account space.

Prior to the transaction processing (mining) a fee would be levied on the contract user for the miners work. The user has to confirm the payment of the fee. In our case, the fee would be charged to the funds of the external account used. Only after confirming the proposed fee charging, and charge collection, would the transaction be inserted into a block, which would then be minded and stored within the block. Figure 4 shows a number of data insertion transactions for some Seller data. (Note that in Fig. 4 each transaction is part of a discrete block indicated by block number, this is a peculiarity of our design, chosen for clear action traceability for this study; in a more general case many transactions would be grouped into the same block).

Retrieval: as each block in a Blockchain contains a set of discrete transactions, it is not inherently possible to retrieve a sub-set of data from the chain by simply referencing the per-record keys explicitly across several contracts (which is possible in case of RDBMS through per-record foreign keys).

Data is retrieved from a blockchain using the address of the smart contract in which the data was stored. The method to retrieve this data is then dependant on the type of storage used inside the smart contract. If a smart contract emits events to the network, we can query these events using filters on any indexed

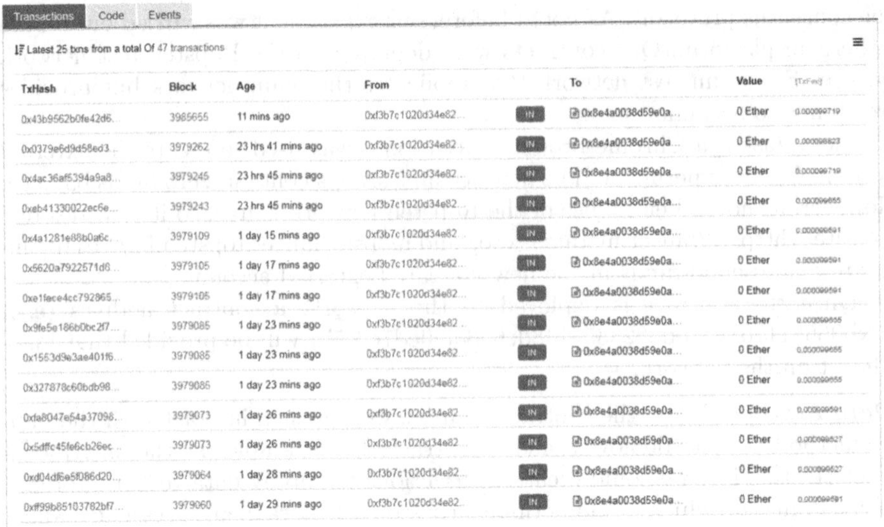
Transactions Code Events

Latest 25 txns from a total Of 47 transactions

TxHash	Block	Age	From		To	Value	[TxFee]
0x43b9562b0fe42d6...	3985655	11 mins ago	0xf3b7c1020d34e82...	IN	0x8e4a0038d59e0a...	0 Ether	0.000099719
0x0379e6d9d58ed3...	3979262	23 hrs 41 mins ago	0xf3b7c1020d34e82...	IN	0x8e4a0038d59e0a...	0 Ether	0.000098823
0x4ac36af5394a9a8...	3979245	23 hrs 45 mins ago	0xf3b7c1020d34e82...	IN	0x8e4a0038d59e0a...	0 Ether	0.000099719
0xeb41330022ec6e...	3979243	23 hrs 45 mins ago	0xf3b7c1020d34e82...	IN	0x8e4a0038d59e0a...	0 Ether	0.000099655
0x4a1281e88b0a6c...	3979109	1 day 15 mins ago	0xf3b7c1020d34e82...	IN	0x8e4a0038d59e0a...	0 Ether	0.000099591
0x5620a7922571d6...	3979105	1 day 17 mins ago	0xf3b7c1020d34e82...	IN	0x8e4a0038d59e0a...	0 Ether	0.000099591
0xe1fece4cc792865...	3979105	1 day 17 mins ago	0xf3b7c1020d34e82...	IN	0x8e4a0038d59e0a...	0 Ether	0.000099591
0x9fe5e186b0bc2f7...	3979085	1 day 23 mins ago	0xf3b7c1020d34e82...	IN	0x8e4a0038d59e0a...	0 Ether	0.000099655
0x1553d9e3ae401f6...	3979085	1 day 23 mins ago	0xf3b7c1020d34e82...	IN	0x8e4a0038d59e0a...	0 Ether	0.000099655
0x327878c60bdb98...	3979085	1 day 23 mins ago	0xf3b7c1020d34e82...	IN	0x8e4a0038d59e0a...	0 Ether	0.000099655
0xfa8047e54a37098...	3979073	1 day 26 mins ago	0xf3b7c1020d34e82...	IN	0x8e4a0038d59e0a...	0 Ether	0.000099591
0x5dffc45fe6cb26ec...	3979073	1 day 26 mins ago	0xf3b7c1020d34e82...	IN	0x8e4a0038d59e0a...	0 Ether	0.000099527
0xd04df6e5f086d20...	3979064	1 day 28 mins ago	0xf3b7c1020d34e82...	IN	0x8e4a0038d59e0a...	0 Ether	0.000099527
0xff99b85103782bf7...	3979060	1 day 29 mins ago	0xf3b7c1020d34e82...	IN	0x8e4a0038d59e0a...	0 Ether	0.000099591

Fig. 4. Caption

parameters (similarly to SELECT statements in SQL). However, these filters are quite limited, with only three indexable parameters per event. Events may also be filtered upon their block number - essentially limiting the search space - but this requires some knowledge of the data stored to be used effectively. If, however, the data is stored directly in the smart contracts storage, this can be accessed directly using calls to read the variables inside the contract.

3 Technological Limitations and Discussion

Having implemented a backend database for a p2p energy trading domain with two alternative technologies, we observe a number of limitations and alternatives, as discussed below.

3.1 Observations on Use of MySQL

MySQL was simple and easy to install and use.

The Management System (MS) in any RDBMS creates a secured application layer around the database. The MS efficiently takes care of role based access on relations, consistency and reliability while inserting and retrieving data and simultaneous request for change-read-update-write operations.

The standard Query Language based on ANSI-SQL provides an efficient and sophisticated way of querying granular data from this database. Additionally, new relationships between existing tables can be defined in an "additive" way, without invalidating previously existing ones.

However, a number of limitations related to the use of the traditional RDBMS also arose:

- Transparency: As the data in the RDBMS is updated or changed, the changes are not visible to the users. This reduces the confidence in the data that is stored in the database.
- Immutability: After the data is inserted into the RDBMS, it can be changed at any time.
- Openness: The RDBMS are not open usually because enterprises own them.
- Data Formats: The data should be engineered (normalised and interlinked via foreign keys) before storing it in RDBMS. This reduces the flexibility. Disparate data sources having different data formats can not use RDBMSs to store the data.

3.2 Observations on Use of Blockchain

Blockchains offer an open, transparent, immutable and distributed platform for storing data, which addresses rather well the above mentioned shortcomings of the RDBMSs. Yet, we also observed a number of limitations of the Blockchain based approach:

- *Querying data from Blockchain*: blockchains don't have any sophisticated data query mechanism to interrogate the data that is stored in them. There are several ways in which a user can get data from a blockchain. Two of these require that the smart contract address is known.
  (a) In the first case "allEvents" quantifier provided by Web3 framework can be used, which returns all the events that are registered with the given Smart Contract since its deployment. Under this option, there is no control over the amount of data that can be obtained from it and on the time it takes to retrieve it. The user must retrieve all data and only then choose the entries relevant to her.
  (b) In the second case, the smart contract specifies data returning functions. This could work well for cases where all data of a particular type is to be returned for every call of this function (e.g., all users registered to this platform). Yet, the flexibility on what can be queried is very limited here (e.g., cannot return only users registered in the current year, unless this specific function is specified prior to the contract deployment). Clearly, inventive solutions could be thought to tackle such lack of flexibility (e.g., instantiate a new smart contract for user registration every year, then annual registrations can be accessed through the annual contract address).

We have previously noted that if a smart contract emits events to the network, we can query these events using filters on any indexed parameters.

These, however, are all pre-designed solutions, as the deployed smart contracts are immutable, and the data to be returned and indexing to be used must all be set pre-deployment. These options lack flexibility of the general SQL-like queries over RDBMSs.

Other ways to get data require explicit knowledge of its transaction hash or block number. However maintaining the transaction hash or Block number for all transactions on a smart contract is not realistically possible.

- *Data Formats*: a smart contract along with its' functions is to be written per data type. However, data types in Solidity (language for smart contracts used in Ethereum) are limited and could cause difficulties if the data source were to evolve/change. However, some generic types also exist, e.g., "String" type could be used to store Json format, which is also a type of string. Nevertheless, this limited type availability requires careful pre-planning for evolution, which cannot always be foreseen.
- Cost: Our experience suggests that the data storage in a blockchain comes always with an incurred transaction cost. The cost is incurred in any network – Public, Private or Consortium - whenever the state of the blockchian is changed via a new transaction, where any data insertion constitutes a new transaction. In our example the, however, publication of the data on generation and consumption, as well as registering as participants on the p2p network does not provide any financial benefits to the participants. It is only the actual trade recording (carried out upon retrial of the previously submitted data) that would lead to financial gains. The parties that publish the row data may not even prosper from the matching. Thus, we suggest that a more flexible pricing model is necessary.
- Technological barriers: two main versions of Ethereum blockchain implementations are currently available: JavaScript based and GOLang based. This experiment is performed mainly using JavaScript based implementations. The tools that are used in both streams are different. JavaScript uses software packages from web3, where as GoLang has its own packages like solc, abigen etc. As of now work done in one stream is not interchangeable/reusable within the another. While doing this experiment we ourselves had frequent mis-communication as collaborators had backgrounds in different streams. We suggest that better integration of the technology streams would improve both the development experience and the quality of the end result.
- The Maturity of Technology: The Blockchain technology used in this approach – Solidity, Web3.js, Ropsten test network, Metamask and Remix Editor are evolving and backward compatibility of features could be an issue.

4   Related Work and Conclusion

Since the emergence of Bitcoin [14] a wide range of research and development activities is under way on using blockchain as a data storage mechanism.

There are a number of areas which relate to the study presented in this paper, some focusing on comparing the utility of blockchain solutions to the centralised databases, some on working on the unification of both technologies. A small selection of such related work is presented below.

In [16] authors analyse which blockchain properties are relevant to various application domains and problem requirements. They review three domains (supply chain management, inter-bank payments and decentralised autonomous organisations) and argue that various types of blockchain would best suite these various domains.

Greenspan [12] studies differences between private blockchains and SQL databases focusing on such issues as trust building and robustness.

A survey on literature describing scenarios where blockchain is applied is presented in [7]. Here the authors attempted to find what factors (i.e., why and how) contributed to the use of blockchain. By comparing blockchain vs a centralised database for such issues as robustness, fault tolerance, performance and redundancy, the paper proposes a decision tree to check whether the use case in hand is advantaged by using a blockchian solution.

Another area of research is in transferring properties of blockchain to centralised databases and/or database properties to blockchains. For instance, BigchainDB [6] integrates properties of a blockchain into a database, while using an Asset as a key-concept. Asset represents a physical or digital entity which starts its' life in BigchainDB with CREATE Transaction and lives further using TRANSFER Transaction. Each Asset contains Metadata to specify details about the Asset. The Life-cycle of a BigchainDB Transaction is described in [8]. Each node in BigchainDB will have a MongoDb [11] instance and maintains same set of data. The Tendermint [15] is used as consensus protocol, which ensures the data safety even if $1/3$ of nodes are down in the network. Traditional database features, like indexing and query support are carried out through the underlying MongoDB.

Hyperledger [5] is a permissioned blockchain system focused on scalability, extensibility and flexibility through modular design. Different consensus algorithm can be configured to this solution (e.g., Kafka, RBFT, Sumeragi, and PoET) while smart contracts [2] can be programmed using platform called Chaincode with Golang [3]. Hyperledger uses Apache Kafka to facilitate private communication channels between the nodes. It can achieve up to 3,500 transactions per second in certain popular deployments. Work to support query [9] and indexing [10] on temporal data in blockchain using Hyperledger is also underway.

In conclusion, we reiterate that this study contributes to better understanding of the issues to be faced when selecting a database solution. We have carried out an exploratory implementation of a particular application (p2p energy trading) using both centralised database and a blockchian-based alternative, and reported the observations emerging from this experience.

References

1. Ethereum project (2019). https://www.ethereum.org/greeter/. Accessed 13 Feb 2019
2. Ethereum white paper: A next-generation smart contract and decentralized application platform (2019). https://github.com/ethereum/wiki/wiki/White-Paper. Accessed 13 Feb 2019
3. The go programming language (2019). https://golang.org/. Accessed 13 Feb 2019

4. Testnet ropsten (eth) blockchain explorer (2019). https://ropsten.etherscan.io/. Accessed 13 Feb 2019
5. Androulaki, E., et al.: Hyperledger fabric: a distributed operating system for permissioned blockchains. In: Proceedings of the Thirteenth EuroSys Conference, EuroSys 2018, pp. 30:1–30:15. ACM, New York (2018). https://doi.org/10.1145/3190508.3190538
6. BigchainDB: Bigchaindb..the blockchain database (2019). https://www.bigchaindb.com/. Accessed 14 Feb 2019
7. Chowdhury, M.J.M., Colman, A., Kabir, M.A., Han, J., Sarda, P.: Blockchain versus database: a critical analysis. In: 2018 17th IEEE International Conference on Trust, Security and Privacy in Computing and Communications/12th IEEE International Conference on Big Data Science and Engineering (TrustCom/BigDataSE), pp. 1348–1353, August 2018. https://doi.org/10.1109/TrustCom/BigDataSE.2018.00186
8. Dhameja, G.: Lifecycle of a bigchaindb transaction - the bigchaindb blog (2019). https://blog.bigchaindb.com/lifecycle-of-a-bigchaindb-transaction-c1e34331cbaa. Accessed 14 Feb 2019
9. Gupta, H., Hans, S., Aggarwal, K., Mehta, S., Chatterjee, B., Jayachandran, P.: Efficiently processing temporal queries on hyperledger fabric. In: 2018 IEEE 34th International Conference on Data Engineering (ICDE), pp. 1489–1494, April 2018. https://doi.org/10.1109/ICDE.2018.00167
10. Gupta, H., Hans, S., Mehta, S., Jayachandran, P.: On building efficient temporal indexes on hyperledger fabric. In: 2018 IEEE 11th International Conference on Cloud Computing (CLOUD), pp. 294–301, July 2018. https://doi.org/10.1109/CLOUD.2018.00044
11. MongoDB: Open source document database — mongodb (2019). https://www.mongodb.com/. Accessed 14 Feb 2019
12. MultiChain: Blockchains vs centralized databases (2019). https://www.multichain.com/blog/2016/03/blockchains-vs-centralized-databases/. Accessed 14 Feb 2019
13. Murkin, J., Chitchyan, R., Ferguson, D.: Goal-based automation of peer-to-peer electricity trading. In: Otjacques, B., Hitzelberger, P., Naumann, S., Wohlgemuth, V. (eds.) From Science to Society. PI, pp. 139–151. Springer, Cham (2018). https://doi.org/10.1007/978-3-319-65687-8_13
14. Nakamoto, S.: Bitcoin: A peer-to-peer electronic cash system (2008)
15. Tendermint: Blockchain consensus - tendermint (2019). https://tendermint.com/. Accessed 14 Feb 2019
16. Wust, K., Gervais, A.: Do you need a blockchain? In: 2018 Crypto Valley Conference on Blockchain Technology (CVCBT), pp. 45–54, June 2018. https://doi.org/10.1109/CVCBT.2018.00011

A Generic Framework for Flexible and Data-Aware Business Process Engines

Steven Mertens[(✉)], Frederik Gailly, and Geert Poels

Faculty of Economics and Business Administration, Ghent University,
Tweekerkenstraat 2, 9000 Ghent, Belgium
{steven.mertens,frederik.gailly,geert.poels}@ugent.be

Abstract. Business Process Management can be applied to improve the efficiency, efficacy and transparency of its processes. This paper focusses on processes that can be characterized as loosely framed and knowledge-intensive (e.g. diagnosis and treatment of a patient in a hospital). Declarative process modeling languages that incorporate decision logic are well suited to model these processes and tools for the automatic discovery of such models from the data in the current IT-systems are starting to appear. However, the resulting models are often difficult for humans to understand, which makes it hard to implement them. Process engines can help to overcome this problem, as they can handle the complexity of the model and support the users to correctly execute it. Process engines are common ground for imperative models, but the offerings on the declarative side are more limited. This paper uses the design science methodology to develop a generic framework for flexible and data-aware process engines. The declarative model supports the direct flexibility needs of the process actor during execution, and it also enables a more general flexibility of the information system as changes to the model can be enacted immediately. An implementation of proposed framework for the DeciClare language was created, DeciClareEngine, and demonstrated with the realistic arm fracture case.

Keywords: Business process engine · Knowledge-intensive processes · Declarative and data-aware process execution · Flexible information systems

1 Introduction

Loosely framed processes are processes that can be executed in a large, but finite, number of ways with all possible activities known in advance [1–3]. Example domains are healthcare (e.g., diagnosis and treatment of a patient), legal (e.g., preparing, arguing and pleading a case), helpdesk (e.g., finding a satisfactory solution) and air traffic control (e.g., deciding the priority for the arriving/departing planes). To model loosely framed processes, declarative process modeling languages are the preferred choice due to their implicit support for process flexibility [1, 3–5]. At the same time, these processes can also be classified as knowledge-intensive (KiP) [2, 3]: they require knowledge workers (e.g., doctors) to leverage their domain knowledge in search for an appropriate process variation for each case. Therefore, declarative modeling language should also incorporate some form of decision logic, as this allows the domain

© Springer Nature Switzerland AG 2019
H. A. Proper and J. Stirna (Eds.): CAiSE 2019 Workshops, LNBIP 349, pp. 201–213, 2019.
https://doi.org/10.1007/978-3-030-20948-3_18

knowledge to be captured that is essential to the execution of these processes. Declarative process models are often difficult for humans to create and to understand [6]. The innate complexity of the processes themselves is the leading cause, however, the absence of a clear path or flow through the models is a strong second. It is easy to lose sight of the overall process when confronted with a large set of constraints, of which each only applies to specific contexts that can vary widely from one constraint to the next. Moreover, it is hard to capture the tacit knowledge of knowledge workers, accumulated during years of experience, in an explicit process model manually (e.g., through interviews). Process mining techniques can be used to overcome this issue by (semi-)automatically creating models from historic data logs of the process, if available. With a model of the process available, whether it be an original or redesigned version of a manually or automatically created model, the next step is to make sure that future process executions are in conformance with the model. However, due to the afore-mentioned understandability issues, doing this manually is challenging.

A Business Process Engine (BPE) enables process actors to correctly execute process models by enacting them [7]. A BPE manages the workflow by monitoring and validating the execution, by showing an overview of the partially executed process instance and the restriction that currently apply based on the model, and by notifying the responsible process actors or automated services when needed. The complexity of the models is less of an issue for BPEs, because computers are well equipped for this type of complexity. Although there exist many BPEs for imperative process models, the offerings for declarative models are much more limited. Even more so if the BPE needs to be able to handle decision logic captured in the models, which represents the knowledge that is so vital to the correct execution of loosely framed KiPs in real-life.

This paper is part of a design science project and, more specifically, a design science cycle to develop the architecture of a business process management system for loosely framed KiPs. In previous work, we have created a modeling language specifically for this type of processes, called DeciClare [3], and developed an automated framework for creating DeciClare models by way of process mining [8]. The contribution of this paper is a generic and high-level framework to support the execution of declarative process models with a data perspective. This is achieved by automatically generating sets of activities that are allowed, conditionally allowed and disallowed as the next activity at each point during the execution of the process. The framework is generic because it does not assume a specific modeling language, but rather a large family of languages that can satisfy the language requirements stated in this paper. Consequently, the actual con-straint validation techniques and corresponding computational complexity are out of scope as they are language depend. The goal is to pave the way for flexible decision- and process-aware support for loosely frame and KiPs.

The remainder of this paper is structured as follows. The next section presents the problem statement as well as the requirements for the solution artifact. In Sect. 3, the generic framework is proposed based on the requirements from Sect. 2. This is fol-lowed by a brief description of the selected process modeling language in Sect. 4. Subsequently, the DeciClareEngine-tool is presented to demonstrate the implementa-tion of the framework in the context of a realistic healthcare process in Sect. 4. Section 6 gives an overview of the related research on this topic and the Sect. 7 concludes the paper and presents directions for future research.

2   Problem Statement and Solution Requirements

Declarative process models consist of many individual constraints and each of these constraints possibly applies to a different context. The result is that it can be very difficult for a user to quickly get an overview and find the process variation suitable for a certain process instance. This is largely due to the inherent nature of the processes being modeled, namely loosely framed KiPs. For example, consider the sheer number of possible diagnoses and treatments to the disposal of an emergency services doctor when a new patient arrives. The decision to follow a specific process variation is taken incrementally by the doctor during the process execution by choosing one or maybe a couple of activities to do next at a time. Because declarative models are hard to read or understand, there is no straightforward way in which they can be enacted directly by users.

A BPE is a software tool that offers supports the execution of a business process model. In this case, it should enact a declarative process model by creating a simplified summary for the users based on the specific process instance context. This summary will need to satisfy the following engine requirements (ER):

1. *The workflow control data containing the current state of each process instance (i.e., the already executed activities and used resources) should be available*
2. *The workflow relevant data of each process instance (e.g., age and gender of patient, presented symptoms...) should be available*
3. *All behavior allowed by the declarative model should be allowed*
4. *All behavior that violates the declarative model should be prohibited*

The four engine requirements above represent the foundation of a BPE. Depending on the expressive power of the declarative modeling language used to create the model, the resulting BPE can incorporate the control-flow, data and resource perspectives of the process. For loosely framed KiPs it remains essential that the freedom allowed by the given declarative model is not reduced by the BPE. The model does not need to be complete and the available constraints should be followed, but it should always present every option available according to the model. The BPE is not an expert system that replaces knowledge workers, but rather a tool to make their job easier.

To make the BPE more user-friendly, it would be useful to provide the user with an explanation of why certain activities are prohibited or will impose future restrictions and with some form of task list or description containing the constraints that still need to be satisfied by executing future activities:

5. *The reasons to why certain activities are not possible at certain times or in certain contexts should be available in the form of the constraint of the declarative model that would be violated*
6. *The restrictions that need to be dealt with later in the execution of the instance should be available to the users (e.g., execute activity X within 5 h)*
7. *A warning should be given for all behavior that potentially could lead to a live- or deadlock (prevention is even better, but not always computationally feasible depending on the used declarative process modeling language)*

BPEs require certain information about the process and its instances to be able to deliver useful results. Early BPEs were only concerned with the activities in a process and the relations between them [9]. Newer BPEs also add information about the resources involved in the process (e.g., personnel). ER3 and ER4 already require the BPE to keep track of the state and specific context of each process instance, but additional requirements are needed on the process model level to be able to create a data-aware declarative BPE. We summarized the informational needs in 8 language requirements (LR). If the process modeling language used to create the process model does not support these LRs, it might be possible to provide this information separate from the model.

1. *A set of all activities of the process*
2. *A set of all resources involved in the process*
3. *A set of all data elements involved in the process*
4. *The capabilities of each resource (e.g., a dialysis machine can be simultaneously used in maximally two process instances)*
5. *The availability of each resource (i.e., how many of this type of resource and when they are available for a process instance)*
6. *The relationships that apply between resources (e.g., a nurse can take on the role of both a scrub nurse and an OR nurse)*
7. *The relationships that apply between the activities and/or the resources (e.g., the patient must be registered before doing an examination and doing an examination requires a doctor and an examination room)*
8. *The decision logic, based on the data elements from LR3, that governs the relationships from LR5 and LR6*

3   Data-Aware Declarative Process Enactment Framework

The first two ERs from Sect. 2 are related to the process instance and are stored on the enactment level. ER1 can be satisfied by keeping a history for each process instance of steps performed and resources utilized. ER2 requires access to the information system of the organization to get the necessary data values and real-time resource usage stats. This is not trivial in real-life, but for the purpose of this paper we will assume that this data is directly available in the same format as defined in the declarative model.

The satisfactory execution of a process instance requires the joined efforts of the BPE and the knowledge workers of the process, because declarative models do not define explicit pathways to follow. The BPE takes on the role of relevant information provider and the knowledge workers use this information to make the decision on what to do next. The framework at the core of the BPE consists of two phases. In the first phase, the BPE uses the workflow relevant and control data (ER1 and ER2) to calculate the parts of the declarative model that apply specifically to the executing instance by looking at the decision logic and preconditions for each constraint (see Table 1). Note that vacuously satisfied constraints [10] should be included (perhaps separately) as they convey important information on possible future restrictions. In the second phase, the BPE calculates which activities are available based on this relevant subset of the process model (see Table 2). It is then up to the knowledge workers to make the actual decision on how to proceed. The decision to execute a certain activity next will prompt an update of the workflow control data and likely generate additional data, which in turn triggers the BPE to redo the two phases. This is repeated until an ending is reached.

The second phase creates five (unsorted) sets of activities, which we will call tiers:

(A) A set consisting of the activities that are available for execution as the next activity without any future restrictions applying.
(B) A set consisting of the activities that are available for execution as the next activity, but with future restrictions applying. These future restrictions come in the form of activities that are required or prohibited to be executed in the future so that the partial instance can be finished correctly.
(C) A set consisting of the activities that are available for execution as the next activity (i.e., tier A or B), but only if the active user is changed to another user.
(D) A set of the activities that are not available now but will be after a specified amount of time has elapsed (and will subsequently move to tier A or B).
(E) A set of the activities that are not available for execution as the next activity.

Table 1. The first phase of the framework of a declarative business process engine

Input: a declarative process model, the current state and current context of a process instance		
#	**Description**	**Req.**
1.	Make a set of all constraints in the declarative model	LR1-8
2.	Check which constraints are active for the process instance by comparing the process instance data with the decision logic of the constraints. Remove the inactive constraints from the list.	ER2
3.	Remove all constraints for which the prerequisites are not satisfied by the history of executed activities and used resources of this process instance.	ER1
	Output: a set of all constraints applicable to the given process instance	

These five tiers give an overview of the allowed and prohibited behavior. ER3 and ER4 are satisfied by allowing only the activities in tiers A and B to be executed next. All activities in tier B are subject to restrictions that need to be dealt with later in the process. In contrast to the activities in tier A, the BPE cannot guarantee that the activities in tier B will not lead to a live- or deadlock. By placing them in a separate tier, this serves as a warning for the user to keep an eye on these restrictions (ER7).

ER5 calls for information to help the knowledge workers executing the process to understand why an activity is in a certain tier. To fulfill this requirement, each activity in tier E will be accompanied with the constraints that would be violated by executing the activity next, which is a byproduct of the second step of the second phase. ER6 relates to the possible restrictions that apply to a certain partial instance and will need to be satisfied before the instance can finish in a correct way (e.g., X needs to be executed because Y has been executed). Fulfilling this requirement is a twofold process. Firstly, the constraints that result in these restrictions must be gathered. This set is already being composed as part of the second step of the second phase: the set of activity-restricting constraints. Secondly, the information needs to be made available to the user. The user needs to be able to view this set of restrictions, both for the current partial trace as well as for each activity from tier A and B (=the restrictions that would apply if this activity is selected as the next executed activity).

Table 2. The second phase of the framework of a declarative business process engine

	Input: a declarative process model and the output of the first phase
1.	Make set of all activities defined in the model, called the potential next-executed activities.

2.	For each activity in the set of potential next-executed activities:
	  For each constraint from the set of applicable constraints:
	    Validate that executing this potential next-executed activity would not violate the constraint.
	      If only satisfied if executed after waiting a finite amount of time, store the constraint in the set of time-violated constraints for this potential next-executed activity.
	      Else if only satisfied if future requirements are fulfilled, store the constraint in the set of activity-restricting constraints for this potential next-executed activity
	      Else if only satisfied if the active resource (=current user of the system) is a different resource than the current active resource, store the constraint in the set of resource-restricting constraints for this potential next-executed activity.
	      Else store constraint in the set of violated constraints for this potential next-executed activity.

3.	For each activity in the set of potential next-executed activities:
	  If the violated constraints set is not empty, add activity to tier E.
	  Else if the time-violated constraints set is not empty, add activity to tier D.
	  Else if the resource-restricting constraints set is not empty, add activity to tier C.
	  Else if the activity-restricting constraints set is not empty, add activity to tier B.
	  Else add activity to tier A.

	Output: tiers A, B, C, D and E

Additionally, some extra information about resource restrictions, time delays and deadlines that apply during the process execution can be added. Each activity in tiers C and D can be annotated with, respectively, the required user and the time delay that needs to be respected before it can move to tier A or B. The delay for a certain activity can be calculated by comparing the remainder of the current time minus the activation time and the delays as specified by the constraints in the set of time-violated constraints for that activity from the second phase. Activities in tiers A and B can be annotated with the deadlines, if applicable, before which each activity needs to be executed. The relevant deadline can be calculated as the lowest deadline from the constraints in the set of activity-restricting constraints from the second step of the second phase, compared to the current time and taking into account the activation time of each of these constraints. Also, the subset of constraints from the full declarative model that apply to the current partial trace and for each activity in tier A and B can be made available, so that the user can review only those constraints that actually matter in this process instance. Again, we would preferably include the vacuously satisfied constraints separately, as these could be interesting when considering future restrictions.

Finally, there is one more possible scenario to be considered. As constraints can have deadlines before which they need to be satisfied, it is possible that a deadline is not satisfied (i.e., the necessary activities are not execute in time). This causes a deadlock. A BPE cannot directly prevent this, as user input is required for executing activities and it is the user's responsibility to monitor the deadlines as shown by the BPE.

4   Process Definition: DeciClare

DeciClare is a mixed-perspective declarative process and decision modeling language that specifically targets loosely framed KiPs [3]. It can be used to create detailed models of the control-flow, data and resource aspects of these processes. This paper uses a direct instantiation (i.e., a temporary visual syntax in a textual format) of the abstract syntax (ars.els-cdn.com/content/image/1-s2.0-S0957417417304414-mmc3.zip), as a real visual syntax has not yet been developed at this time. The foundation of DeciClare is the Declare language and most of its extensions [11–13], which are either incorporated in a direct or generalized way. Therefore, Declare models can be easily converted to equivalent DeciClare models [3]. Additionally, more perspectives were added as well as concepts from the DMN language [14]. The latter makes the resulting language 'data-aware', because data values can be used to (de)activate constraints based on the specific execution context, and capable of modeling the decision logic that typically governs KiPs. DeciClare supports 36 constraint templates (i.e., types of constraints) spanning four template classes: existence, relation, resource and data. 26 of these templates have time parameters expressing the time interval in which the constraint applies. For a complete explanation of DeciClare, we refer the reader to [3].

The current implementation of the DeciClareEngine-tool presented in this paper supports the 18 most important constraint templates of DeciClare (Supported templates and examples at github.com/stevmert/DeciClareBPMS/blob/master/engine/support.pdf). A DeciClare model can contain all the information necessary to satisfy LR1-8 from Sect. 2. Activities, resources and all their relations can be fully modeled, and the constraints can be enriched with activation and deactivation decisions, based on the data elements, to allow for a level of detail that closely matches reality.

5   Demonstration: DeciClareEngine

The DeciClareEngine tool (github.com/stevmert/DeciClareBPMS/blob/master/engine/releases/DeciClareEngine.jar, the code can also be found on this GitHub) has been developed to demonstrate how the generic framework from the previous section can be implemented. It is a data-aware declarative BPE that takes a DeciClare model as input. This means that it supports the control-flow, decision logic, time restrictions, resource authorizations and resource usages of the given process model.

When starting the BPE, the user first needs to select the role he or she will take on during the process instance before the main interface opens. At the top of the screen (left side of Fig. 1), the current time and user (=current resource) can be found as well as the current partial trace. The tiers A to E are displayed in the middle of the screen. And at the bottom of the screen, all data elements used in the model are listed with the option to add or change them for the current instance. The user can execute an activity from tier A or B by clicking on it. This prompts a screen where the user can enter the duration of the activity and change the data elements as part of the activity execution (right side of Fig. 1). The 'Explanation'-button next to the activities in tiers B, C, D and E presents the user with a set of the specific constraints that caused the activity to be placed in that specific tier (i.e., future restrictions or violations). Note that delays and

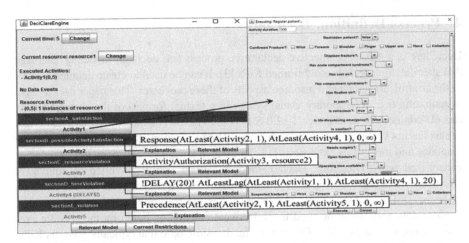

Fig. 1. The main interface (left), with added explanations, and activity execution dialog (right)

deadlines are signaled next to the activity name and that their current status can be checked at any time as part of the explanation. To get the subset of constraints that are currently active, the user can click on the 'Relevant model'-button at the bottom of the screen or next to the corresponding activity. Vacuously satisfied constraints are included in this summary, although they are not yet display separately.

As the example model, we will use the healthcare process for treating arm-related fractures (github.com/stevmert/DeciClareBPMS/blob/master/engine/models/ArmFrac-tureCase_DeciClareModel.txt) presented in [3]. It is a realistic, but simplified, representation of the registration, diagnosis and treatment of patients with one or more (possible) fractures of the fingers, hands, wrists, forearms, upper arms, shoulders and collarbones in an emergency department of a hospital. The DeciClare model contains 229 constraints, of which 183 are supported by the current version of the tool. The process instance used to demonstrate the tool is of a 24-year-old woman who enters the emergency services with pain in her wrist after a bicycle accident. Every activity of the process is listed in the first column of Table 3. The other columns are snapshots (Sx) (i.e., 0–13) showing in which tier each activity was placed by the BPE at that time in the process. S0 is the moment that the patient walks in the emergency room, with the receptionist as active user. The receptionist is not authorized to execute 7 of the 8 available activities, all of which come with future restrictions. The triage nurse takes a quick peek at the patient and concludes that her condition is not life-threatening, triggering the corresponding data event. This reduces the number of available activities to just one (S1), because only in the worst cases it is possible to skip the registration at the start. Next, the patient is registered at the reception, during which the receptionist sets the four data attributes relevant to the process (i.e., been to this hospital before, older than 14 years old, not bedridden and conscious) and the used resources (i.e., receptionist and reception desk). The user is currently asked to input the duration, data events and resource events of the executed activity (right side of Fig. 1), but in real settings this data should be extracted directly from the applications used to capture this data. Once registered, 7 activities become available, but the receptionist is only authorized to unregister the patient (S2). At this point, the active user is switched to a doctor, who is authorized to execute the 6 other activities (S3). By looking at the future restrictions that apply to the current partial instance, the doctor can see that several activities are now mandatory for this instance: unregistering the patient, taking a medical history, doing a clinical examination, taking an X-ray, applying ice, choosing a treatment and giving some pain relief. The doctor decides to proceed by letting a nurse take the patient's medical history, triggering two more data events (i.e., no current cast or fixation on the wrist in question) and one resource event (i.e., nurse used). Taking the medical history of the patient unlocks an additional activity in tier B: doing a clinical examination (S4). This is also the activity the doctor chooses to do next, which in turn triggers four more data events (i.e., suspected fracture of wrist, swollen, in pain and not an open fracture) and two resource events (i.e., uses doctor and exam room). S5 has 18 available activities. Because the doctor indicated that the patient is in pain, she can now receive some pain relief. After giving her a NSAID painkiller, 17 activities become available (S6). Note that prescribing anticoagulants is in tier D because there must be at least 12 h between receiving NSAID painkillers and receiving anticoagulants. 12 h later, this activity would move back to tier B.

Table 3. An overview of the activities and the tier in which they were placed for each snapshot

	Receptionist		Doctor										Receptionist	
	0	1	2	3	4	5	6	7	8	9	10	11	12	13
Register patient	B	**B**	E	E	E	E	E	E	E	E	E	E	E	E
Take medical history of patient	C	E	C	**B**	B	B	B	B	B	B	B	B	C	E
Clinical examination of patient	C	E	E	E	**B**	B	B	B	B	B	B	B	C	E
Doctor consultation	E	E	E	E	E	E	B	B	B	**B**	B	B	C	E
Take X-ray	E	E	E	E	E	E	B	B	**B**	B	B	B	C	E
Take CT scan	E	E	E	E	E	E	B	B	B	B	B	B	C	E
Prescribe NSAID painkillers	E	E	E	E	E	**B**	B	B	B	B	B	B	C	E
Prescribe SAID painkillers	E	E	E	E	E	B	B	B	B	B	B	B	C	E
Prescribe anticoagulants	E	E	E	E	E	B	D	D	D	D	D	D	D	E
Prescribe stomach protecting drug	E	E	E	E	E	B	B	B	B	B	B	B	C	E
Prescribe rest (=no treatment)	E	E	E	E	E	B	B	B	B	B	B	B	C	E
Apply ice	C	E	C	B	B	B	**B**	B	B	B	B	B	C	E
Apply cast	E	E	E	E	E	E	E	E	B	B	B	B	C	E
Remove cast	E	E	E	E	E	E	E	E	E	E	E	E	E	E
Apply splint	C	E	C	B	B	B	B	B	B	B	**B**	B	C	E
Apply sling	C	E	C	B	B	B	B	B	B	**B**	B	B	C	E
Apply fixation	E	E	E	E	E	E	E	E	B	B	B	B	C	E
Remove fixation	E	E	E	E	E	E	E	E	E	E	E	E	E	E
Apply bandage	C	E	C	B	B	B	B	B	B	B	B	B	C	E
Apply figure of eight bandage	E	E	E	E	E	E	E	E	B	B	B	B	C	E
Perform surgery	E	E	E	E	E	E	E	E	B	B	B	B	C	E
Apply intra-compartmental pressure monitor	E	E	E	E	E	B	B	B	B	B	B	B	C	E
Let patient rest	C	E	C	B	B	B	B	B	B	B	B	B	B	E
Stay in patient room	E	E	E	E	E	B	B	B	B	B	B	B	C	E
Unregister patient	E	E	B	C	C	C	C	C	C	C	C	C	**A**	E

By taking another look at the future restriction that currently apply, the doctor can see that three activities are still mandatory for this instance: unregistering the patient, applying ice and taking an X-ray. The former is straightforward, but the latter two are due to the specific context of the case. Ice treatment is needed because the wrist is swollen and the X-ray to take a closer look at the patient's wrist. The doctor decides to do the ice treatment first. S7 offers the same options as the previous one and now the X-ray is selected, triggering two more resource events (i.e., nurse and X-ray room used). This results in four additional activities becoming available (S8). A doctor consultation to discuss the scan is now a mandatory, as stated in the current restrictions, so the doctor does this consultation next. During the consultation (using a doctor and an exam room), the doctor confirms the suspected wrist fracture by looking at the X-ray photo but, luckily, also that it is not a displaced or unstable fracture. This means that surgery is not required. The same activities are available in S9, yet it is now mandatory to apply a sling and a cast/splint in the future. The doctor decides to apply a splint next, which triggers another resource event (nurse used). Again, the same activities are available afterwards (S10). So now the doctor applies a sling to support the splinted wrist of the patient. In S11, the same activities are available, but the only current restriction now is that the patient will need to be unregistered in the future. The doctor decides that the patient can go home, so she is asked to go and unregister at the reception. The active user is now switched to the receptionist again (S12), which moves unregistering the patient from tier D to tier A (and 19 others from B to D). This means that no restrictions will remain after its execution. Finally, the receptionist unregisters the patient, triggering two more resource events (receptionist and reception desk used). No activities are available in S12, and the instance is in a conforming state according to the process model, so the user gets a message that the process has ended successfully.

6 Related Research

The existing BPEs can be classified according to the predictability-spectrum of the processes for which they are best suited. In this section, the differences between the DeciClareEngine-tool, used in the demonstration of this paper, and each of the existing BPEs that target loosely framed processes will be highlighted in more detail.

The DECLARE framework is based on the Declare language [11], for which efficient techniques for the actual validation of (MP-)Declare constraints have been proposed [16]. Everything that can be expressed in Declare, can be expressed in the DeciClare language used in this paper [3]. Yet, the opposite is not true as DeciClare adds a data and resource perspective as well as an explicit concept of time in the form of deadlines and delays. So, compared to the DECLARE framework, DeciClareEngine additionally takes decision logic, resources, deadlines and delays into account. More recently, a BPE for the MP-Declare language was proposed that maps the constraints to Alloy and uses the corresponding satisfiability solver [15]. This approach can prevent live- and deadlocks. However, it is only feasible for very small models (e.g., 10 constraints) due to the computation complexity that results from the state space explosion. DeciClareEngine has no support for this yet, but this feature will be revisited in the future. Models of loosely framed KiPs are typically big and complex. Therefore, we will focus on investigating partial or heuristic versions of these features in future work.

ReFlex is a BPE that uses a graph-based rule engine to overcome certain limitations of Linear Temporal Logic (LTL), as is used by the Declare language. It uses 7 types of edges that correspond to 6 constraint templates of Declare and 1 extra type of constraint. DeciClare, and therefore DeciClareEngine, also supports these 7 types of constraints and additionally offers support for time delays and deadlines, and a data and resource perspective. The selling point of ReFlex is also the detection of live- and deadlocks.

DCR Graphs have an online platform that includes a BPE as part of the graph editor (for simulation). The DCR language has 6 relations (roughly equivalent to the Response and Precedence templates of DeciClare) and a clear visual syntax with support for hierarchical modeling. The simplicity of DCR Graphs is good for human understanding but limits its expressive power, although a data perspective [17] and some time-concepts (in DCR 2.0) have been added recently. DeciClare has additional support for more complex constraints, general context data elements, changing values of data attributes during the process execution and deadlines. On a functional level, the DCR Graphs BPE is quite similar to the prototype presented as demonstration of this paper, albeit based on a less expressive language and with a much more polished interface. There is no academic description of how the DCR Graphs BPE works internally, although a demonstration is provided in [18]. The contribution of our paper is the generic framework to base this kind of BPE on, which has not been published before.

7 Conclusion and Future Research

This paper proposes a generic framework for creating data-aware declarative BPEs and demonstrates it by applying it to create a BPE for the DeciClare process modeling language. A BPE based on the proposed framework can support the execution of a real-life loosely framed KiPs, taking into account the control-flow, data and resource perspectives and corresponding decision logic governing them.

Due to the complexity and understandability issues of declarative languages, declarative models are seldom useful during the execution of processes. A BPE can be used to support the process actors during the execution of the process model by offering a process-aware view on what has been done already, what can or cannot be done next and what will need to or cannot happen in the future. The main advantage of using a BPE for the execution of a process is, of course, the certainty of conformance to a predefined process model. However, it can also be the foundation for a truly flexible information system, because it enables the rapid deployment of process changes in dynamic environments. Just make the necessary changes to the underlying process model. The BPE allows for these changes to be communicated to all process actors and at the same time enforce that the changes are being implemented correctly.

In addition to offering runtime support, BPEs are also an essential tool for process simulation. Simulation makes it possible to analyze the impact of different runtime decisions or changes to the process model itself on the process outcome or characteristic. Another way to use model simulation, would be to validate a model that is the result of process mining or interviews. Historical or fictitious process instances can be simulated using the BPE, allowing domain experts to validate the process model in specific and more relatable contexts. This type of model validation is similar to how [19] uses Alloy to simulate OntoUML models to validate that the model allows all wanted interpretations, while excluding the unwanted ones. It is also a powerful tool for educational purposes. The current education for doctors and other medical personnel leans heavily on internships so that the trainee can learn on the job from more experienced personnel. An educational simulator offers the trainee an additional tool to learn how things are done in a certain hospital and gain valuable experience in a risk-free environment. By using a mined process model that includes decision logic, it even has the potential to reveal (some of) the tacit knowledge of experienced colleagues to the trainee without a need for any direct interaction with those colleagues or patients.

The current design cycle of our research project is not finished yet. DeciClareEngine will be further refined by: (1) Adding support for the missing constraint templates and deactivation decisions, (2) Adding support for dynamic resource availabilities on process instance level, (3) Adding support for parallel execution of activities and (4) Investigating partial live- or deadlock detection or prevention mechanisms. The next step in this project is to make the runtime support of DeciClareEngine smarter. A first experimental iteration of this step has been performed in [20] and is being repeated with DeciClare and the DeciClareEngine tool. Where DeciClareEngine presents the user with unsorted set of possible next activities, an additional layer will rank and annotate the activities according to historic probabilities or specific optimization goals.

References

1. van der Aalst, W.M.P.: Business process management: a comprehensive survey. ISRN Softw. Eng. **2013**, 1–37 (2013)
2. Di Ciccio, C., Marrella, A., Russo, A.: Knowledge-intensive processes: characteristics, requirements and analysis of contemporary approaches. J. Data Semant. **4**, 29–57 (2015)
3. Mertens, S., Gailly, F., Poels, G.: Towards a decision-aware declarative process modeling language for knowledge-intensive processes. Expert Syst. Appl. **87**, 316–334 (2017)
4. Goedertier, S., Vanthienen, J., Caron, F.: Declarative business process modelling: principles and modelling languages. Enterp. Inf. Syst. **9**, 161–185 (2015)
5. van der Aalst, W.M.P., Pesic, M., Schonenberg, H.: Declarative workflows: balancing between flexibility and support. Comput. Sci. - Res. Dev. **23**, 99–113 (2009)
6. Haisjackl, C., Barba, I., Zugal, S., Soffer, P., Hadar, I., Reichert, M., et al.: Understanding declare models: strategies, pitfalls, empirical results. Softw. Syst. Model. **15**, 1–28 (2014)
7. Dumas, M., van der Aalst, W.M.P., ter Hofstede, A.H.M.: Process-Aware Information Systems: Bridging People and Software through Process Technology. Wiley, Hoboken (2005)
8. Mertens, S., Gailly, F., Poels, G.: Discovering health-care processes using DeciClareMiner. Heal. Syst. - Spec. Issue SIG-Health Des. Innov. Impact Healthc. IT. **7**, 195–211 (2018)
9. van der Aalst, W.M.P.: Three good reasons for using a petri-net-based workflow management system. In: Wakayama, T., Kannapan, S., Khoong, C.M., Navathe, S., Yates, J. (eds.) Information and Process Integration in Enterprises. SECS, vol. 428, pp. 161–182. Springer, Boston (1998). https://doi.org/10.1007/978-1-4615-5499-8_10

10. Maggi, F.M., Montali, M., Di Ciccio, C., Mendling, J.: Semantic vacuity detection in declarative process mining. In: La Rosa, M., Loos, P., Pastor, O. (eds.) BPM 2016. LNCS, vol. 9850, pp. 158–175. Springer, Cham (2016). https://doi.org/10.1007/978-3-319-45348-4_10
11. Pesic, M.: Constraint-based workflow management systems: shifting control to users (2008)
12. Westergaard, M., Maggi, F.M.: Looking into the future: using timed automata to provide a priori advice about timed declarative process models. In: Meersman, R., et al. (eds.) OTM 2012. LNCS, vol. 7565, pp. 250–267. Springer, Heidelberg (2012). https://doi.org/10.1007/978-3-642-33606-5_16
13. Jiménez-Ramírez, A., Barba, I., del Valle, C., Weber, B.: Generating multi-objective optimized business process enactment plans. In: Salinesi, C., Norrie, M.C., Pastor, Ó. (eds.) CAiSE 2013. LNCS, vol. 7908, pp. 99–115. Springer, Heidelberg (2013). https://doi.org/10.1007/978-3-642-38709-8_7
14. Object Management Group: Decision Model and Notation (DMN1.0) (2014)
15. Ackermann, L., Schönig, S., Petter, S., Schützenmeier, N., Jablonski, S.: Execution of multi-perspective declarative process models. In: Panetto, H., Debruyne, C., Proper, H., Ardagna, C., Roman, D., Meersman, R. (eds.) On the Move to Meaningful Internet Systems. LNCS, vol. 11230, pp. 154–172. Springer, Cham (2018). https://doi.org/10.1007/978-3-030-02671-4_9
16. Burattin, A., Maggi, F.M., Sperduti, A.: Conformance checking based on multi-perspective declarative process models. Expert Syst. Appl. **65**, 194–211 (2016)
17. Mukkamala, R.R.: A Formal Model For Declarative Workflows (2012)
18. Marquard, M., Shahzad, M., Slaats, T.: Web-based modelling and collaborative simulation of declarative processes. In: Motahari-Nezhad, H.R., Recker, J., Weidlich, M. (eds.) BPM 2015. LNCS, vol. 9253, pp. 209–225. Springer, Cham (2015). https://doi.org/10.1007/978-3-319-23063-4_15
19. Benevides, A., et al.: Validating modal aspects of OntoUML conceptual models using automatically generated visual word structures. J. Univ. Comput. Sci. **16**, 2904 (2010)
20. Mertens, S., Gailly, F., Poels, G.: Generating business process recommendations with a population-based meta-heuristic. In: Fournier, F., Mendling, J. (eds.) BPM 2014. LNBIP, vol. 202, pp. 516–528. Springer, Cham (2015). https://doi.org/10.1007/978-3-319-15895-2_44

Building Information Systems Using Collaborative-Filtering Recommendation Techniques

Phuong T. Nguyen[✉], Juri Di Rocco, and Davide Di Ruscio

Department of Information Engineering, Computer Science and Mathematics,
Università degli Studi dell'Aquila, Via Vetoio 2, 67100 L'Aquila, Italy
{phuong.nguyen,juri.dirocco,davide.diruscio}@univaq.it

Abstract. IoT-technologies allow for the connection of miscellaneous devices, thereby creating a platform that sustains rich data sources. Given the circumstances, it is essential to have decent machinery in order to exploit the existing infrastructure and provide users with personalized services. Among others, recommender systems have been widely used to suggest users additional items that best match their needs and expectation. The use of recommender systems has gained considerable momentum in recent years. Nevertheless, the selection of a proper recommendation technique depends much on the input data as well as the domain of applications. In this work, we present an evaluation of two well-known collaborative-filtering (CF) techniques to build an information system for managing and recommending books in the IoT context. To validate the performance, we conduct a series of experiments on two considerably large datasets. The experimental results lead us to some interesting conclusions. In contrast to many existing studies which state that the item-based CF technique outperforms the user-based CF technique, we found out that there is no distinct winner between them. Furthermore, we confirm that the performance of a CF recommender system may be good with regards to some quality metrics, but not to some others.

Keywords: IoT · Recommender systems · Collaborative-filtering · Book recommendation

1 Introduction

The proliferation of IoT-technologies in recent years has enabled numerous applications and introduced a vast amount of information. Such source of information can be properly managed and mined only if there are suitable tools and machineries. Otherwise, given that huge amount of information, users would struggle

The research described in this paper has been carried out as part of the CROSSMINER Project, EU Horizon 2020 Research and Innovation Programme, grant agreement No. 732223.

© Springer Nature Switzerland AG 2019
H. A. Proper and J. Stirna (Eds.): CAiSE 2019 Workshops, LNBIP 349, pp. 214–226, 2019.
https://doi.org/10.1007/978-3-030-20948-3_19

to look for and approach the sources that meet their demand, in the hope of transforming them to practical knowledge. In other words, *"we are drowning in information but starved for knowledge."*[1] In this sense, the deployment of flexible information systems, which exploit existing data to improve user experience is of paramount importance. To this end, the realization of techniques and tools to build such systems has attracted a lot of attention from the research community recently.

The inspiration for our work arose from the need for a flexible system that collects and processes information of readers' preferences coming from various sources as shown in Fig. 1. The ultimate aim is to assist new readers in finding books which best match their preferences. In a nutshell, our system helps readers find books that are most relevant to those in their profile. This is a step towards building a digital library working in the IoT infrastructure [25].

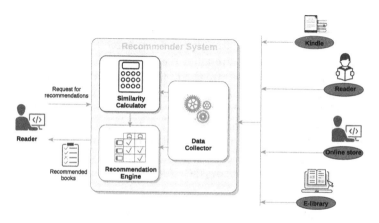

Fig. 1. A book information system in the IoT context.

In recent years, research in Recommender Systems (RSs) has empowered several applications. RSs are a means to provide users with highly relevant information to their profile as well as current context. For instance, RSs have been deployed to recommend a wide range of things, such as movies [9], music [15,17], books [21], to name a few. Among others, collaborative-filtering (CF) techniques keep gaining popularity due to their simplicity but effectiveness: CF recommendation is still among the most successful and widely used techniques for building recommender systems [13], as by Amazon [14]. A CF recommender system works on the basis of a user-item ratings matrix [24]. Specifically, in the matrix a user is represented by a row, an item is represented by a column and each cell in the matrix corresponds to a rating given by a user for an item [19]. Given a customer, a CF recommender system suggests products that customers with similar preference have already purchased. The representation using a user-item ratings

---

[1] ***John Naisbitt***, *researcher of future studies.*

matrix allows for two main ways to compute missing ratings [2,19], namely the user-based CF [30], hereafter ubCF and the item-based [24] CF techniques, hereafter ibCF. Through a careful observation, we end up adopting both techniques since they work on the premise that *"if customers agree about the quality or relevance of some items, then they will likely agree about other items"* [26], and thus being suitable for our purpose.

In this sense, our paper has the following contributions: *(i)* Presenting a comprehensive evaluation of an information system for recommending online books; *(ii)* Comparing the performance of the user-based CF and that of the item-based CF technique. The paper is organized as follows: In Sect. 2, we summarize the related work. Section 3 recalls the two CF techniques, i.e., ubCF and ibCF. The whole evaluation is described in Sect. 4. Finally, Sect. 5 concludes the paper.

2 Related Work

Recommender engines are a staple element of several information systems, serving to introduce products that match well with customers' expectation [14]. The development of such systems has brought in several well-defined recommendation techniques which in turn demonstrate their effectiveness also in related domains, e.g., entertainment industry [6,10]. We summarize the most notable studies that address the related issues in Table 1. This table lists information concerning datasets as well as the evaluation metrics. Due to space limits, we depict only the alias of datasets as well as metrics, and interested readers are referred to the original papers for a complete description. We also recall the technique that gains a better performance (**Better CF**). As can be seen, most of the studies

Table 1. Summary of some notable related work.

Study	Dataset	Metrics	Better CF
Karypis et al. [13]	Ecommerce, Catalog, Ccard, Skills, Movielens	Success rate	ibCF
Cacheda et al. [5]	Movielens, Netflix	MAE, RMSE, Coverage, GIM, GPIM	ibCF
Sarwar et al. [24]	Movielens	MAE	ibCF
Papagelis et al. [22]	Movie Recommendation System (MRS)	MAE	ibCF
Deshpande et al. [8]	Ctlg1, Ctlg2, Ctlg3, Ccard, Ecmrc, Em, Movielens, Skill	Success rate, ARHR	ibCF
Jalili et al. [12]	Movielens, Epinions, LastFM, BookCrossing, Jester	Accuracy, Diversity, Novelty, Unified Metric	none

find out that ibCF gains a superior performance compared to ubCF [5,13,22]. For instance, *Papagelis et al.* [22] conduct an evaluation on a movie dataset with 2068 ratings for 641 movies by 114 users, the authors found out that ibCF has a superior quality than that of ubCF with respect to Mean Absolute Error (MAE). Only *Jalili et al.* [12] have a different conclusion where they discover that none of ubCF and ibCF gains a distinctly better performance.

3   BookRec: A Book Recommender System

The core of CF techniques is a matrix that stores all the ratings given by all users, thus yielding the name user-item ratings matrix. To compute missing ratings, memory-based algorithms make use of the whole matrix [5], and depending on the information exploited for the recommendation process, there are two types of memory-based algorithms, i.e., ubCF and ibCF. In particular, ubCF computes missing ratings by exploiting the row-wise relationships among similar users, whereas ibCF does the same task by using the column-wise similarities among items.

3.1   User-Based Collaborative Filtering

Figure 2(a) depicts a user-item matrix with u_a being the active user. An asterisk (∗) represents a known rating, whereas a question mark (?) represents an unknown rating and needs to be predicted. By ubCF [11,30], the preference of u_a for additional items is deduced from users similar to u_a.

The horizontal rectangles in Fig. 2(a) imply that the row-wise relationships between u_a and the similar users u_1, u_2, u_3 are exploited to compute the missing ratings for u_a as follows [22]:

$$r_{u_a,b} = \overline{r_u} + \frac{\sum_{u_i \in\ topsim(u_a)}(r_{u_i,b} - \overline{r_{u_i}}) \cdot sim(u_a, u_i)}{\sum_{q \in\ topsim(u_i)} sim(u_a, u_i)} \qquad (1)$$

where $\overline{r_{u_a}}$ and $\overline{r_{u_i}}$ are the average rating of u_a and u_i, respectively; u_i belongs to the set of *top-k* most similar users of u_a, denoted as $topsim(p)$; $sim(u_a, u_i)$ is the similarity between u_a and a user u_v, and it is computed using Eq. 2. Different from conventional approaches that compute similarity using the

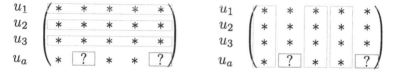

(a) User-based CF technique   (b) Item-based CF technique

Fig. 2. Collaborative-filtering techniques.

Pearson or Spearman indices [22], we adopt the approach in [9] to compute similarities as follows. Given that user u has rated a set of books $(b_1, b_2, .., b_n)$, the features of u are represented by a vector $\overrightarrow{\phi} = (\phi_1, \phi_2, .., \phi_n)$, with ϕ_j being the weight of node b_j. It is computed as the term-frequency inverse document frequency function as follows: $\phi_j = f_{b_j} * log(\frac{|U|}{a_{b_j}})$; where f_{b_j} is the number of occurrence of b_j with respect to u, it can be either 0 and 1; $|U|$ is the number of users; a_{b_j} is the number of users that rate b_j. The similarity between users u and v with their corresponding feature vectors $\overrightarrow{\phi} = \{\phi_j\}_{j=1,..,n}$ and $\overrightarrow{\omega} = \{\omega_j\}_{j=1,..,n}$ is computed as given below [9]:

$$sim(u, v) = \frac{\sum_{i=1}^{n} \phi_j \times \omega_j}{\sqrt{\sum_{j=1}^{n}(\phi_j)^2} \times \sqrt{\sum_{j=1}^{n}(\omega_j)^2}} \tag{2}$$

3.2 Item-Based Collaborative Filtering

Similar to Fig. 2(a), the vertical rectangles in Fig. 2(b) represent the column-wise relationships between the active book b. The following formula is exploited to predict if u_a should like b or not [22]:

$$r_{u_a,b} = \overline{r_b} + \frac{\sum_{c \in rated(u_a)}(r_{u_a,c} - \overline{r_{ua}}) \cdot sim(b, c)}{\sum_{c \in rated(u_a)} sim(b, c)} \tag{3}$$

where $sim(b, c)$ is the similarity between book b and c; $rated(u_a)$ is the set of books that have been rated by user u_a. The final outcome of the recommendation process is a ranked list of books that are relevant to the active user. We built BookRec, a recommender system to provide booklovers with highly relevant items, exploiting both CF techniques mentioned above. To facilitate future research, we made available the tool and the datasets used in our evaluation in GitHub.[2]

4 Evaluation

At a certain point in time, we came across the question: Which technique is the most suitable one for recommending books? According to our investigation, it seems that ibCF obtains a better performance as shown in several existing studies [5,8,13,22,24]. However, we believe that there is still the need to study the suitability of the two techniques for the book domain. In particular, we conduct an empirical study on two datasets: BookCrossing [31] and Goodbooks [29]. To thoroughly study the performance, we make use of different quality indicators, i.e., accuracy (precision, recall, and nDCG), diversity (entropy, coverage), and novelty (EPC) [16].

This section explains our evaluation in detail. We describe the datasets used in Sect. 4.1. A set of quality indicators is introduced in Sect. 4.2. Section 4.3 presents the experimental results. Finally, Sect. 4.4 outlines some lessons learned from the evaluation.

---

[2] https://github.com/BookRec/BookRec/.

4.1 Datasets

We collected two datasets for the book domain: `BookCrossing`[3] and `Goodbooks`[4]. By the former, there are $278,858$ users, $271,379$ books, and $1,149,788$ ratings. By the latter, there are $53,424$ users, $10,000$ books, and $5,976,479$ ratings. Sparsity is computed as $1 - nR/nI * nU$, where nR, nI, and nU are the number of ratings, items, and users, respectively [22]. The user-item matrices by both datasets are extremely sparse as most users rate a small ratio of the books. To foster an efficient evaluation, we downsized the matrices by selecting users with a considerably high number of ratings and we got two subsets as described in Table 2.

Table 2. Statistics of the datasets.

	BookCrossing	Goodbooks
# of users	$11,692$	$10,325$
# of books	$143,183$	$9,907$
# of ratings	$295,390$	$982,986$
Sparsity	99.98%	99.03%

Furthermore, to exploit users' profiles and facilitate the computation of the quality indicators mentioned in Sect. 4.2, we map five-star or ten-star scores to binary ratings. In practice, this means we are interested in whether a user likes or does not like a book. Given a user u with the mean rating $\hat{r}(u)$, the ratings are normalized by means of the following formula [9]:

$$
profile(u) = \begin{cases} (b_j, v_j)|v_j = 1, (u, b_j) \geq \hat{r}(u) \\ (b_j, v_j)|v_j = -1, otherwise \end{cases}
$$

4.2 Metrics

It is necessary to utilize a set of *quality indicators* to quantify various aspects of the recommendation results [13,24]. For the book domain, besides accuracy, we believe that the ability to provide diverse and novel recommendations is important. We call $REC(u)$ as the *top-N* items recommended to u. It is a ranked list in descending order of real scores, with $REC_r(u)$ being the recommended book at position r; k is the number of neighbour users considered for the recommendation process. Given a testing user u, a half of the rated books is extracted and used as the ground-truth data, or as *gt(u)*; $match(u) = gt(u) \bigcap REC(u)$ is the set of items that match with those in *gt(u)*. Thus, the metrics utilized to measure the recommendations are explained as follows.

---

[3] http://www2.informatik.uni-freiburg.de/~cziegler/BX/.
[4] https://github.com/zygmuntz/goodbooks-10k.

Accuracy. The ability to return accurate items is important for Information Retrieval applications [23]. Considering a list of *top-N* books, *precision@N* and *recall@N* together with *Normalized Discounted Cumulative Gain* are utilized to measure the accuracy of the recommendation results.

Precision and Recall precision@N is the ratio of the *top-N* recommended items belonging to the ground-truth dataset, whereas recall@N is the ratio of the ground-truth items appearing in the N recommended items [7,11,17]:

$$precision@N(u) = \frac{|match(u)|}{N} \tag{4}$$

$$recall@N(u) = \frac{|match(u)|}{|gt(u)|} \tag{5}$$

Normalized Discounted Cumulative Gain. Precision and recall reflect well the accuracy, however they neglect ranking sensitivity [4,20]. nDCG has been devised as an effective measure to remedy this, for binary ratings, it is computed with this formula:

$$nDCG@N(u) = \frac{1}{iDCG} \cdot \sum_{r=1}^{N} \frac{rel(u,r)}{log_2(r+1)} \tag{6}$$

where iDCG is a normalized factor; $rel(u,r) = 1$ if $b_r \in gt(u)$, 0 otherwise. nDCG reveals if a system is capable of presenting highly relevant items on the top of the list.

Diversity. In business, it is important to improve the coverage as also the distribution of products across customers, thus increasing the chance that products get sold by being introduced [28]. In the scope of this paper, we employ coverage and entropy to gauge diversity. Let B be the set of all books available for recommendation, $\#rec(b)$ denote the number of users getting b as a recommendation, i.e., $\#rec(b) = count_{u \in U}(|(\cup_{r=1}^{N} REC_r(u)) \ni b|)$, $b \in B$, *total* denote the total number of *top-N* recommendations across all users, the metrics are defined as follows:

Coverage. The ability to provide a wide range of items is not only expected but helpful [13]. However, accuracy does not reveal coverage since a system can recommend accurate items but the set of recommendations may be small. To this end, coverage measures the percentage of items being recommended:

$$coverage@N(u) = \frac{|\cup_{u \in U} \cup_{r=1}^{N} REC_r(u)|}{|B|} \tag{7}$$

Entropy. The metric is used to evaluate if the recommendations are concentrated on only a small set of items or spread across a wide range of items [1]:

$$entropy@N(u) = -\sum_{b \in B} \left(\frac{\#rec(b)}{total}\right) ln \left(\frac{\#rec(b)}{total}\right) \tag{8}$$

this implies that a lower entropy value indicates a better distribution and vice versa.

Novelty. In business, the *long tail effect* implies that a few of the most popular products are extremely popular, while the rest, so-called the long tail, is obscure to customers [3]. Recommending products in the long tail is beneficial both to customers and to business owners [28]. Expected popularity complement (EPC) is utilized to quantify novelty [18,27,28]:

Expected popularity complement EPC measures if a system is able to recommend unpopular items, i.e., those that have been rated by a small number of users:

$$EPC@N(U) = \frac{\sum_{u \in U} \sum_{r=1}^{N} \frac{rel(u,r)*[1-pop(REC_r(u))]}{log_2(r+1)}}{\sum_{u \in U} \sum_{r=1}^{N} \frac{rel(u,r)}{log_2(r+1)}} \tag{9}$$

where $pop(REC_r(u))$ is the popularity of the item at the position r in the *top-N* recommended list. It is computed as the ratio between the number of projects that receive $REC_r(u)$ as recommendation and the number of projects that receive the most ever recommended book as recommendation [18]. EPC increases if the system recommends more unpopular books.

We perform ten-fold cross validation and for each testing user, a half of her ratings is randomly selected as query, the other half is saved as $gt(u)$. By performing the evaluation with the consideration of the quality metrics, we aim at addressing the following research questions:

RQ_1: Which CF technique performs better? Many existing studies [5,8,13, 22,24] demonstrate that ibCF outperforms ubCF. In contrast, a recent work [12] shows that there is no clear winner between ubCF and ibCF. We investigate which technique obtains a better performance in the book domain.

RQ_2: Does an increase in the number of neighbour users help improve recommendation outcomes? Increasing the number of neighbours means adding more computational complexity. Thus, it is essential to study if it is beneficial to recommendation with respect to various quality indicators mentioned above.

4.3   Results

RQ_1: Which CF technique performs better? We answer this question by investigating each of the quality indicators in Sect. 4.2.

Accuracy. Figure 3(a) and (b) show the precision-recall curves (PRCs) for both datasets. Given two PRCs, the one closer to the upper right corner represents a better accuracy [7]. Thus, we see that for both BookCrossing and Goodbooks, a better accuracy is obtained when more neighbor users are incorporated into the user-item matrix. In particular, the accuracy for the two datasets when $k = 20$ is better than that when $k = 5$. Furthermore, it is evident that ubCF outperforms ibCF for both test configurations, i.e., $k = 5$ and $k = 20$ and by all datasets. The difference in performance of ubCF and ibCF is more visible by the BookCrossing dataset.

The nDCG-recall curves obtained by performing experiments on the datasets are depicted in Fig. 3(c) and (d). By `BookCrossing`, `ubCF` obtains a better ranking-sensitive accuracy than `ibCF` does. It means that using `ubCF` the system is able to recommend more highly relevant items at the top of the list. This holds for both configurations, i.e., $k = 5$ and $k = 20$. By the `Goodbooks` dataset, the difference in nDCG obtained by `ubCF` and `ibCF` is almost negligible. This implies that using `ubCF` and `ibCF` on the `Goodbooks` dataset yields almost the same ranking-sensitive accuracy. Still, for this dataset incorporating more neighbours brings a better accuracy. Altogether, we conclude that `ubCF` has a better accuracy than `ibCF`.

Diversity. Figure 4(a) and (b) show that the difference in entropy obtained by `ibCF` and `ubCF` is very small. With the `Goodbooks` dataset, we get the same entropy for both recommendation techniques. Since a lower entropy value corresponds to a better coverage (see Eq. 8), the entropy obtained by `ibCF` is better than that of `ubCF` by `BookCrossing`. As shown in Fig. 4(c) and (d), Coverage is proportional to recall. This is understandable since recall increases when more items in the ranked list are recommended. We see that `ibCF` outperforms `ubCF` in terms of coverage as its corresponding curves are in a upper position. However, for `Goodbooks`, none of the techniques outperforms the other. In summary, for the diversity metric, `ibCF` gains a superior performance compared to `ubCF`.

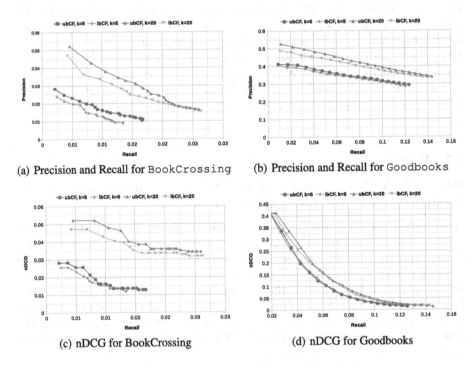

(a) Precision and Recall for `BookCrossing`   (b) Precision and Recall for `Goodbooks`

(c) nDCG for BookCrossing   (d) nDCG for Goodbooks

Fig. 3. Accuracy for `BookCrossing` and `Goodbooks`.

Novelty for `BookCrossing`, it is evident that `ubCF` has a considerable lower novelty compared to that of `ibCF` when more neighbours are used for recommendation as shown in Fig. 5(a). However, for the `Goodbooks` dataset, `ibCF` clearly outperforms `ubCF` for both configurations, i.e., $k = 5$ and $k = 20$. The novelty of the recommendations by `ibCF` substantially improves when more neighbour users are incorporated, i.e., $k = 20$. By `ubCF`, the novelty does not increase when we change k to 20. To summarize, we see that `ibCF` helps obtain a much better novelty than `ubCF` can do.

RQ_2: Does an increase in the number of neighbour users help improve recommendation outcomes? We see that for `BookCrossing`, increasing the number of neighbour users from $k = 5$ to $k = 20$ helps improve accuracy (precision, recall, nDCG). However, this makes coverage and EPC decrease considerably (see Fig. 4(c) and 5(a)). For `Goodbooks`, we witness the same trend as accuracy, entropy, and EPC improve if $k = 20$. However, by `ubCF` there is no improvement in EPC at all. In summary, we see that an increase in k is beneficial to some metrics but harms the others.

4.4   Lessons Learned

The first conclusion drawn from the experimental results on the two book datasets is that, considering the quality indicators mentioned in Sect. 4.2, `ubCF` fosters accuracy (precision, recall, and nDCG); meanwhile, `ibCF` is beneficial to diversity and novelty. The performance difference is more visible for the `BookCrossing` dataset where the user-item matrix is extremely sparse, i.e., Sparsity $= 99.98\%$ (see Table 2). When data becomes denser, the difference between `ubCF` and `ibCF` considerably reduces and can be negligible for most of the considered quality metrics. This is the case with the `Goodbooks` dataset where there are less items but more ratings, i.e., Sparsity $= 99.03\%$ (see Table 2).

Taking into consideration the work by *Jalili* et al. [12], where the authors discovered that each of the collaborative-filtering algorithms mentioned in this paper performs well in some but not all settings, we come to the second conclusion that general speaking, a *panacea* does not exist among `ubCF` and `ibCF`. In other words, there is no algorithm that always outperforms the other in all datasets. Our finding contradicts those of many existing studies [5,8,13,22,24], which declare that `ibCF` clearly outperforms `ubCF`.

Furthermore, we confirm that the performance of a recommender system may be good with respect to some evaluation metrics, but may be poor by others [12]. Therefore, it is highly advisable to take into account various quality indicators when designing a new recommender system. More importantly, one needs to be sure in the first place: Which quality aspects does s/he aim for?

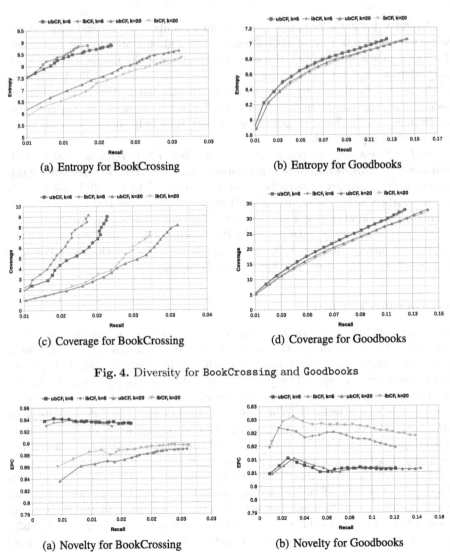

Fig. 4. Diversity for BookCrossing and Goodbooks

(a) Novelty for BookCrossing

(b) Novelty for Goodbooks

Fig. 5. Novelty for BookCrossing and Goodbooks.

5   Conclusions and Future Work

This paper introduced a thorough evaluation for the book domain using two considerably large datasets, exploiting various quality metrics. Our experimental results show that there is no clear winner between two collaborative-filtering techniques, i.e., ubCF and ibCF. Furthermore, the difference in performance between the two techniques becomes negligible when more data is available. We plan to extend the evaluation by incorporating more data, as well as using additional quality indicators. Moreover, we are going to investigate the effect of adding more neighbour users to build the user-item matrix.

References

1. Adomavicius, G., Kwon, Y.: Improving aggregate recommendation diversity using ranking-based techniques. IEEE Trans. Knowl. Data Eng. **24**(5), 896–911 (2012)
2. Aggarwal, C.C.: Neighborhood-based collaborative filtering. Recommender Systems, pp. 29–70. Springer, Cham (2016). https://doi.org/10.1007/978-3-319-29659-3_2
3. Anderson, C.: The Long Tail: Why the Future of Business is Selling Less of More. Hyperion (2006)
4. Bellogín, A., Cantador, I., Castells, P.: A comparative study of heterogeneous item recommendations in social systems. Inf. Sci. **221**, 142–169 (2013)
5. Cacheda, F., Carneiro, V., Fernández, D., Formoso, V.: Comparison of collaborative filtering algorithms: limitations of current techniques and proposals for scalable, high-performance recommender systems. ACM Trans. Web **5**(1), 2:1–2:33 (2011)
6. Davidson, J., et al.: The youtube video recommendation system. In: Proceedings of the Fourth ACM Conference on Recommender Systems, RecSys 2010, pp. 293–296. ACM, New York (2010)
7. Davis, J., Goadrich, M.: The relationship between precision-recall and ROC curves. In: Proceedings of the 23rd International Conference on Machine Learning, ICML 2006, pp. 233–240. ACM (2006)
8. Deshpande, M., Karypis, G.: Item-based top-N recommendation algorithms. ACM Trans. Inf. Syst. **22**(1), 143–177 (2004)
9. Di Noia, T., Mirizzi, R., Ostuni, V.C., Romito, D., Zanker, M.: Linked open data to support content-based recommender systems. In: Proceedings of the 8th International Conference on Semantic Systems, I-SEMANTICS 2012, pp. 1–8. ACM (2012)
10. Gomez-Uribe, C.A., Hunt, N.: The netflix recommender system: algorithms, business value, and innovation. ACM Trans. Manage. Inf. Syst. **6**(4), 13:1–13:19 (2015)
11. Isinkaye, F., Folajimi, Y., Ojokoh, B.: Recommendation systems: Principles, methods and evaluation. Egypt. Inform. J. **16**(3), 261–273 (2015)
12. Jalili, M., Ahmadian, S., Izadi, M., Moradi, P., Salehi, M.: Evaluating collaborative filtering recommender algorithms: a survey. IEEE Access **6**, 74003–74024 (2018)
13. Karypis, G.: Evaluation of item-based top-N recommendation algorithms. In: Proceedings of the Tenth International Conference on Information and Knowledge Management, CIKM 2001, pp. 247–254. ACM, New York (2001)
14. Linden, G., Smith, B., York, J.: Amazon.com recommendations: item-to-item collaborative filtering. IEEE Internet Comput. **7**(1), 76–80 (2003)
15. Nanopoulos, A., Rafailidis, D., Symeonidis, P., Manolopoulos, Y.: MusicBox: personalized music recommendation based on cubic analysis of social tags. IEEE Trans. Audio Speech Lang. Process. **18**(2), 407–412 (2010)
16. Nguyen, P.T., Tomeo, P., Di Noia, T., Di Sciascio, E.: An evaluation of SimRank and personalized PageRank to build a recommender system for the web of data. In: Proceedings of the 24th International Conference on World Wide Web, WWW 2015 Companion, pp. 1477–1482. ACM (2015)

17. Nguyen, P.T., Tomeo, P., Di Noia, T., Di Sciascio, E.: Content-based recommendations via DBpedia and freebase: a case study in the music domain. In: Arenas, M., et al. (eds.) ISWC 2015. LNCS, vol. 9366, pp. 605–621. Springer, Cham (2015). https://doi.org/10.1007/978-3-319-25007-6_35

18. Niemann, K., Wolpers, M.: A new collaborative filtering approach for increasing the aggregate diversity of recommender systems. In: Proceedings of the 19th ACM SIGKDD International Conference on Knowledge Discovery and Data Mining, KDD 2013, pp. 955–963. ACM (2013)

19. Di Noia, T., Ostuni, V.C.: Recommender systems and linked open data. In: Faber, W., Paschke, A. (eds.) Reasoning Web 2015. LNCS, vol. 9203, pp. 88–113. Springer, Cham (2015). https://doi.org/10.1007/978-3-319-21768-0_4

20. Noia, T.D., Rosati, J., Tomeo, P., Sciascio, E.D.: Adaptive multi-attribute diversity for recommender systems. Inf. Sci. **382–383**, 234–253 (2017)

21. Núñez-Valdéz, E.R., Lovelle, J.M.C., Martínez, O.S., García-Díaz, V., de Pablos, P.O., Marín, C.E.M.: Implicit feedback techniques on recommender systems applied to electronic books. Comput. Hum. Behav. **28**(4), 1186–1193 (2012)

22. Papagelis, M., Plexousakis, D.: Qualitative analysis of user-based and item-based prediction algorithms for recommendation agents. In: Klusch, M., Ossowski, S., Kashyap, V., Unland, R. (eds.) CIA 2004. LNCS (LNAI), vol. 3191, pp. 152–166. Springer, Heidelberg (2004). https://doi.org/10.1007/978-3-540-30104-2_12

23. Saracevic, T.: Evaluation of evaluation in information retrieval. In: Proceedings of the 18th Annual International ACM SIGIR Conference on Research and Development in Information Retrieval, SIGIR 1995, pp. 138–146. ACM (1995)

24. Sarwar, B., Karypis, G., Konstan, J., Riedl, J.: Item-based collaborative filtering recommendation algorithms. In: Proceedings of the 10th International Conference on World Wide Web, WWW 2001, pp. 285–295. ACM, New York (2001)

25. Fortino, G., Rovella, A., Russo, W., Savaglio, C.: Towards cyberphysical digital libraries: integrating IoT smart objects into digital libraries. In: Guerrieri, A., Loscri, V., Rovella, A., Fortino, G. (eds.) Management of Cyber Physical Objects in the Future Internet of Things. IT, pp. 135–156. Springer, Cham (2016). https://doi.org/10.1007/978-3-319-26869-9_7

26. Schafer, J.B., Frankowski, D., Herlocker, J., Sen, S.: Collaborative filtering recommender systems. In: Brusilovsky, P., Kobsa, A., Nejdl, W. (eds.) The Adaptive Web. LNCS, vol. 4321, pp. 291–324. Springer, Heidelberg (2007). https://doi.org/10.1007/978-3-540-72079-9_9

27. Vargas, S., Castells, P.: Rank and relevance in novelty and diversity metrics for recommender systems. In: Proceedings of the Fifth ACM Conference on Recommender Systems, RecSys 2011, pp. 109–116. ACM (2011)

28. Vargas, S., Castells, P.: Improving sales diversity by recommending users to items. In: Eighth ACM Conference on Recommender Systems, RecSys 2014, Foster City, Silicon Valley, CA, USA, 06 October 2014, pp. 145–152 (2014)

29. Zajac, Z.: Goodbooks-10k: a new dataset for book recommendations. FastML (2017)

30. Zhao, Z.-D., Shang, M.-S.: User-based collaborative-filtering recommendation algorithms on hadoop. In: Proceedings of the 2010 Third International Conference on Knowledge Discovery and Data Mining, WKDD 2010, pp. 478–481. IEEE Computer Society, Washington, DC (2010)

31. Ziegler, C.-N., McNee, S.M., Konstan, J.A., Lausen, G.: Improving recommendation lists through topic diversification. In: Proceedings of the 14th International Conference on World Wide Web, WWW 2005, pp. 22–32. ACM, New York (2005)

Author Index

Printed in the United States
By Bookmasters